RISK &
REWARD

RISK & REWARD

An Inside View of the
Property/Casualty Insurance Business

Stephen Catlin

with James Burcke

ISKABOO PUBLISHING

First published in 2017
by Iskaboo Publishing Ltd
22C Lady Margaret Road
London NW5 2XS
www.iskaboo.co.uk

Design and typesetting by Emperor
Printed in the United Kingdom by CPI Colour Ltd

The statements and views expressed in this book are solely those of the authors and do
not represent the statements and views of the XL Group Ltd group of companies
or any other persons affiliated with XL Group Ltd or its subsidiaries.

A CIP record for this book is available from the British Library

ISBN 978-0-9575595-5-4

To all those who contributed
to the success of Catlin Group Limited

CONTENTS

FOREWORD

Nikolaus von Bomhard,
Former chairman of the board of management, Munich Re

Stephen Catlin and I first met back in the early 2000s. At that time, he was already a well-known figure, not just at Lloyd's but also in the global insurance world. My first impression of Stephen was strong; he came across as very determined, technical and always mindful of the insurance industry as a whole. The fact that we are both truly passionate about politics and opera enthusiasts certainly helped to bring us closer together.

Over the years, we have come to know each other increasingly well and have become friends. Consequently, when Stephen asked me if I would be willing to write the foreword of his book, I accepted immediately. When he sent me the draft of *Risk & Reward*, I knew I had made the right decision, since I felt compelled to keep reading down to the final page.

Risk & Reward is in part a history of the Catlin Group and, as Catlin is inextricably connected to Stephen Catlin, it is also a history of his unprecedented lifetime achievements. Having started as a small Lloyd's syndicate without a fax machine or a photocopier, Catlin became a multi-billion-dollar company employing 2,500 people in 25 countries. That is what I call a successful start-up! And over time, Stephen has become a highly esteemed insurance heavyweight to whom the industry rightly listens.

At Munich Re, Catlin (now XL Catlin) is respected as a competitor and highly valued as a client, with whom we have built a long-standing client relationship. The atmosphere of trust and respect between our companies has, of course, to do with individuals, and Stephen Catlin tops that list.

In this book, Stephen also presents his views on the developments within Lloyd's and on the challenges currently facing the insurance industry. Many of the opinions he puts forward in this book coincide with my own. This refers, for example, to what he has written about the paramount importance of risk management and the art of underwriting. Unsurprisingly, I also completely agree with his remarks on the usefulness of reinsurance, but as a reinsurer myself, much less so with regard to the value of arbitrage in reinsurance, which he mastered so well as an underwriter at Lloyd's. And I sincerely hope that his call to more vigorously address new risks – such as cyber – in order to remain relevant for our customers will be heard throughout the insurance industry.

In my view, the strongest parts of this book are those where Stephen recollects and visualizes personal encounters. He transports the readers back in time and allows them to participate in the discussions and decisions which led to the growing success of Catlin and, at the same time, provides a much better understanding of Lloyd's eventful history over the last 45 years. Anyone who has had the privilege of discussing issues with Stephen knows that he gets to the point in comprehensible, direct language without hiding behind convoluted phrasing and technical terms, of which there are plenty in the insurance world. So, you really do not have to be an insurance expert to understand and enjoy *Risk & Reward*.

With my final remark, I cannot resist disagreeing with one of Stephen's theses. He writes that the insurance industry is doing a poor job explaining what it does and why. This is not true. You would like proof? Then turn the page and start reading!

With my warmest regards,
Nikolaus von Bomhard

PREFACE

As the old saying goes, you can't judge a book by its cover. I hope that holds true in the case of this book. Many readers may think that *Risk & Reward* is my autobiography. It's definitely not.

Risk & Reward is my attempt to draw on more than 40 years of experience in the property/casualty insurance industry to discuss some of the most important practices and concepts underlying the insurance business. Along the way, I will use examples from my life to illustrate these issues, but this book is about insurance and the insurance industry, not me.

I hope the book will be valuable to those who are interested in learning how to build an insurance business from the ground up. After working at Lloyd's of London for more than a decade, I decided in 1984, at the tender age of 29, to establish a managing agency and an underwriting syndicate. Catlin Underwriting Agencies Limited began business with two employees: an assistant underwriter and me. It had paid-up capital of £25,000, some of it secured against my home, and a silver inkwell that had been given to me by Brian Evens, my former boss. During our first year of operations, Syndicate 1003 wrote just £2.5 million in gross premiums.

Over the years, the managing agency grew and developed to become the publicly traded Catlin Group Limited, to which I will refer in this book as simply 'Catlin'. As many of you know, Catlin was acquired by XL Group during 2015 in a transaction that valued Catlin at more than $4 billion. At the time of the transaction, Catlin wrote annual gross premiums of $6 billion through 55 offices in 25 countries around the world. We employed 2,500 people.

I served as Catlin's chief executive officer at the group level during the entire history of the company.

* * *

I had never contemplated writing a book until shortly after XL acquired Catlin. I met with Mike McGavick, XL's chief executive officer and my new boss, to discuss my responsibilities as executive deputy chairman of the merged companies. Much to my surprise, Mike encouraged me to write this book.

"Look," he said, "you have been in this business as long as practically anyone, and you have a great story to tell."

After a couple of days, I began to see his logic, although perhaps with a bit of a different spin.

If you search in a bookstore or on a website such as Amazon for books on property/casualty insurance – particularly commercial insurance as opposed to personal lines coverage – you won't find much. You'll find lots of books about other sectors of the financial services industry, such as banks or stockbrokers, but not very many books about insurance. Many of the insurance books you will find are at least 20 years old, and most of them are theoretical volumes written by university professors. You will find few books based on the real-life experiences of people who actually worked for an insurance company or an insurance broker.

I must admit that I knew nothing about insurance when I got my first job at Lloyd's in 1973. I learned primarily from experience and by asking as many dumb questions as I could. I also began taking the courses required to earn the Advanced Diploma in Insurance (ACII) designation from the Chartered Insurance Institute in London. I passed all of the required examinations within two years bar one: 'Marine, Aviation and Risk Assessment'. That was a bit surprising as I was just starting to underwrite marine insurance. I think I failed that exam five times. My boss finally told me that I should just give up.

The reason I could not pass the exam, even though it was probably my specialty subject, was because I could not manage to provide the theoretical answers that were necessary to get sufficient marks. Instead, I provided real-life answers, which were not what the people who graded the paper were looking for.

I finally received my ACII designation in 2011, through a then-new assessment method that allows candidates to utilize their previous experience rather than only exam results.

So, you won't find a lot of theory in the following pages. Instead, I hope to draw on my own experience – as an insurance underwriter, as an entrepreneur and as a corporate chief executive officer – to discuss some of the most important issues relating to commercial property/casualty insurance and reinsurance.

* * *

I have divided *Risk & Reward* into four sections. The first, 'Insurance Fundamentals', offers my views on the essential workings of commercial property/casualty insurance and reinsurance. Again, these chapters are not intended to serve as a textbook. Instead, they are an attempt to discuss what I consider to be important aspects of how the insurance business operates. Much of the material in these chapters will be familiar to anyone with a decent knowledge of the insurance industry, but such a person may be interested in my viewpoints regarding these subjects.

The second section, 'Building a Business for the Future', tells the story of Catlin from my introduction to the insurance industry in 1973 through the company's origins in 1984 to its acquisition by XL in 2015. We learned many lessons as a business during the company's journey from a two-man Lloyd's agency to a major multinational insurer and reinsurer. I hope others can benefit from our experience.

As I have worked in the London market – especially at Lloyd's – for my entire career, I wanted to offer my impressions of the important events that have shaped the London market during the past 40 or so years. I hope this third section, 'Lloyd's and the London Market', does just that.

As I look back, there are many other important topics that relate to business in general and the insurance industry in particular. These subjects are of great interest to me and, hopefully, you the reader will share some of that interest. The fourth section of this book, 'Important Issues', provides my view on matters as diverse as leadership, interacting with regulators, attracting new talent and establishing a cohesive corporate brand.

Readers outside the United Kingdom might find this book somewhat London-centric. I began my career in London, and for the first 15 years of its existence Catlin's sole office was in the City of London. The company then began to expand globally, and by 2010 Catlin was organized into six underwriting hubs: London, US, Bermuda, Europe, Asia-Pacific and Canada. So, while I have significant experience doing business in insurance markets around the world, the bulk of my experience was rooted in London, particularly at Lloyd's.

To help compensate for the emphasis on London, I have chosen to write this book using American spellings of most words. I know some of my colleagues in London will be shocked and appalled, but I want the book to be useful to as many people in as many countries as possible.

Finally, a note about currencies. While Lloyd's and most companies in London use sterling as their functional currency, roughly half of the business written by Lloyd's is US-based and a substantial amount of non-US business is denominated in US dollars as well. As the sterling-US dollar exchange rate has swung greatly over the past 40 years (and is still doing so as I write this), I have used both sterling and US dollars in this book. I hope readers don't find this confusing, but attempting to convert all figures into just one currency would probably be misleading.

I hope that you find *Risk & Reward* interesting, stimulating and, at times, controversial. As those who have met me know all too well, I am not shy about expressing an opinion.

Stephen Catlin
June 2017

PART I
INSURANCE FUNDAMENTALS

1. THE VALUE OF INSURANCE

If insurance did not exist,
someone would have to invent it

The world as we know it today wouldn't work very well without insurance. If there was no insurance, you wouldn't be able to drive a car. You couldn't fly in an airplane. You couldn't travel on a ship, nor could a ship carry cargo. You couldn't attend a sporting event. In most countries, it would be impossible to obtain a mortgage on a house.

Insurance is truly an intrinsic part of today's economic order. If insurance did not exist, someone would have to invent it.

However, it is also true that insurance – no matter what its benefits – is a 'need to have' product, as opposed to something most people really *want* to buy. For that reason, the insurance industry, particularly property/casualty insurers, are probably resented by the population as a whole because there's no particular pleasure in buying an insurance product. People enjoy buying food, clothes, electronic gadgets and, occasionally, cars. Very few people enjoy a visit to their insurance agent or broker.

Why is the value of property/casualty insurance so unappreciated?

One of my theories is that the insurance industry has been poor – really, really poor – at communicating what it does, how it does it, and how insurance can add value for people and businesses. In my view, the industry has probably been the worst communicators and lobbyists in the financial services sector.

I must admit that I was ready to quit my first job at Lloyd's after a few months. I wasn't sure whether I was working in an insurance market or a big gambling casino. However, once I realized that there was true value in insurance and that the insurance industry was a crucial part of the international financial infrastructure, I could satisfy myself that I was no longer a croupier in training. I was actually adding some sort of social value. With that thought, I really got stuck into it and asked myself, "Okay, how can we do this better?"

* * *

Of course, insurance has no real value to a policyholder – whether the buyer is an individual or a business – until that policyholder suffers a loss. Then, insurance comes in very handy, although there's always a possibility that the policyholder will not really appreciate the fact that the loss has been covered by the policy.

All too often following a claim, insurers mishandle this golden opportunity to confirm their worth. Too many times, insurers do not respond to the claimant with a smile, a handshake and a check. Instead, they inappropriately deny the claim and issue a reservation of rights letter. Rather than be helpful and responsive to customers, insurers are frequently adversarial. Insurers often send the wrong message at a time when clients really need their help. While there may be a valid reason to dispute the claim, these types of actions are certainly not customer-friendly.

A 2012 Gallup Survey asked Americans which category of professionals was the most honest and trustworthy. Nurses came out on top, with 85 per cent rating the nursing professionals as having 'high' or 'very high' ethical standards. Insurance salesmen did not fare as well: only 15 per cent said honesty and ethical standards in insurance were high or very high. At least our industry did not come out at the bottom of the league. While bankers and lawyers were rated more favorably than the insurance industry, insurance salespeople were ranked ahead of stockbrokers, senators and congressmen.

There's some comfort in the thought that the survey respondents were probably referring to personal lines insurance agents. I sincerely hope that commercial insurance brokers and underwriters would fare better!

Seriously, I think respect for the insurance industry has gone up, not down, during the past 40 years. I further believe that the level of competence has increased, as has the quality of people involved in the industry at a senior level. Nowadays, we as insurers can go head to head with other professionals – such as bankers, lawyers or accountants – and hold our heads up high. I'm not sure that was the case when I first started my insurance career; at that time the insurance sector was certainly regarded as being inferior to other financial services businesses.

* * *

Another reason that people do not appreciate the value of insurance is the notion that 'it could never happen to me'.

Most policyholders, whether individual or commercial, do not really contemplate that a loss is probable or even possible. Most people don't believe they will have an auto accident or that their house could possibly burn to the ground. However, bad things do happen despite what people want to believe. Who would have thought that someone would have such a demented personality that he would order his followers to hijack jetliners and crash them into skyscrapers? Once or twice a year, an event occurs that is truly unforeseen, such as the tragedy we now call 9/11. Even though that loss was never contemplated, insurers eventually paid claims amounting to around $40 billion.

While it is easy to bash the insurance industry for any number of reasons, insurance plays an essential role in helping society recover from catastrophes, just as it saves an individual from financial ruin when his or her house is destroyed by a fire. Take 2011 as an example. That year saw an unprecedented series of natural disasters worldwide, including the earthquake and subsequent tsunami in Japan; two earthquakes in Christchurch, New Zealand; several devastating tornadoes in the United States; and a flood in an industrial area near Bangkok the size of Birmingham, England. All told, insurers paid out more than $100 billion in catastrophe claims in 2011, further demonstrating the value of insurance.

* * *

Insurance is part of the financial services industry, and therefore it is only natural to compare insurers with banks. I will go into some detail later regarding the differences between insurers and banks, but it is fair to say that most people would rather deal with a bank than an insurance company. The banking product – and by that I mean debt in its various forms – is more appreciated by most people than insurance. Debt allows a person or a company to do things that they would not ordinarily be able to do, such as purchasing something that they could not afford immediately (such as a home) or allowing them to make the cash they do have work more flexibly.

However, in many cases, you can't obtain a loan without insurance.

In some cultures, insurance is viewed as a tax. I can remember when I first went to China, more than 25 years ago. I spent much of my trip explaining what insurance was, how it worked and the benefits it provided. I was mainly met by blank stares. On my second trip, several years later, there was a better understanding, but most people questioned the need to buy insurance. The assumption seemed to be that if there is a loss, the government should pay for it because of the taxes that citizens pay. However, even in China, there are many instances where the government will not reimburse a company for a loss.

To this day, it is against public policy in Shanghai for a bank to insist that a mortgage holder purchase insurance on a property. Just think of the uninsured losses that could arise when a windstorm hits the Pudong business district of Shanghai, as it inevitably will.

* * *

Insurance companies can provide value in addition to the coverage they sell: they can provide risk management expertise. It is in insurers' interests that the companies which they cover employ the best practices possible to prevent losses from happening in the first place. Of course, companies with bad risk management practices must pay higher premiums than well-managed policyholders, but it is in everyone's best interests to avoid a loss whenever possible.

Consider British Petroleum, now officially BP plc. As an energy underwriter during the 1980s, I knew BP's company secretary, Judith Hanratty, very well. Judith was a talented risk manager, and she rightly concluded that the insurance industry was not able to provide the type of 'Armageddon' coverage that she sought for BP – simply because insurers did not have enough capital to write such high coverage limits. At the time, BP had a market capitalization of about £35 billion, while the proxy for capital of all Lloyd's syndicates then was only about £5 billion. Even had we had the capacity, the premium that insurers would have had to charge would have been more than BP was prepared to pay. There were simply not enough sufficiently large insurers in those days to spread the risk adequately.

Fast-forward about 25 years to 2010, when the Deepwater Horizon oil rig exploded, killing 11 people and creating the largest accidental maritime oil spill ever recorded. The rig, while owned by another company, had been leased to BP, which still did not buy most types of insurance. Subsequent investigations into the disaster revealed that BP's risk management practices were not as robust as one would have thought. If BP had bought commercial insurance to cover their drilling risks, insurers would have likely insisted on more stringent risk management practices. To date, Deepwater Horizon is thought to have cost BP more than $50 billion in clean-up costs, compensation and fines. Insurance, if purchased, might have contributed only about $10 billion at most, but on the other hand the disaster might never have happened because insurers would have likely demanded better risk management from BP.

* * *

One problem that the insurance industry faces – and one that cannot easily be solved – relates to timing. Insurance is a product that people really do not enjoy purchasing, and something bad must happen for it to have any perceived value. A car crash is a bad thing. Two ships colliding is probably worse. So is an airplane crash. And two jetliners crashing into two buildings in New York's financial district is simply horrific. While the insurance product can significantly mitigate the economic impact of a disaster, it can't change the fact that its value can only be really appreciated when something bad happens.

One of the things I learned from starting an insurance business from scratch is that a good reputation for claims-paying capability – and perhaps, more importantly, claims-paying credibility – is something an insurer earns over a long period of time. An insurer must demonstrate time and time again that it will pay valid claims fairly and on a consistent basis. The best judge of an insurer's claims-handling abilities is a broker because a broker sees claims occurring on a daily basis, while most policyholders suffer claims relatively infrequently.

One of the great differentiators between Catlin – and now XL Catlin – and most other insurers has been the ability to manage and efficiently handle difficult claims quickly and fairly. Even when a claim is not clear-cut, we have learned that it is better to get all parties around a table to discuss their issues in order to reach a fair compromise rather than simply to deny the claim.

If I could change one thing about our industry, I would drive home the insurance value proposition so that clients, regulators and even governments could clearly see the true worth that insurance actually provides. We must find ways of telling the world how much value the industry can provide following a loss. The most significant part of that value proposition is claims handling, which really is our shop window.

2. The Meaning of Risk

What risk is and why it must be managed

"What does 'risk' mean to you?"

I have been asked that question on several occasions. To me, the best way to define risk is to consider what a person or a business could lose if a fortuity were to happen that is unexpected, unforeseen but plausible. What would be the physical and financial outcome if such an event happened?

But, in the insurance industry, risk can have a different meaning. As we are essentially selling a promissory note against potential events in the future, there is always the risk that an insurer will not have the assets to honor its promise to pay. Insurers must make certain that we don't overexpose ourselves and that we have sufficient assets to meet future liabilities. In other words, insurers need to have a comprehensive understanding of the *downside risk to capital*.

That understanding has improved dramatically over the 40 years that I have worked in the insurance industry. Risk modeling, which is still not perfect, has greatly contributed to our insights. Insurers and brokers should, just by the sheer size of their databases, have a far greater knowledge of risk and various outcomes than an individual client. The client is, by and large, limited to its own data and perhaps some sector-specific information. I believe that insurers must share our knowledge of risk, our knowledge of the probability of risk and indeed our knowledge of the possible severity of risk. We must share our ability to model risk and to mitigate it.

Unfortunately, I don't think 'risk' is a concept that is given a priority by many businesses, even banks. To understand why, we must return to the 'it cannot happen to me' mentality. If you have little or no understanding of risk and a truly serious event occurs, then you learn the hard way. Too few companies actually ask their insurers – or possibly even their brokers – to help them identify and quantify their risks.

Several years ago, I was privileged to meet with the management of a long-time Catlin policyholder that was also one of the largest shipping companies in the world. I had previously met with the CEO; now I was speaking to the risk manager. He said to me, "Stephen, first and foremost, I want you to help me understand the risks that I have and then, secondly, how those risks can be mitigated. Can they be managed better? Thirdly, is there an insurance product that makes sense as part of that mitigation? My primary interest is to understand my risk. How can you help me understand my risk better from the experience that you have within the insurance industry?"

This was a sensible chap! If an insurance company is going to add value to its clients, the first thing we should be doing is helping them understand their risks more effectively and, where appropriate, suggest types of coverage that can transfer risk to the insurer at an appropriate price.

I think insurance too often is bought for the wrong reason. A client shouldn't purchase insurance just for the sake of it; a company should buy insurance to transfer the risks it finds difficult to manage itself at an appropriate cost.

The businesses that I believe have a good understanding of risk are those companies where risk management is taken seriously in the executive suite. If a company is properly aware of risk and the value of risk management, you can be certain that the CEO is helping to drive that awareness. If the CEO worries about risk, then he or she will very possibly employ a risk manager who can identify risk and has an in-depth knowledge of what insurance products are appropriate to purchase based on the risk appetite of the business.

* * *

People's attitudes to risk can vary greatly, mostly based on their understanding.

Here is a personal story that never ceases to amaze me. When my father-in-law died, it fell to me to sort out his household insurance details on behalf of my wife's mother. My father-in-law was a schoolteacher and was not a wealthy man. He had purchased three insurance policies. He bought a policy to cover his house, most probably because he had a mortgage and therefore the bank required insurance. Another policy covered his car; he had to buy this policy because he couldn't legally drive the car without it. Finally, he bought a separate policy to cover his television, a common purchase at that time.

The household insurance cost roughly £35 per year at the time. As he had the policy for many years, he was hopelessly underinsured, probably for only a third of the house's value. If there had been a loss, the insurer would have paid only one-third of his claim due to the concept of 'average'[1].

---

1 'Average' is the principle used in insurance to calculate a claims payment in cases where the limit of the policy is less than the actual value of the property or good insured (in other words, the property or good is underinsured). If a partial loss occurs, the claims payment will be proportionate to the percentage of the underinsurance.

By comparison, the policy covering the television was costing about £25 per year.

When I pointed this out to my mother-in-law, basically saying that she should spend £100 per year on household insurance rather than £35, she refused. However, she gladly accepted a £10 increase in the television insurance premium because the TV had broken down the previous year, and the insurer had paid the claim. The fact that she could easily afford to buy a replacement television from her savings, but couldn't afford a replacement home, wasn't the point for her. The TV policy had more value to her because she had received a claim payment, even though the risk posed by the potential loss of her home was far greater.

I have seen large companies follow that same philosophy, and it's just mind-boggling that they don't consider the downside risk to their own capital. They don't look at what could happen to them if things went terribly wrong. But, as I said earlier, people – and even businesses – seldom believe they are going to suffer a loss.

* * *

I believe the concept of downside risk to capital is much better understood by the insurance industry than it is by the banking industry. More than a decade ago, I was invited to meet one of the top executives of Lehman Brothers, the investment bank. I was told by one of Catlin's non-executive directors that I might learn something new by talking to this guy. So, we had a so-called informal lunch in one of Lehman's boardrooms, where we were served sandwiches by white-gloved waiters.

We were talking about risk, and I soon got the sense that the banker and I were not using the same language. We did not seem to have the same understanding. So, I asked him to define the word 'risk', and he looked at me like I was barking mad. After a bit of hesitation, he started to describe risk in terms of credit risk, credit swaps and credit derivatives. Then he stopped; that was it.

I began to smile, and he asked why. I said with a laugh that half of the insurance industry does not understand credit risk, and the half that does understand it is unable to charge for it explicitly. When the insurance industry thinks about risk, I explained, we think of downside risk to capital. We consider what could possibly occur to force us to cease being able to trade and therefore not be able to pay our obligations to our policyholders.

Once again, the Lehman director looked at me as if I was truly crazy.

A few days later, I called the Catlin non-executive director who had suggested going over to Lehmans. I advised him to sell any Lehman shares that he may own because the bank's senior management didn't seem to understand risk; they didn't contemplate risk in terms of what could happen to their balance sheet should an unforeseen circumstance occur.

To this day, I don't think many banks have really thought about risk in the same way that insurers do.

* * *

If there is one thing that most people agree about risk, it is that events are very difficult to predict. Sometimes luck plays a role, but at the end of the day, good risk management can really help mitigate the impact of a loss.

Consider, for example, the Qantas A380 'super-jumbo' airliner that suffered an uncontained engine failure on November 4, 2010, during a flight from Singapore to Sydney. The airplane, which suffered extensive damage, was able to return to Singapore and make an emergency landing.

Shrapnel from the exploding engine had punctured part of the wing and damaged the fuel system, causing leaks and a fuel tank fire. In addition, the hydraulic systems and the anti-lock braking system were disabled, the landing flaps were damaged, and two of the other engines were degraded. In short, it was a catastrophe waiting to happen.

However, Qantas was fortunate that five pilots were on board: the three pilots who would normally have been responsible for flying the airplane, as well as a 'check pilot' whose job it was to check the competency of the crew. A fifth pilot was on board to train to become a check pilot. Together, these five pilots formed a first-rate risk management team.

Fortunately, the crew was able to control the aircraft despite the damage and flew a holding pattern close to the Singapore airport while checking systems. Using the programs aboard the plane, the crew discovered that the airplane could be landed, although the programs indicated that there would be only 150 metres of the 4,000 metre long runway to spare.

By working together, identifying risks and then striving to mitigate them as best they could, the team of pilots managed to land the A380 safely. There were no injuries reported among the 440 passengers and 29 crew on board the airplane.

Interestingly, this incident occurred about six months after the explosion of the Deepwater Horizon oil rig in the Gulf of Mexico and the resulting oil spill, an incident that consisted of a chain of events. Each part of the chain in and of itself wasn't significant, but the combination of events was disastrous.

A large number of things happened sequentially, but unlike the case of the A380, no one appeared to have reacted to the aggregating problem until it was too late.

3. Underwriting

Insurance starts with a policy ... or at least it should

Is underwriting an art or a science? Who knows? It's probably a bit of both, with a little luck thrown in for good measure.

Back in the 1970s, when I began my insurance career, underwriting was much more of an art. Over the years, however, underwriting has become a lot more scientific. Underwriters can now base their decisions on much better data than we had 40 years ago. They can use complex underwriting models – either bespoke or purchased from one of several reputable modeling agencies – to support their decision-making. Actuaries now play a prominent role in the underwriting process at most insurance companies.

However, in my opinion, models cannot completely replace humans as underwriters. Models can certainly support underwriting decisions, but I believe that the best underwriting is a product of the ability to price business from grass-roots principles, an incisive understanding of downside risk to capital and a lot of old-fashioned common sense.

A good underwriter must have a number of different qualities. He or she must have good judgment. One has to be reasonably numerate. A good underwriter should be able to think outside the box and consider the unexpected. Keeping in mind that the underwriter also acts as a salesperson of sorts to the broker, an effective underwriter must also have excellent communication skills and what doctors call 'a good bedside manner'.

That bedside manner can manifest itself differently among different people. Paul Brand, who worked with me at Catlin for nearly 30 years and later became chief underwriting officer of insurance at XL Catlin, has a very different bedside manner to mine. I'm perhaps better at dealing with a new client than he is, but he is probably better than me when it comes to managing an existing client. 'Brando', as Paul is commonly known in the market, engenders a feeling of thoughtfulness, trust, fairness and stability. Those are all important qualities for an underwriter to possess.

* * *

13

Of course, there were no rating models whatsoever when I began my underwriting career at Lloyd's in 1973. I had already been working at B.L. Evens & Others Syndicate 264 for five years when it was decided that the syndicate would begin to underwrite an energy insurance account and a reinsurance account. I would be the underwriter of both of these business portfolios.

Further complicating matters for me, I had to learn nearly everything about underwriting the energy and reinsurance accounts on my own. I soon realized there was very little rhyme or reason to underwriting in those days.

So, I tried to apply common sense whenever possible. When I finally took a step back, I discovered that underwriting isn't really that difficult once one thinks about it. An underwriter assumes risk, with the intention of charging a premium appropriate to the underlying exposure. For example, an underwriter makes money when he or she is paid 10-to-1 for a 5-to-1 risk, provided he or she has an adequate spread of different types of business in the portfolio. In other words, if you break insurance and reinsurance down to the basics, an underwriter is actually considering the odds that a loss will occur and charging a premium that is hopefully higher than those odds would warrant.

While this explanation is somewhat simplistic, it's exactly how I went about it when I began underwriting back in 1978: I calculated, to the best of my ability, the probability that a claim would arise on each policy I wrote.

Years later, we used this same principle at Catlin when we underwrote our first terrorism policy, just two days after 9/11. Somebody asked me, "How in the hell can you price that?" I replied that he should just think about me as a bookie. Provided I get enough money in, I can spread my portfolio of risk. I would charge a certain rate for a school in Ohio and a lot more for a stadium in New York. And, in those days, we had seven days' notice of cancellation if we had second thoughts about the rate we had quoted.

* * *

In the London market, most policies are written on a subscription basis. One Lloyd's syndicate or company is selected by the policyholder's broker as the 'leader', and this underwriter calculates the rate and agrees the details of the coverage. Once the leader decides what percentage of the policy he or she wishes to underwrite, the broker then goes around with a 'placing slip'[2] to other syndicates and companies; these are known as 'followers'.

---

2   A placing slip is a document created by a broker that contains a summary of the terms of a proposed insurance or reinsurance contract which is then presented to underwriters.

They follow the rate, policy language and conditions set by the leader. This process continues until the policy is fully subscribed.

To my mind, an underwriter must be a leader – or at least aspire to be a leader – to be taken seriously in the marketplace. To me, simply being a follower means that you represent passive capacity. You are not really adding value.

Of course, the leader has to do a lot more than a follower does. A leader has to be able to assess a risk accurately and negotiate a price to the satisfaction of the broker and the client. Then, when a claim arises, it's the leader's syndicate or company that handles the management of the claim.

However, being a successful leader means that you have captured the respect of both brokers and your fellow underwriters. No one wants to follow a leader if that underwriter is proven to be a fool. To me, being a recognized leader is a sign of respect. When I began underwriting the energy insurance and reinsurance portfolios in the late 1970s, I wanted to lead business wherever possible. That was tricky, however, because our syndicate did not lead much business in those days; we simply followed the lead underwriter.

When I established my own syndicate in 1984, we were the 432nd syndicate in the Lloyd's marketplace. By 2004, there were only 64 syndicates, while the number of syndicates rose to 97 by the end of 2015. Looking at these numbers, one would think there are fewer leaders today than there were 30 years ago. The same holds true in the company market (i.e. the portion of the London insurance market written by insurance companies outside of Lloyd's).

In fact, the number of leaders in percentage terms has risen because the market has contracted. Increasingly, it's difficult to survive if you are not a leader. Why should brokers take the time to talk to you if they have a choice, other than when the price is too cheap or when they are placing distressed risks?

Some syndicates that don't normally lead a lot of business usually do have some area of specialization where they are known to be an expert. A Lloyd's syndicate can attract business if it is truly a niche specialist, although it will be interesting to see whether these types of syndicates can survive as the cost of doing business continues to increase.

* * *

I have been asked many times what it was like to be an underwriter in the 'old days', before the introduction of computers and rating models. While a lot of underwriting at Lloyd's is now done in an agency's own offices, in those days almost all underwriting was done from the syndicate's 'box' (in reality, a set of desks) in the Lloyd's Underwriting Room. Most of the information the underwriter possessed – and there was not much compared with today – came from the placing broker. How was an underwriter able to calculate the correct rate?

Underwriters in those days worked from common sense, grass-roots principles and gut instinct. A good underwriter had – and probably still has – a nose that can differentiate between business that's good and business that smells. It's a shame that some of today's underwriters have never really developed the instincts that were needed to succeed 30 or 40 years ago.

Fortunately for those of us underwriting in those days, the margins were much greater and the market was not so competitive, so an underwriting error was not as costly as it can be today. The more competitive the market becomes, the tighter the margins. An underwriter today, therefore, must pay greater attention to detail to succeed.

Today's underwriting models are fantastic tools that can be used to support a decision made by an underwriter, but I do not believe that they should drive a decision. At Catlin, I told our underwriters that they could make decisions that were contrary to what a model indicated so long as they understood the model's limitations as well as their own. At the end of the day, a model does not make money for an insurer. What makes the money is getting the most appropriate margin possible from a good piece of business.

Do I prefer today's marketplace in terms of disclosure, information and technical approach? Yes, it's much better. However, those inputs are not what make an insurer money: they underpin underwriting decisions, and those decisions must also take into account a variety of soft issues that the model may not consider, including any long-standing relationships between the insurer and the client.

Likewise, actuaries play a significant role in the underwriting process today. Catlin was one of the first – if not the first – syndicate at Lloyd's to employ a full-time actuary. However, actuarial support does not automatically mean success. Actuarial analysis is only as good as the information and data on which it is based. Sometimes the information is very robust, and sometimes it isn't.

During the period between 1998 and 2000, actuaries made huge mistakes in the pricing of US casualty business because they were looking at the past, not at what was happening in the American civil justice system at the time.

They didn't take into account current trends that were driving up claims costs because they were too focused on what had previously happened. Many insurers, including Catlin, had to strengthen casualty reserves significantly in the early 2000s for US casualty business underwritten in the late 1990s.

Don't misunderstand me: I'm a great believer in actuaries in principle, but actuaries have limitations. I believe it's the underwriter who should be making the final decision, not the actuary. The actuary should absolutely test the underwriter, and if the underwriter can't respond with a rational reply, there's probably a problem.

Of course, if an insurer has robust actuarial data and therefore a more robust pricing model, the insurer will probably produce lower margins. That's because the competition most probably has similar data and can come to similar conclusions. Better margins tend to be produced when there is some actuarial uncertainty. In those instances, an underwriter must take his or her own view of the risk, which may not be duplicated by competitors. In such a situation, when an underwriter is going it alone, he or she can often seek a bigger margin. As an underwriter, I've always been interested in areas where some actuarial uncertainty exists because those are the areas in which an underwriter can truly use his or her judgment.

*   *   *

An underwriter must be able to analyze probabilities because that is what really drives the rate on a particular piece of business, whether it's insurance or reinsurance. What are the odds that a certain policy or contract will produce a loss? Once an underwriter has analyzed the probabilities, he or she must charge at least 50 per cent more than the odds to make a decent margin. There are brokerage commissions and other distribution costs to pay (which on average consume 20 to 25 per cent of the gross premium). There are other overheads like salaries, rent and taxes.

Credit risk must also be considered by the underwriter when setting a rate. Even if an underwriting portfolio is protected by reinsurance *(see Chapter 6)*, an underwriter must factor in the possibility that reinsurers will either refuse, or be unable, to honor their commitment to pay certain losses. While insurers talk about gross exposure (before reinsurance is considered) and net exposure (after collecting reinsurance), the insurer is responsible for the gross amount of a claim should its reinsurers fail to pay.

*   *   *

Back in 1990 a new underwriter joined the Catlin syndicate to write the marine hull account. At our annual underwriting conference, she said she expected to make a profit the next year, which was 1991. The hull market was in terrible shape at the time, settling at a 150 to 160 per cent loss ratio, so Paul Brand and I told her that we did not expect a profit; we just did not want to suffer too large a loss on the account. Pull back a bit, we told her.

Due to the lousy state of the market, insurers were exiting the marine hull class en masse. It was clear that rates should be increased significantly – perhaps doubled – for hull risks, while at the same time the amount of risk retained by a policyholder should be increased by up to a factor of four to get rid of wear-and-tear claims. I decided that we should entirely re-underwrite our hull book of business.

Brando was concerned. He did not see how anyone could turn a 160 per cent loss ratio into a profit in a year. I replied that I didn't think we could make a profit, but I thought we could approach break-even, which was a pretty good stepping stone to profitability. Brando still had his doubts, and while I did not often act without his agreement, this time I took a chance.

Catlin managed to break even on the hull book that year. Competitors did not try to undercut our rates because the results had been so appalling. Our strategy had been based on common sense, gut instinct and an awareness of what was happening in the marketplace. We couldn't model it, as we would do today, because we didn't have the data to do it.

To this day, when I hear underwriters say they did not write a piece of business because the model said they couldn't, I shudder. To me, a model is a support mechanism to underpin a decision you have taken personally. If you make decisions solely based on a model, you will probably be wrong when you think you are right, and you will probably be right when you think you are wrong. That's because the model *de facto* is incomplete; the data in the model cannot cover every situation.

An underwriter must understand the limitations of any model to utilize it properly. And underwriters must be very careful when using models purchased from one of the major modeling agencies because, in my opinion, they can create systemic risk. If everyone uses the same model, often because regulators say one must, there is a chance that everyone will get it right. However, there is also a chance – if the model is flawed or there's incomplete data – that everybody will get it wrong! If you look at it that way, models can increase – rather than decrease – risk.

I still say that if something doesn't smell right and doesn't feel right, then don't underwrite it. If your gut instinct says 'no', listen to your gut.

* * *

A good underwriter will also be careful to maintain good relationships. You never know when a relationship will come in handy.

The largest account that Catlin ever led as an underwriter was the reinsurance program for the International Group of P&I Clubs, whose members write protection and indemnity insurance (a form of marine liability insurance) covering around 90 per cent of the world's ocean-going tonnage. It is the largest marine reinsurance contract in the world, and Catlin would have never won that account in 2003 if it were not for relationships made much earlier.

The International Group contract had been led by a Lloyd's syndicate managed by Janson Green Ltd., now part of QBE Insurance Group, for more than 50 years. However, ahead of the 2003 renewal, the relationship between the client and the lead underwriter had broken down, partly due to a substantial premium increase which many following underwriters believed had not been properly explained by the lead underwriter to the client. The leadership of the program was up for grabs.

Miller Insurance Services, the International Group's long-time broker, came to me – along with several other Lloyd's underwriters – with a rate proposal. "Would you support something at this level?" they asked. I, of course, said I would discuss it with Paul Brand and others. While I would have preferred a slightly higher rate on a technical basis, I told Brando that this was a great opportunity for Catlin as the International Group had been proved to be a loyal, long-term client. "If there's a loss, they will pay back the money over time as rates are increased," I reasoned, which is exactly what an underwriter would want to happen.

Of course, Catlin was not the only underwriter bidding to lead this prestigious account. There were others, particularly the late Ian Agnew, a good friend who at the time was chairman of Wellington Underwriting plc (a company that Catlin would acquire in 2006).

When I told Millers that I would be willing to lead the International Group account along the lines of the broker's proposal, I also told them that the most important criterion in selecting the leader should be the potential for a long relationship. I said, "Think about how the leader is going to behave in the future. This is the kind of contract that for nine years is easy to lead, but there will be lots of problems during that tenth year because you could have a large, very difficult claim. There could be a quite difficult negotiation that requires measured behavior."

It probably did not hurt that Millers' CEO, Graham Clarke, had been a good friend of mine for at least 25 years. However, the person who would make the final recommendation to the client was Millers' chairman, Iain Webb-Wilson, and that's where relationships really came into play.

A few years earlier, I had attended an insurance industry conference at the Greenbrier Resort in West Virginia, and I ended up playing golf with Iain and his wife. Now, I'm a lousy golfer on the best of days, but I played particularly poorly that day. However, I managed to keep my cool. I tried to be sociable despite driving the ball all over the course, and I was happy to pick up my ball when I was delaying the others.

I later learned that when it was time to make the decision, Iain told Graham Clarke, "I think we should go for Stephen because he's got strength of character. The way he held it together while playing the most disgusting round of golf at the Greenbrier really impressed me."

This is an example of how an underwriter builds relationships over time and how he or she is paid back. This is why it's worth being seen doing the right thing and acting with integrity. Brokers and clients have choices. When the deciding factor is not necessarily price, it can often come down to the quality of the business relationship.

And here's a postscript. Throughout this process, other underwriters – also vying for the lead – were bad-mouthing Ian Agnew and particularly me, saying that the Catlin syndicate was not qualified to lead such a big account. However, once Catlin was selected as the leader, every single one of them not only followed our lead, but offered to increase their line on the account.

* * *

While an underwriter has control over the rate he or she wishes to charge for a piece of business, one phenomenon over which even the best underwriter has little or no control is the underwriting cycle.

Insurance is a cyclical business and has been so for as long as I can remember. Cycles are not uniform. Sometimes, the cycle for a certain class of business – aviation, for example – will have little similarity to the cycles for most other classes of business. But at certain points in time – as happened in the early 1980s, the early 1990s and again in the late 1990s – the downward cycles for nearly all types of business converge, creating a true buyer's market ... as well as lots of headaches and financial pain for insurers.

Cycles are naturally going to occur because of supply and demand, pure and simple. If insurers have had several good years financially, capital will come flooding into the marketplace. Soon, there is much more capital than the market requires, so underwriters begin lowering rates to attract business away from competitors to utilize their capital. That's okay if everyone is still making a profit. However, one of two things usually happens during the downward portion of a cycle: either the market continues to soften and rates begin to deteriorate below technical benchmarks until the pain gets too great, or a huge loss (or series of losses) occurs, draining capital from the marketplace and forcing underwriters to raise rates, quickly and substantially, thus turning the cycle. For example, Hurricane Andrew triggered an abrupt correction in 1992.

* * *

Of course, an underwriter does not work in isolation. Each day, an underwriter will do business with many brokers, whose duty is to get the best deal for their clients. The role of the broker is so important that I will cover it more fully in Chapter 7.

Underwriters and brokers must work closely together. To do so, there must be mutual trust between an underwriter and a broker. Sometimes, though, that does not occur. Brokers at times do not fully explain the risks that they are asking the underwriter to insure. The underwriter must make sure that he or she understands the risk properly and has as much information as possible before providing a quote.

There are two major types of brokers: retail brokers and wholesale brokers. Retail brokers work directly with a client. Wholesale brokers work as intermediaries between retail brokers and specialty insurers; they usually do not have regular contact with the policyholder. Wholesale brokers often possess specialized expertise in a specific class of business or a specific market (such as Lloyd's) and usually deal with difficult-to-place risks.

As wholesale brokers can only really justify their worth to the retail brokers (and thus to the policyholder) based on the price they negotiate, there is usually more pricing pressure when a wholesale broker is involved.

For example, in the early 1990s a well-known lead underwriter negotiated a 1.5 per cent rate on line[3] on an energy insurance program being placed on behalf of a major oil company. He expected the rest of the market to follow his lead.

I was incensed because while he had negotiated a 1.5 per cent rate against the policyholder's physical assets, which was probably a fair price, there was a lot more coverage included in the policy than simply physical damage;

---

3 Rate on line is the amount of premium paid for a policy stated as a percentage of the limits of the policy. For example, a $2 million premium for a $100 million policy would represent a 2 per cent rate on line.

there was also coverage for cost of control and business interruption, which I believed had been effectively given for free.

I did not understand how the underwriter could rate the program in such a manner. Why did he do it? I guessed that he simply accepted the rate the broker had suggested without considering that there was much more coverage included in the package. Of course, the broker would have been happy that the underwriter was none the wiser.

I discussed the matter with Paul Brand and with Doug Howat, who in those days was one of Brando's assistants and is now chief executive, Global Lines, Insurance, for XL Catlin. I asked them to get hold of the placement, to analyze it exposure-by-exposure and then to price each exposure to get to the true rate. It took them three or four days to do it. Their work showed that the 1.5 per cent rate on line was woefully insufficient. The actual rate on line charged by the lead underwriter, when all exposures were considered, was closer to 0.15 per cent.

After having reassessed the exposure, it did not take long for the following underwriters to appreciate that our analysis was correct. The underwriters then demanded that they should see coverage details similar to the analysis that Brando and Doug had produced before following a quote on such a complex policy.

Of course, now the brokers were really hacked off, saying that what I had done was unfair. I said to the brokers: "Tell me why it's bad news for underwriters to understand the downside risk to the policies they have written?" After a lot of gnashing of teeth, the brokers accepted my argument, helped by the fact that this episode had occurred right at the bottom of an underwriting cycle and soon, as the market hardened, they would have a tough time placing difficult business.

The lesson to be learned here is *caveat emptor*. An underwriter should always start with *caveat emptor*. Judging a risk is a bit like reading a holiday brochure. Don't just look at the glossy pictures, but rather consider carefully what you're not being told.

*　*　*

As the insurer does not have a great deal of contact with the client – that's the broker's job – it is often difficult for an underwriter to explain rating decisions to the policyholder. A complicating factor can be the transaction costs involved in placing the coverage, especially when one or more wholesale brokers are involved. The amount paid to intermediaries can range from 15 to 50 per cent of the total premium paid by the policyholder.

Unfortunately, some brokers do not always give their clients a clear view of these transactional costs.

I have always believed that there should be absolute transparency regarding brokerage costs, especially on big-ticket business where there may be several brokers in the chain. In recent years, this situation has improved, and there is now often a negotiated fee pertaining to transaction costs for many of the larger risks.

A policyholder's loss experience obviously has a bearing on the rate charged. If the policyholder was not responsible for the loss – for example, the insured suffers a loss from a storm even though it has ensured that the property was maintained properly – the rate charged on renewal would not rise by as much as with a situation in which the policyholder's actions (or inactions) helped create the loss. In other words, good risk management can pay off for a policyholder, whether by mitigating a loss initially or reducing its impact if a loss does occur.

If a loss results solely from poor risk management, the underwriter should question whether he or she should renew the account, because another loss is probably on its way.

My first boss, Brian Evens, told me years ago: "Remember, you're underwriting whoever's name is on top of the slip. If you don't trust them or you don't think they have good risk management, don't write them." I would far rather underwrite coverage for a well-run company with a good risk management program at 90 per cent of the perceived rate than for an average company with sloppy risk management and questionable leadership at 110 per cent.

That same principle applies to reinsurance transactions, a subject which I will address in detail in Chapter 6. Sloppy underwriters should, and do, pay a lot more for their reinsurance protection than good underwriters.

* * *

As in most disciplines, two pairs of eyes during the underwriting process are usually better than one. Peer review is an important element in underwriting. It's not that one person cannot be successful, but having someone looking over your shoulder is always helpful. For a really complex risk, four pairs of eyes are probably better than two.

In Catlin's early days, Paul Brand and I would generally come within 5 per cent of each other when we would price the same piece of business. When we fell outside the range, it usually meant that one of us – or sometimes both – had made a misjudgment somewhere along the way. Even though our methodologies and thought processes were different, they were both rational, and I believe that taking two approaches when underwriting a complex piece of business can be a very good discipline.

Of course, you don't always have the luxury of having someone else prospectively review every underwriting decision. Underwriters are traders, and one must allow the traders to trade. However, retrospectively, an insurer must check every underwriter to ensure that he or she is following the business plan and to take note of any errors that may have been made during the underwriting process. Nowadays, internal audit plays a valuable role.

It's important that peer review takes place as quickly as possible, because the quicker an error or misjudgment is discovered, the quicker something can be done about it. For example, if a problem policy is found during peer review, an insurer can purchase facultative reinsurance[4] to protect its bottom line.

I can clearly remember writing a 10 per cent line on a property risk because I thought it made sense. Brando came up to me afterwards and said just one word to me, "California". To which I replied, "Yikes!" I had forgotten to factor in that the policyholder had significant operations in California that were exposed to earthquake risk. How did I ever miss that?

I called the broker immediately. "Look, I'm terribly sorry," I said. "I made a mistake that is my fault entirely. Is there any chance of me putting a dot between the one and the zero?" The broker asked why I would want to do that. "Because I missed some of the exposure," I replied. "It's not your fault, it's entirely my fault. I'm not complaining about your broking. I missed something, and I'd quite like to see if I can rectify it." And he said, "Yeah, all right, Guv." I was allowed by the broker to reduce my line from 10 per cent to 1.0 per cent by putting a dot between the one and the zero.

While I had significantly reduced my potential upside should the policy run loss-free, I had reduced my downside risk, which to me was much more important. The other lesson is to reinforce the importance of the underwriter-broker relationship. If I had not been on good terms with that broker, he probably would not have let me change my line.

* * *

The wording of any policy is an important part of the underwriting process. When a claim arises, it is crucial that there is a clear understanding of

---

4   Facultative reinsurance is a form of reinsurance whereby the insurer negotiates an individual reinsurance agreement for a specific policy. See Chapter 6.

exactly what is covered and what isn't. Of course, that is easier said than done, and arguments regarding policy wordings have kept many a lawyer in business. Just think of the mess – and the resulting litigation – that followed 9/11 because the wordings of the property insurance policies covering the World Trade Center were not clear. Different layers of coverage had different wordings.

It was always the case, especially when I first began writing energy insurance back in the late 1970s, that it was thought to be in a policyholder's best interest to have a manuscript policy wording – i.e. not standard form – for a complicated risk. With a manuscript wording, so the theory went, the policyholder could get exactly the coverage it wanted. However, the trouble with a manuscript wording is there is usually no case law to underpin the wording. Insurers adopt standard wordings for a reason: they have been written and examined by experts. The safest option for any client, in my view, is to have a standard wording. If the client wants something extra for good reason, then the client can purchase an endorsement to the policy. In that case, if there is doubt, it will be regarding the endorsement, not the entire policy.

Again, in the old days, it would be standard practice for the underwriter to write such an endorsement himself. But I learned when Catlin first employed a syndicate lawyer, Daniel Primer, who for years was Catlin's general counsel, that the smart thing to do was for the underwriter to draft the endorsement in his own language – so the intent was clear – and then hand it to a lawyer to make sure the wording actually matched that intention on a legal basis.

There is no doubt that the shorter the wording, the safer it is from the underwriter's point of view. The more words used, the more that is open to challenge.

Wordings and what became known as 'contract certainty' – the need to finalize policy wording before the policy period begins – were a problem long before 9/11. Traditionally, the Lloyd's market has been very sloppy with regards to policy wordings, and other markets haven't been that much better.

I recall in the 1980s taking over the lead of an energy package policy, which included business interruption coverage. As normal practice, the main points of the policy were spelled out on the slip, but that isn't what you want if there is a policy dispute that goes to court. When the policy was renewed a year later, the broker – whose responsibility it was – had still not presented me with the policy wording from the year before. I asked the broker, "What are you on? If there is a loss, we are now guaranteed to go to court: you, me and the client. By the way, you may well end up being the most exposed because I believe you could be charged with dereliction of duty."

It fell on deaf ears with the placing broker, so eventually I sent a letter to the CEO of the broker to communicate my utter dismay and disgust at the broker's poor performance. It took four to six weeks to get a reply to that letter, and the broker was still prevaricating about the wording. So, then I did something that I have never done before or since: I rang up another broker who had experience with that particular type of business and suggested that he contact the client, attempt to explain the situation and see if he could win the account from the other broker.

The second broker won the business, and the matter was soon settled. Naturally, the original broker was up in arms. I told him, "It's your own fault. If you want to stop doing business with me, go right ahead. By the way, if anybody asks why you are no longer doing business with me, I will explain to them what I did and why I did it."

The new, and current, broker then said to me, "Look, there is now distrust from the client. Because of what has happened, I think the only way we are going to get from A to B is for you and me to go see the client ourselves. We will sit around the table and thrash it out once and for all, including the expiring policy."

I did it, even though the client was based in the Asia-Pacific region and it meant two 20-hour flights for what I thought would be an afternoon's meeting. Actually, it took a day and a half, but we resolved the problem regarding the wording in a professional way. Once it was agreed, the client said he wanted to show me something. We went into another room, and he showed me three shelves full of ring binders and files. "This is the communication about the wording with the previous broker, and we never got to an agreement. Thank you very much, Stephen."

By the way, I am not talking about a small matter here. The premium for the policy was $5 million to $10 million, and that was several decades ago.

This is an extreme example, but it illustrates how difficult it can be to achieve contract certainty, especially when dealing with issues such as business interruption, which by its nature is hard to define what is covered, what is not covered, how a claim should be adjusted and on what basis. For example, if the policy covers loss of 'profits', what exactly does the word 'profits' mean?

Insurers and brokers have become much better at contract certainty, not the least because of regulatory requirements, but we were certainly sloppy in the past. It's no wonder that the insurance industry gets a bad reputation when a client buys a policy, but no one knows precisely what it covers.

4. Claims

Why do some insurers make the claims process so difficult?

As I pointed out earlier, when discussing the value of insurance, claims payment should be considered the shop window of any insurance carrier. The most powerful way an insurer can impress a client is to pay valid claims quickly, fairly and without hassle. If a claim is covered, morally it's the right thing to do.

The funny thing is that, through the years, many insurers have consistently ignored good claims management practices and have even disparaged the role of the claims professional.

When I started out in the insurance industry, the claims adjuster was on the lowest rung of the insurance ladder. Perhaps underwriters and brokers were thought to be on a higher level because, when you think about it, they bring in the money, while the claims professional pays it out.

When I began working at Lloyd's at the age of 19, I owned two suits: a blue suit and a dull green suit. A couple of months later, I asked my mother if I could borrow some money to buy another suit. She asked what was wrong with the two that I owned. I replied, "I can't wear the green one to work because everybody would think I was a claims broker."

That's a silly story, but it's true. Claims handling traditionally had been held in very low esteem in the insurance industry – and that is probably one of the reasons that insurers have such a poor reputation. Insurers simply don't handle claims as well as they should.

For far too long, many insurers have spent the least amount of money possible on claims operations. I observed it early on while working at Lloyd's and, as I became familiar with other insurance markets around the world, I saw the same lack of investment. That's led to some fairly incompetent behavior.

The good news is that the industry's attitude towards claims has changed greatly. Talented claims professionals are now making as much money as underwriters and placing brokers, and that is appropriate. I firmly believe that good claims people can be as valuable in retaining clients and producing new business as good underwriters.

Many years ago Catlin was just another company as far as claims management went. In other words, we weren't very good at it. However, as I began to realize how insurance really works and how it provided value to policyholders, I also realized that it was time for Catlin to invest in claims expertise. In 2003 we brought on board Nick Sinfield, an attorney by trade who was truly passionate about claims excellence. With the support of Paul Jardine – who at the time was CEO of our London operations and, as a former director of Equitas *(see Chapter 16)*, knew a great deal about good claims management practices – Nick transformed the Catlin claims team into something special. This didn't happen overnight, and it cost a considerable amount of money. However, it was well worth the effort and expense.

Starting in 2009, Gracechurch Consulting interviewed London market brokers to determine which insurers are thought to have the best claims operations. I am proud to say that Catlin finished at the top of the pack every year, sometimes by a large margin. And, as Catlin established offices around the world, we made sure that the commitment to claims excellence that we had nurtured in London was shared in each and every location. By the time that Catlin was acquired by XL in 2015, we had earned the reputation of being one of a handful of insurers whose claims performance was considered by many as truly excellent.

I am extremely proud of that fact.

* * *

What qualities does a good claims professional possess? Actually, it's pretty simple. To do his or her job well, a claims professional needs to be intelligent and diligent and must display the highest levels of integrity. However, what makes one claims person better than another is the ability to put oneself into the shoes of the claimant and work out exactly how the claimant feels about the loss.

A good claims person has the ability to make the claimant's circumstances better, not just financially but emotionally as well.

A claims handler's job is complicated by the fact that we as insurers sell a product that covers events that are often unexpected or even unforeseen. Some of these events were never fully contemplated by the underwriter and/ or broker when the policy was written, and the policy wording is all too often ambiguous. Some claims are simple and are relatively easy to handle; others are quite complex. Does the policy wording actually cover the claim? Did the insurer's promise to pay include that eventuality? Does the contract wording cover the series of events at issue?

These types of situations are problematic for insurers, but I believe it is wrong to simply deny claims that are not clear-cut. I believe that the insurer must go back to the time the policy was written and try to recall the underwriter's intent. The insurer must ask: "If I had thought about the circumstance now before me, would I have intended the policy to cover this event?" If the answer is 'yes', the insurer and claimant should work together to resolve the issue.

Insurers, in my opinion, should do the right thing. Litigation should be one of the last ports of call. Instead, insurers should sit down with the claimant and work through what happened and when it happened. If it is not clear whether the event is covered – if a grey area exists – the insurer should work with the claimant to reach a fair and reasonable resolution.

Lawyers are occasionally needed to clarify finer points of law. However, I am against calling in the lawyers too soon. I have nothing against lawyers, but all too often lawyers can mean litigation, and litigation is costly. Sometimes it costs more for an insurer to fight a claim than to pay it.

The broker can make the claims settlement process easier. The claimant may want representation in claims negotiations, which is only natural. A good claims broker can help make this process seamless. Sometimes, of course, a broker will take the side of his or her client come hell or high water. That's probably natural. Unfortunately, if the claimant is making an unfair claim and is supported by the broker, the insurer will find itself in a very difficult situation. It is those cases that often can only be resolved by arbitration or in the courts.

Likewise, the policyholder will sometimes know that a claim is not covered, but lawyers will think they can find a hole in the policy wording that will allow the claim to be paid. Insurers should fight these cases with all the tools available to them.

Some claims scenarios are unbelievably complex. I won't name the companies involved due to confidentiality agreements, but Catlin was once involved in a situation where we had written liability coverage for two parties that blamed each other for the event that gave rise to a very large claim. It was an unbelievably complicated situation, and we were caught in the middle. However, by acting with the utmost professionalism and good faith, our claims team managed to negotiate a settlement between the parties, and the claim was paid in full within six months without litigation. The reputation of both parties remained intact without any undue publicity. My guess is that had the case gone to litigation, it could have taken possibly seven or eight years longer to resolve at the cost of tens – if not hundreds – of millions of extra dollars.

Unfortunately, I can think of similar cases – in which a claim could have, or even should have, been resolved quickly – that have gone on for years, producing huge legal fees, simply because the insurer would not sit down and negotiate with the client. Those kinds of cases give the insurance industry a very bad reputation.

5. RESERVES

How much is enough, but not too much?

Reserves – the amount of money that an insurer sets aside to cover its obligations – are as important to an insurer's success as underwriting and claims management.

There are different types of reserves. For example, insurers establish reserves for unearned premiums. Unearned premiums represent the amount of money an insurer would have to repay to a client if a policy is canceled before it expired. That type of reserve is relatively easy to calculate.

Insurers must also establish loss reserves, which represent the cost of all claims, plus associated expenses, that must be paid in the future in connection with policies that have already been underwritten. That's not so easy to calculate.

The art of loss reserving is under continual development, and I am happy to say that standards for reserving are far, far higher today than they were 40 years ago.

I first became involved with the reserving process shortly after I started working for a Lloyd's syndicate when I became interested in the process of calculating the 'reinsurance to close'. Lloyd's syndicates have historically operated under a system of three-year accounting. At the end of any year, the accounts are left open for another two years to allow time for claims to be filed. At the end of the third year, an amount of money is paid into the next year's account to cover any claims that may arise after the three-year period has passed. This 'reinsurance to close' allows the syndicate to 'close' its books for a given year.

Of course, in those days we had no actuarial support to determine the amount of reinsurance to close; it wasn't required. We could do almost whatever we wanted so long as the independent auditor approved (this would subsequently cause huge problems in the Lloyd's market). All the auditor wanted to know was that the reinsurance-to-close premium appeared to be sufficient, not whether it was necessarily accurate.

After several years, our syndicate had built up such a large surplus through the reinsurance-to-close process that we could have reported profits that far exceeded the syndicate's actual performance in any given year.

Those days are long over. Or are they?

From the 1990s, all Lloyd's managing agents have been required to have independent actuarial reviews of their loss reserves, and such reviews became commonplace throughout the insurance industry worldwide. Catlin hired its first actuarial employee in the late 1990s; now all insurers have in-house actuarial support.

Today, an insurer's reserves are scrutinized by many third parties: actuaries, regulators, securities analysts and rating agencies. The rules governing loss reserving – whether at Lloyd's or in any other insurance market – are both complex and stringent.

When it comes to reserves, there is no single correct figure. Actuaries can be seen as somewhat difficult characters because they seldom give you a straight answer. Paul Jardine, who became well-known in the insurance market as the chief actuary at Equitas, the Lloyd's 'lifeboat' established in 1996, and who went on to become a top executive at both Catlin and XL Catlin, often answered questions with the caveat 'within an actuarial range'.

When setting loss reserves, you are dealing with various uncertainties. How many claims will arise in the future against the policies you have written in a certain year? What will be the rate of inflation? Will courts become more generous when awarding damages covered by liability policies? So, when setting reserves, you must look at a range of outcomes and then select some value between the two endpoints.

Over an entire portfolio of business, I would defy anybody to set their reserves with an accuracy better than plus or minus 1 per cent of ultimate costs. At Catlin, over the years, we released an average of about 2 per cent from our reserves annually, which shows that we reserved appropriately. Of course, you never get it all correct. During most years we would have to strengthen reserves for some classes of business, but would produce larger-than-average releases from other classes that offset the reserve strengthening.

* * *

Another thing that has changed regarding reserving – and this is a major change – is that once upon a time the size of an insurer's loss reserves had no impact on its capital requirements. Today, the larger an insurer's loss reserves, the more capital it is required to hold. While one might think that over-reserving is a good thing (although the tax man would probably disagree if over-reserving is used to hide taxable profits), insurers now get hit with a larger capital requirement if their reserves are excessive.

The best way of judging how well an insurer is managed is to look at its reserving practices. If a company must frequently increase its reserves retrospectively, an observer could wonder whether the insurer has been declaring profits that did not actually exist, whether it does not have enough knowledge about the business it has written or whether it's just plain unlucky.

Over Catlin's 31 years of existence, we had to strengthen reserves on a net basis in only three years. Once was in the mid-1990s, when all Lloyd's syndicates had to contribute to the funding of Equitas. The other two occasions were in the early 2000s, when we had to increase casualty reserves arising from policies underwritten in the late 1990s. That happened because actuaries failed to realize that the size of judgments made by US courts were rising much more quickly than previously thought and that in some instances case law had changed. Most insurers that wrote US casualty business also increased their reserves in those years.

The reserving process can really help an insurer's management understand whether the company is producing an adequate profit margin. I think it is beneficial for anyone wanting to enter insurance company management to have some experience of reserving, just as underwriting and claims experience is also helpful. It is somewhat sad that, today, insurance companies tend to specialize management roles. I think underwriters become better at their jobs if they must deal with their dirty laundry, either through claims management or the reserving process.

* * *

Two important terms in the reserving process are 'incurred losses' and 'incurred-but-not-reported losses', known in the industry as simply 'IBNR'. Incurred losses refer to the total amount of paid claims and loss reserves associated with a particular time period for known losses that have not yet been paid. IBNR is an estimate of the claims arising from events that have already taken place but have not yet been reported to the insurer; in some cases, no one may have realized that such events had occurred. Together, incurred losses and IBNR combine to form the estimate of an insurer's total claims liabilities for a given year.

Back when I became interested in reserving back in the 1970s, we had some data that was rock-solid. We knew the gross and net premiums per class of business for each month, and we also knew the paid gross and net loss ratios. However, what was not so robust was the incurred loss data and the IBNR. With the incurred loss data, the problem was communication. We had to rely on brokers to report claims activity to the lead underwriter, which often was months in arrears. Then, as a largely following syndicate, we had to wait for the lead underwriter to tell us what was going on. So calculating incurred losses was often largely guesswork. We didn't have the models now available to calculate IBNR, so we had to make significant assumptions there, too. But, amazingly, we were never that far off.

As Catlin grew from a small Lloyd's syndicate to a major multinational insurance group, and as loss reserving practices became much more sophisticated, I still kept close watch on the reserving process. In later years, I got really involved as year-end approached.

I would first try to look at reserves from a helicopter viewpoint to get comfortable with the overall picture from a common-sense perspective. Before getting involved with the actuarial work, I'd take one step back and say, "Does this feel right?" Because if it didn't feel right, you wanted to find out damned quick why it didn't. I had to retain that high-level view throughout the process because, if I didn't, I risked getting buried in the weeds.

I probably drilled down into the reserving process and individual business classes more than many other CEOs would, however, possibly due to my underwriting background. I was usually looking for a greater than 10 per cent spread in ultimate loss ratios, either between our underwriters' estimates and those of our internal actuaries or between our own actuaries' estimates and those of the external actuaries. If there was anything greater than a 10 per cent spread, I'd want to know what was going on.

Everyone involved in the reserve review was an intelligent, rational professional, and there would always be differences of opinion because reserving is based on a range of outcomes. If a market is hardening or if policy conditions have tightened, an underwriter would naturally expect the loss ratio to decrease. Conversely, an underwriter would expect the loss ratio to rise in a soft market when he or she is broadening coverage or lowering deductibles. Actuaries generally are more cautious than underwriters in their assessments.

However, when there was more than a 10 per cent difference in estimates of ultimate loss ratios, I would tell the team to do the work again. Almost without exception, somebody – or occasionally several people – involved in the process had got something wrong.

I believe that it was important for me as a CEO to become involved in the reserving process because, as the adage goes, good numbers often continue to get better, but bad numbers only get worse. The last thing you want in reserving is a lot of bad numbers. Some of the biggest mistakes I've made in my life have occurred when I haven't followed my instincts.

The greatest area of uncertainty in the reserving process is usually tied to US casualty coverages. Some of these policies are what insurers regard as long-tail; claims are sometimes only known many years after the coverage was written. Property coverage and many forms of casualty coverage are relatively short-tail; the underwriter knows the quantum of claims to expect relatively quickly. An underwriter writing long-tail US casualty coverage not only has to cope with the delays that are inherent with the long-tail, but he or she may also be at the mercy of the American civil justice system, which can defy rhyme or reason. Long-tail casualty claims from the US have caused many insurers to become insolvent, and asbestos and pollution claims in particular nearly caused Lloyd's collapse during the 1990s.

Underwriting long-tail casualty business is inherently risky. It's difficult to price this type of coverage correctly in the first place, and bad things can happen as time passes. Inflation can rise, increasing claims costs. Interest rates can fall, meaning the insurer receives a lower rate of return on its investments. Courts can change how they compensate plaintiffs. And sometimes, like with asbestos and pollution claims, the underwriter may not have fully contemplated the nature of the risk at the time the policy was written.

If a class of business is difficult to underwrite, it's also probably difficult to reserve for it with precision. However, if an insurer can accurately set the range of outcomes, the underwriters can reprice policies they write in the future to recoup past losses.

I have always maintained that an insurer should write a balance of long-tail and short-tail business. The long-tail book gives the insurer cash flow to pay for short-term claims as they arise. If a catastrophe occurs, the short-tail book reprices virtually overnight, while it often takes much longer to reprice the long-tail book because the underwriter must wait for trends to emerge. In a worst-case scenario, an insurer under-reserves for casualty business for many years.

If reserving is linked to pricing, which is what almost always happens, the insurer may have under-reserved for many years. By the time the insurer has realized its errors, it could be insolvent. If you look at many insurer insolvencies both in the US and the UK – Transit Casualty, Mission, Ideal Mutual, Reliance, H.S. Weavers and Independent Insurance, to name just a few – you will see the same story over and over again: underpricing leading to poor reserving practices and vice versa.

* * *

35

It's not possible to discuss reserving without mentioning the 'cheating phase', a term coined by V.J. Dowling, the respected American securities analyst specializing in the insurance industry. According to Dowling, some insurance companies – despite the actuarial rigor that is now part of the reserving process – build up a pot of excess loss reserves during profitable underwriting years. They then empty the pot as underwriting conditions turn sour. This, Dowling says, is the 'cheating phase'. These insurers are still reporting decent profits, but their financial results do not reflect the actual state of the market.

I agree with Dowling that, looking back ten years or so, many insurers at one time or another 'cheated'. However, the ability to cheat has diminished as greater restrictions have been imposed by regulators and rating agencies on how far an insurer can set its reserves from the actuarial best estimate.

As I write this, the marketplace is entrenched in a competitive cycle in which rates for most classes of business are already low and still falling. Yet, some companies are still releasing a generous amount of reserves. Are they in the 'cheating phase'? Possibly. However, it is also true that insurers' attritional loss ratio (the ratio of losses to premiums, excluding natural catastrophe and large man-made losses) has held remarkably steady during the current cycle even though rates are falling. One would expect the attritional loss ratio to rise during the downward portion of a cycle.

Either risk management has greatly improved, reducing losses, or the industry has been reserved much better than anyone thought. Maybe the industry is just plain lucky. It's too early to tell which is correct, but for the moment I'm sticking with luck.

6. REINSURANCE

Think of it as a bookie, laying off some of his bets

The concept of reinsurance is often misunderstood by the outside world, so I would like to contextualize what reinsurance is, how it works and why insurers buy it[5]. Insurance professionals who understand reinsurance probably do not need to read this chapter, but I believe some explanation will help non-practitioners to see just how core reinsurance is to the insurance industry.

Reinsurance is exactly what it says on the tin: it's insurance purchased by an insurer. Reinsurance is a mechanism by which an insurer can spread risk, and it can do that in several different ways.

The two main types of reinsurance are treaty reinsurance and facultative reinsurance. Treaty reinsurance allows an insurer to automatically transfer risk to a reinsurer under the terms of an agreement with a reinsurer, called a treaty, most often negotiated annually. There are two types of treaty reinsurance: proportional and non-proportional, which I will explain later. In a facultative reinsurance transaction, an insurer purchases reinsurance protection on a policy-by-policy basis. Facultative reinsurance can also be structured proportionally or non-proportionally.

Through a reinsurance contract, the insurer 'cedes' risk to a reinsurer. For that reason, insurers participating in reinsurance contracts are sometimes known as 'ceding companies' or 'cedants'.

Proportional treaty reinsurance

The simplest form of reinsurance is proportional or pro-rata reinsurance, through which an insurer cedes either its whole portfolio or a certain portion of its portfolio to a reinsurer on a straight pro-rata basis. The reinsurer agrees to follow the same conditions of coverage as written in the primary policy, which is known as 'following the fortunes'.

---

5 For those looking for a comprehensive but easy-to-understand explanation of how reinsurance works, I suggest a publication by Munich Re: *RE.IN.SURANCE: A Basic Guide to Facultative and Treaty Reinsurance*. It can be downloaded at: https://www.munichre.com/site/mram/get/documents_E96160999/mram/assetpool.mr_america/PDFs/3_Publications/reinsurance_basic_guide.pdf.

Typically, the insurer will receive a fee (sometimes known as a ceding commission or 'overrider') to cover its expense of underwriting the underlying policies in the first place. The insurer would also normally be entitled to a profit commission that is based on the overall profitability of the treaty. Quite often, a proportional treaty would also include a 'deficit clause' so that losses in previous years of a relationship must be repaid to the reinsurer through premiums before any profit commission is paid in subsequent years.

There are many ways an insurer and reinsurer can structure a proportional treaty.

Non-proportional (or excess-of-loss) treaty reinsurance

Non-proportional reinsurance and excess-of-loss reinsurance mean virtually the same thing. Through non-proportional reinsurance, an insurer transfers risk from losses that arise from the same event, such as an earthquake, hurricane or some other natural disaster. Due to this common usage, non-proportional reinsurance is often called 'catastrophe reinsurance'.

This reinsurance is written on an excess-of-loss basis, rather than a proportional basis. For example, an insurer may retain $50 million of risk from one natural peril and then reinsure any losses exceeding that amount up to the limit of the treaty. This type of reinsurance is primarily a mechanism to provide capital relief to the ceding insurer by limiting its exposure to a catastrophic event. If the insurer didn't buy this coverage, the aggregation of many different claims arising from the same catastrophe could create too much stress on the insurer's balance sheet.

Facultative reinsurance

Facultative reinsurance, which I mentioned in Chapter 3, allows an insurer to reinsure a specific policy or risk. Think of it as a one-off form of reinsurance. Sometimes facultative reinsurance is written on a follow-form basis, but sometimes it simply reinsures one of the specific risks covered by a policy.

For example, if an insurer writes a policy with a $100 million limit, it may wish to enter into a facultative reinsurance agreement whereby the insurer retains the first $50 million of exposure for any one loss against the policy and cedes any loss exceeding that amount. Alternatively, using the same example, the contract could retain an aggregate amount of $50 million of losses against the policy (even if they stem from multiple events), with the reinsurer assuming any losses exceeding $50 million in the aggregate.

Sometimes, particularly in a competitive or 'soft' market, an insurer can structure a facultative facility that allows it to cede on a 50/50 basis any risk the insurer writes. Underwriters may buy such reinsurance for capital reasons: e.g. the insurer wanted to assume a bigger position on an account than its balance sheet can withstand, so a facultative facility allows the insurer to offload part of the risk to reduce its potential liability to a more manageable level for capital purposes

If an insurer writes a package policy (lots of different types of coverages included in one policy), it can use facultative reinsurance to transfer certain types of exposures (e.g. casualty) while retaining others with which the insurer is more comfortable (e.g. property). This type of mechanism also allows an insurer to balance his portfolio among the different classes of coverage it writes.

* * *

Reinsurance has been around for a long time. The first recorded reinsurance contract was written in 1370 when the insurer of a shipment from Genoa, Italy, to Bruges in Belgium transferred part of the risk to another insurer. The first specialist reinsurance company was Cologne Re, now ultimately owned by Berkshire Hathaway, which was founded in 1846. Reinsurance is an intrinsic part of the insurance industry, and many insurance companies write both insurance and reinsurance policies.

In a perfect world, reinsurance provides value to both the insurer and the reinsurer. If the buyer is in profit because it has effectively transferred significant losses to the reinsurer, the buyer would be expected over time to help pay back the reinsurer by continuing to renew contracts, possibly at a higher rate to reflect the insurer's adverse loss experience. Alternatively, if the ceding company has a clean loss history, it would expect over time to be charged a lower rate, plus it may receive substantial profit commissions.

* * *

There is one other reinsurance-related term that I would like to define: 'retrocession'. It sounds complicated, but it's really pretty simple. A retrocession is simply a reinsurance transaction in which the ceding company is a reinsurer rather than an insurer. In other words, a retrocession is simply the reinsurance of reinsurance! Retrocessions are usually written to transfer catastrophe reinsurance risk. Retrocessions allow reinsurers, just as insurers, to spread the risk they assume and to manage their capital.

However, there have been some instances, such as the so-called 'LMX spiral' of the 1980s, which had the opposite effect and concentrated risk among just a few underwriters. In those days, risk was ceded several times from one reinsurer to another. In other words, Reinsurer A retroceded risk to Reinsurer B, which then retroceded to Reinsurer C, which then retroceded back to Reinsurer A ... you can get the picture and now realize why it is called a spiral. Such a spiral can produce concentration of risk – rather than diversification, which is what is intended – because often only a handful of reinsurers underwrite high-layer retrocessions. In other words, when a spiral occurs, fewer companies become the ultimate payers of the underlying catastrophe exposure.

At this point, let's leave the subject of reinsurance to rest for a while. Don't be disappointed, though: I will return to the subject soon enough.

7. The Broker-Insurer Relationship

We need each other, but can we actually get along?

If you look at insurance as a value proposition from the client's point of view, you should probably start with the broker.

A commercial insurance buyer hires a broker before any insurance is purchased. It is the broker who represents the client, not the insurer. A broker should not only act as an intermediary, but should also serve as a consultant as well, discussing with the client the risks it faces and the methods that can potentially be used to mitigate or transfer these risks. The broker works for the client, not the insurer, and that's the way it should be.

Most brokers do their jobs well. A small number don't, but I could say the same thing about insurers.

Insurers underwriting commercial property/casualty business in most parts of the world couldn't survive without brokers because it is the broker that actually produces the business for the insurer. Many insurers are not equipped to acquire accounts on their own. That's the way the system works, and it would be difficult – if not impossible – to change it.

However, there are problems inherent in the broker-insurer relationship. In most cases, brokers are not remunerated by fees paid by the client, as is the case in most other sectors of the financial services industry. Instead, insurance brokers are most often remunerated by the insurer through commissions. The broker's goal – as it should be for the sake of the broker's own investors – is to maximize commissions; the insurer, of course, wants to keep commissions as low as possible, while still maintaining access to a supply of quality business.

In addition, there can be many brokers involved in a complex, big-ticket policy, such as those underwritten at Lloyd's. When coverage is complicated or hard to place, the retail broker will often call on a wholesale broker, who has expertise in certain areas that the retail broker lacks. If coverage is to be placed at Lloyd's, the wholesale broker will then contact a London broker to place the coverage with Lloyd's syndicates. That's at least three brokers in the chain, and all of them will want a piece of the commission. That obviously causes brokers to seek higher commissions from the insurers with which the coverage is placed.

This is a relatively simple example. Sometimes there can be four or more brokers in the chain.

When there is a chain of brokers as I have described, I don't like it when the brokers in the middle collect money from the transaction in an opaque manner. I think that is not only wrong; I think it's morally reprehensible. The client should know just how many brokers are in the chain and what each is getting in terms of commission. That's simply common decency and good business practice.

* * *

I am a strong supporter of brokers – and I have been since I started in the insurance industry – because I believe that the broker system offers efficient 'distribution'[6] for insurance carriers and offers choice for the buyer. Working at Lloyd's, I learned quickly that it was impossible for an underwriter to become accessible to clients around the world that are looking for many different types of insurance. Trying to do so would be cost-prohibitive, while a broker – who deals with large numbers of insurers – should be able to provide this type of distribution at a much more reasonable cost.

Brokers provide choice to a client, again something about which I feel strongly. If a client dealt solely with a single carrier, the client would be in a position where it had to accept whatever the insurer offered. It would be difficult for the client – unless it was very large – to solicit quotes from different insurers for different classes of business and then make informed decisions. A broker does just that. Because the broker is an expert, it can advise its clients not only about how their insurance should be placed, but also about risk management. A broker can advise a client, for example, that it may be cheaper to retain some risk than to buy insurance to cover everything. As a client's risk management issues become more complex, the more it probably needs a broker.

The really constructive part of the broker's role is explaining what is available to the client from the insurance industry. Brokers can do that on an independent basis because they have access to many different carriers.

It's the broker's job to get the best deal for its client. However, some critics complain that brokers all too often look for the best deal for themselves.

* * *

---

6   Distribution is the term commonly used in the insurance industry to describe the method used by an insurer to reach its policyholders. For example, through brokers, through agents representing only one insurer or through direct contact with the client (a direct-writing insurer).

In most cases, once the coverage is placed, the placing broker deducts the agreed commission from the premium paid by the client. As the premium makes its way from the client to the insurer, each of the brokers along the way takes its share of the commission before the insurer ever gets paid.

A lot of clients probably do not have any idea how much money is paid from the premium to the brokers in the middle. To use a simplistic example, a client pays £100 annually for a property policy and after four years has a claim for £200. The client cannot see a problem; it has been paying £100 annually for four years, so the insurer still is making a profit. However, if the insurer is only getting 70 per cent of the premium and still has its own overheads to pay, the insurer is not actually making any money. People often think that insurance is not good value, and if you look at it this way, it probably isn't due to the cost of process *(see Chapter 8)* and intermediation.

There are occasions, especially during a hard market, where an underwriter will quote a premium net of commissions. The underwriter is essentially saying, "Okay, here's what I want for the risk; what you take out on the way through is up to you." There's some validity in that process as the underwriter is getting an agreed amount of premium. The trouble, in my opinion, is that there is absolutely no control whatsoever over what's taken out in the middle. I believe the client should know what the underwriter receives net of commissions for the coverage. I wonder whether many clients realize that often 30 to 40 per cent of the premium it has paid is being collected by brokers rather than the underwriter?

In some cases, an underwriter must pay a higher rate of commission because business is written by a managing general agent (MGA) or some other form of coverholder[7], which does a lot of the work the insurer would normally do. Obviously, an insurer must pay a higher commission upfront to a coverholder as it has additional duties compared with a broker. But I also think that much of a coverholder's additional remuneration should be paid by the insurer through profit commissions based on how much money the business written by the coverholder makes for the insurer. While dealing with coverholders does increase an insurer's acquisition costs, it should lower its corporate costs because the coverholder is responsible for some of the work the insurer ordinarily must perform.

*　*　*

7　A coverholder is an insurance intermediary authorized by an insurer or Lloyd's managing agent to enter into contracts of insurance in the name of insurers or syndicates, subject to certain written terms and conditions. A coverholder is often described as having 'binding authority' for an insurer because it is able to 'bind' the insurer to a certain risk.

One of the more telling conversations I ever had was with a newly appointed CEO of an insurance broker who had previously worked as an investment banker. It was his first week on the job, and he knew very little about the insurance industry. We chatted for about 90 minutes and agreed that we would meet again in six months, once he had learned more about the business and could measure up some of the things I had told him.

When I saw him again, I asked what during the past six months had surprised him most about the insurance industry. He replied that it was brokers' lack of ability to persuade a client to pay a fee to the broker. I then asked him how many people at his company could do that. A handful? The CEO said he had only found two people who could sell a fee to a client. Just two. Of course, nearly all employees in the investment bank, where the CEO had previously worked, are taught how to sell a fee to a client and how to demonstrate the value added by the bank to justify the fee.

Any client can go to a bank and pay a $1 million fee for a piece of work. The same client can go to an insurance broker and get the same sort of work done for no fee. That doesn't make any sense at all, and the system as it exists can lead to bad selling and bad purchasing.

In my opinion, insurance brokers have not historically differentiated to a sufficient extent between good insurers and bad ones. And, by a bad one, I mean an insurer that either does not place enough emphasis on quality claims practices or simply thinks the best way to make money is to dispute claims whenever possible. In recent years, this situation has improved because brokers have finally realized that they will probably lose an account if claims are not handled properly. The broker could even be sued. Whereas, if you're dealing with a good carrier that does pay valid claims appropriately and proactively, the broker will likely retain the account.

A broker must help a client select from among good insurers and bad insurers; the broker should be able to tell them apart, while most clients – through no fault of their own – wouldn't have a clue.

Using this same logic, insurers must rely on brokers. We spent 30 years at Catlin establishing our reputation as being a prompt and fair payer of valid claims. We believed that was the right thing to do, and we were proud of our efforts. However, we had to rely on brokers to communicate that value proposition to the policyholder. Would they do that? Would they sometimes sacrifice quality for perhaps a larger commission? You be the judge.

* * *

Each year in September, the leaders of the insurance/reinsurance industry gather in Monte Carlo for the *Rendez-Vous de Septembre*. The *Rendez-Vous* consists of several days of high-level meetings among insurers, reinsurers and brokers to discuss relationships and to set the stage for year-end renewals. It can be a lot of fun, but it's also hard work. A typical day starts with a business breakfast at 7 a.m., includes more than a dozen one-on-one meetings and ends at midnight or later after a business dinner.

A couple of years ago, Paul Brand and I had met during the *Rendez-Vous* with two high-ranking executives of a major broker. Basically, the broker's top management team asked for the meeting because they wanted to extract more commissions from Catlin. I had already had a conversation regarding this topic with the No. 2 guy, but now he was trying again by bringing his superior along.

I decided that I had to defend Catlin's turf. So I asked the No. 2 guy a series of questions for the benefit of his boss.

I began: "When was the last time you came to see me to complain about the way Catlin mismanaged a claim?"

"I can't remember. I'm not sure if I ever have," replied the No. 2 guy.

"How many other carriers can you say that about?" I asked.

"I'm not sure. I'm not sure I can," was his response.

"When was the last time that you came to me and complained that we'd behaved badly on an endorsement or some other matter?"

"I can't remember. I'm not sure I ever have."

"How many other carriers can you say that about?"

"I'm not sure. I'm not sure that I can."

"When have we ever given you cause to inform your E&O (errors and omissions) underwriters about an issue on a policy placed with Catlin in case a lawsuit against you arises?"

"I'm not sure; I don't know that I ever have."

"How many other leading underwriters can you say that about?"

"Maybe one or two."

"How many times has your company lost business because of our behavior?"

"Um ... I don't know that I can think of any situation."

"So, in the round, would you say that we actually give you a pretty good service?"

"Yes, you're one of our preferred carriers because you give good service, you're consistent and you're fair," he said.

"When have you ever paid me for that service, just so I understand?" I asked.

"We don't pay for that service, but we do try to show you good business."

"I'm very appreciative of that. So, just to be clear, you're asking me to pay you an increased commission, which you're asking of all insurers, including the following market, and you're asking for the same level of payment from everyone, even though many of these insurers offer you no added value. We keep creating business opportunities for you, we honor our promise to pay and we try to make certain that you never lose a piece of business due to our performance. So, if you want to talk about me paying you an extra commission along with the rest of the market, maybe I should ask you to pay me for all those things I do for you for nothing."

He turned silent.

I then said to him, "When I look at our largest brokers, the growth in income to Catlin from your company is the lowest over the past three reporting periods. So, let's look at this: you're not growing as quickly with us as others are; we're giving you the best service in the marketplace by your statement, not mine. And now you want me to pay you more money at a time when margins are really tight. Why would I want to do that? Maybe the best thing for me to do is to stop giving you all those good services, and just give them to your competitors."

The top guy was lost for words. He asked his No. 2 if I had told the truth. "Yeah, it is true," he said. The CEO closed the meeting by saying that the broker would rethink the request.

Following the meeting, an assistant who helped me manage my meetings in Monte Carlo, commented: "What on earth happened at that meeting? Most people walk out of here smiling. Those two walked out with their shoulders sloped down; they were thoroughly depressed."

While the main purpose of my conversation was to avoid paying the additional commission, I also wanted to ask whether the broker actually valued the service that Catlin as an insurer provided to it.

However, you can also look at it another way. It illustrates how insurers, including Catlin, have not been able to promote sufficiently their value-added capabilities.

Brokers rate insurers primarily on things like turnaround time, product innovation and price. They overlook the true differentiator among insurers: how well they back up their promise to pay. As clients don't have that many claims, many brokers don't take notice. However, when you think about it, paying valid claims is what insurance is all about.

* * *

The balance of power between the broker and insurer oscillates through market cycles, as you'd expect. Sometimes the insurer has the upper hand, and sometimes it's the broker which can call most of the shots. As I write this we are in a soft market, and it currently feels as if brokers are winning more than insurers, but that will even out over time.

Unfortunately, by its nature, the broker-insurer relationship can – and does – become adversarial. Brokers can – and will – do almost anything to make sure they get the best deal for their clients while maximizing commissions. Brokers in the past threatened to cease doing business with Catlin if we refused to cave in regarding a certain issue, even if that would be a severe disadvantage for us.

Personally, I was never reluctant to take on a broker in such a situation. After enduring the trials and tribulations of setting up my own business, there's not a broker in the world who was going to frighten me, and no one broker ever had absolute power over me or my company. I have also found that brokers sometimes make empty threats. It's a question of the underwriter having the courage to say "no". Is the underwriter prepared to lose a piece of business to make a point? Brokers must have discipline, but so must underwriters.

The balance of power becomes dangerous when an individual broker places so much business with a certain insurer that the broker can begin to exert undue influence. I've always worked hard to make certain that Catlin had significant trading relationships with many brokers, making sure that no one broker ever brought in more than about 20 per cent of our business. If our largest broker would suddenly stop doing business with us, we would certainly feel the pain, but we would not collapse. Once a broker knows that he cannot exert that kind of influence, it will back off when the underwriter says "no" because it's probably in the broker's best interest to continue doing business with the insurer, especially if the insurer is a quality company.

* * *

Brokers are a key player in another type of challenge facing the insurance industry, but I will discuss that in the next chapter.

8. THE PROCESS PROBLEM

Data handling is a do-or-die issue for the insurance industry

If I look back at the property/casualty insurance industry over the past 40 years, tremendous progress has been made in so many different areas: modeling, claims handling, capital management, professionalism, the level of talent ... the list is long.

The one area that hasn't moved on much during that 40-year period is what I call 'process': how insurers and brokers obtain data, handle data and process data. Frankly, we are still pushing paper around to a ludicrous extent. In London, brokers show up at the Lloyd's Underwriting Room or insurers' offices carrying huge files of paper. We are still entering the same data at nearly every point from initial quote to policy issuance. The whole 'process' is unbelievably inefficient.

The difference between property/casualty insurance compared with nearly any other sector of the financial services industry is that the capture of data is extremely variable. By that I mean that if you do solve the data capture problem for a certain class of business, that does not mean you have solved the problem with the remaining classes. My guess is that on average there is only about 50 per cent data commonality between two classes of business. The set of data required for a property insurance policy is very different from what you would need for a D&O (directors' and officers' liability) policy.

Therefore, we must establish systems that are able to collect data differently according to the class of business to be underwritten. In other words, one size does not fit all. This leads to a level of complexity that you don't see, for example, among stockbrokers, where probably 95 per cent of the data is common from one client to another.

* * *

To someone not familiar with the insurance industry, what is meant by 'process'? Here's an example.

A client contacts a broker to obtain coverage for certain exposures. The client provides the broker with information about the exposures so the broker can then make a proposition to underwriters on behalf of the client. This information is often given to the broker in the form of paper documents, which the broker enters into its system. The broker then produces what in London is known as a 'slip', which is a precis of the proposed policy based on that data.

After negotiating the price and terms of the policy, the coverage is agreed among the insurers, the broker and the client. The broker must then issue a policy on behalf of the underwriter, and the broker also must then send an invoice or a debit note to the client to pay the premium. The premium is paid to the broker, is entered into the broker's ledger and is eventually passed on to the insurer with the commission deducted.

That's a lot of process.

If there is an endorsement to the policy, a similar process is followed. Then, should there be a claim against the policy, yet another similar process is followed backwards and forwards between the client and the insurer, with the broker in the middle. Of course, as I pointed out in the previous chapter, there is often more than one broker involved in a relationship – for example, a retail broker, a wholesale broker and a London wholesale broker – and the data and the process must flow through each of these parties.

All too often, each broker will be required to manually input data because of system incompatibility, sometimes creating quadruple entry when – in this day and age – single entry is all that should be necessary. Not only is this duplication costly and time-consuming, errors can and do happen at each step of the process.

The process problem exists worldwide. It is less pronounced for personal lines and small commercial business, which is more straightforward and most often handled by just one broker. The problem grows larger as risks become more complex and more brokers become involved. It is particularly pronounced at Lloyd's, which is a subscription market where many underwriters can participate on a single policy.

The crux of the problem is that the same data is entered several times rather than just once: what is known as single data entry. What we need is one version of the truth. However, insurers use the same data for underwriting, for actuarial pricing, for actuarial reserving, for claims, for finance. We have fallen into the trap of collecting the same data in four or five different ways, which means we often have four or five versions of the truth.

When you think about how people communicate, one person probably communicates about 80 per cent of what he or she means to say to another person. If data is communicated – or entered – four or five times as part of the process, it's easy to see that the insurer – as the party at the end of the chain – may only be getting half of the truth.

I can't understand why, in this day and age, the premium for a policy goes from the client to the retail broker to the wholesale broker to the London broker and finally to the underwriter? How is that an efficient process? There are costs associated all the way. While interest rates are currently low, the time value of money is now a lot less than it once was. However, if interest rates should rise, each party in the chain would be increasingly tempted to hang on to that premium a bit longer. That's what happened 20 years ago, when a much greater percentage of broker revenues came from investment income on money actually owed to insurers or clients.

*   *   *

When you consider the insurance process problem, you can point your finger in a lot of directions because there are certainly many contributors.

The process is primarily driven by brokers, which serve as the interface between the policyholder and the insurer. Brokers have historically believed that part of their value-added proposition is managing the process and, indeed, owning the process helps brokers retain business – or at least that is the perception. Thus, brokers have been very keen to keep control of the process.

The information that must be communicated by the client to insurers is transmitted through the broker. In the same way, if there is a claim, information flows from the insurer or claims adjuster through the broker (or brokers) to the policyholder. If you look at it this way, potentially half of a broker's responsibilities relates to process rather than the actual placement of policies.

A big problem, however, is that the broker doesn't actually pay for the cost of the process. You could argue that the insurer pays for it or you could say that the client pays for it, but no one – neither the insurer nor the client – holds the broker accountable for the frictional processing costs.

In 2014, Catlin's last full year of operations as an independent company, we spent nearly $1 billion – or about 24 per cent of net premiums earned – on what are known as 'policy acquisition costs', basically money paid to brokers. That means we probably paid brokers approximately $500 million for process, with little or no accountability. Insurers establish key performance indicators (KPIs) for auditors, consultants and almost any other counterparty. But we do not generally hold brokers to KPIs, even though we pay them nearly a quarter of net premiums earned.

As a consequence, there's never been any real incentive for the broker community to become efficient at processing. As brokers are remunerated through commissions, if processing costs are more than brokers anticipate, they simply seek to increase commissions. Again, whether the insurer or the client pays the added cost is not totally clear.

If we as an industry don't sort out this issue in a reasonably short time frame, let's say five years, someone else will. There are companies, such as Google or Microsoft, whose *modus operandi* is utmost efficiency. Companies such as these look at the insurance industry and must think we are absolute Luddites. I fear that these companies are becoming interested in sorting out the process problem for us. If this happens, it could cause great disruption for the commercial insurance business.

For brokers, controlling a major portion of the process gives them better control of the client. Would brokers want to give that up? Brokers currently do not reserve for ongoing process costs and expenses, such as long-tail claims-related expenses. If brokers were no longer remunerated by insurers for their contributions to process, they would have a strain on their balance sheets due to costs that they will incur in the future.

Why shouldn't a company like Microsoft or Google simply replace the broker? That would not be good for the client, in my opinion, because a 'processor' would not be able to offer the value-added services that an insurance broker can provide to its clients: advising on alternative markets, loss control engineering, claims advice, etc. We shouldn't eliminate the broker from the process because the broker clearly does add value in many different ways.

From an underwriter's perspective, giving one company control over the process for the industry, rather than splitting it among competing brokers, could put huge pressure on insurance pricing.

*   *   *

One of the industry's biggest problems is that most of the data we use is collected and manipulated manually. You would think by now a proposal form for coverage would be electronically completed by a client, passed seamlessly to the broker, which would then pass it on electronically – untouched – to the insurer. Wrong! At each step of the way, the data is often re-entered, partly because of system incompatibility.

Why hasn't the industry done anything to solve the process problem, I hear you ask. There are several reasons. First, there has been a lack of appetite to address the issue. Underwriters have essentially paid brokers to provide much of the process, but the broker does not provide underwriting capital. If you are not accountable for something (i.e. you do not have a financial stake in the ultimate result), you're never as efficient as if you are accountable for it. That's a fact of life. There's little incentive on the brokers' part to sort the process problem out; if brokers think they're not making enough money, they can always attempt to charge more commission.

Secondly, underwriters find it difficult to agree with each other, and likewise brokers find it hard to concur with competitors. So, there exists what I believe is a false sense of competitive advantage; no one wants their rivals to use the same systems. This has now become a competitive disadvantage for everybody involved.

What's the solution? Utopia, most people would argue, is what is called market reform. All of the process would go through a central, streamlined system based on single data entry. That should make everybody happy. Or would it? To achieve true market reform, many different counterparties would have to agree to sit around a table, hold hands and agree on a solution. While many of these players say they could do that in principle, in reality insurers and brokers do not like to change the way they currently do things It gets too personal.

While I would support any form of market reform in principle, I must be honest and say that I am far from convinced that true market reform is easily achievable.

The other option is that the process problem will eventually be solved on a business-to-business basis. In other words, a select number of insurers and brokers will individually find solutions to the problem, bypassing smaller players. This, of course, would lead to a contraction of the marketplace because each insurer would only want to deal with a certain number of brokers and, likewise, brokers would not want to deal with more insurers than absolutely necessary. Such a B-to-B relationship would still require a common standard for data entry, and the market appears to be miles away from that at the moment. And, of course, this type of solution is complicated by the need for different types of data for different classes of business.

The process problem has been kicked into the long grass time and time again. Lloyd's spent five years and a reported £70 million on Project Kinnect, a proposed electronic trading platform, only to walk away from it in 2006. But the process problem is becoming less and less sustainable; the costs are just too high. The insurance industry must deal with it or, as I said earlier, it could be solved by parties outside the industry.

If that happens, we cannot complain if we don't like the solution.

PART II
BUILDING A BUSINESS FOR THE FUTURE: THE CATLIN STORY

9. Beginnings

How I found myself working in insurance …
and growing to like it

I began working at Lloyd's in 1973, but I don't think it's fair to say that I joined Lloyd's. It's more like I fell into Lloyd's.

My father was a doctor, and he wanted me to follow in his footsteps and study medicine. I didn't want to do that, however. I was not into academia as a teenager living in Essex, and so my father and I made a deal. I would not try to become a doctor; I would become a dentist instead.

That might have been fine, except I didn't get the grades necessary to be accepted by a dental school. I failed twice. I was adrift and didn't really know what I wanted to be or to do. In fact, I knew more about what I didn't want to do. I surely didn't want to be stuck in an office all day. I had no desire whatsoever to go to a university and get a degree for the hell of it. I could never, in those days, study for the sake of studying.

I liked the outdoors, so doing something that would allow me to be outside could have been attractive. I was good with my hands. My friends probably won't believe this, but as a student I had built a boat, a hi-fi cabinet, fruit bowls and table lamps. I could take a Morris Minor engine apart and put it back together again. I considered becoming a policeman, I considered joining the army and I thought about going to Cornwall to work in the clotted cream business for friends of my father, something I had previously done during summer vacations.

Deep down, I also had a hankering to run my own business. My grandfather, my father's father, had run a successful printing business during and after the Second World War. I had always admired him.

Then I met a guy sailing, which was one of my hobbies. He told me that he needed a boy in his box at Lloyd's. I didn't have a clue as to what a box was or, for that matter, Lloyd's. I didn't know the difference between Lloyd's of London and Lloyds Bank. But, as I wasn't doing anything else, I agreed to go for an interview. My mother thought I was being silly because she thought I would never be able to endure an office job.

My hair had grown down to my shoulders, so I had it cut off. I wore a suit that was bright blue with flared trousers. I put on my only proper shirt, which was yellow with a huge collar, along with a kipper tie and my only pair of leather shoes, which were brown with stacked heels. I thought I was conforming!

* * *

The interview was at Anton Underwriting Agency Limited, which at the time was owned by Antony Gibbs & Sons, the merchant bank, which also had an insurance brokerage arm. A few days later, I was offered a job at a salary of £950 per year as what was known as a 'scratch boy' for Lloyd's Syndicate 264[8], a marine syndicate which was managed by Anton. I was to begin work on October 1, 1973, reporting to Brian Evens, the syndicate's active underwriter[9].

Lloyd's was then a very different place to what it is today. The box at which I worked was located in the Lloyd's Underwriting Room in what is now remembered as the 1958 Lloyd's Building, across Lime Street from the current Lloyd's headquarters (The building was demolished some years ago to make way for the current Willis Building.) The atmosphere in the Underwriting Room was that of a male-only club; women weren't allowed. There were no computer screens; they did not appear for another decade. Eight people worked in the box, and we shared one desktop electronic calculator among us. A calculator cost a lot of money back in those days, £140 or so, which would be worth about £1,500 today. All it did was add, subtract, multiply and divide.

If it were today, I wouldn't have been hired. The job of scratch boy no longer exists at any Lloyd's managing agency. I spent my days photocopying, filing and acting as an entry boy, writing down the decisions that the underwriters had taken. (When an underwriter agrees to underwrite a policy, he initials – or scratches – the paperwork supplied by the broker, hence the term 'scratch boy'.) Everything was entered by hand in those days.

The guy who got me the job resigned from the syndicate soon afterwards to become a broker. I got his job, although I still had to do my old job for about 18 months or so. He was still regarded as an assistant, but he got the cream of the ledger work and he was allowed to underwrite business that

---

8 Lloyd's is not an insurance company but rather a marketplace composed of many individual underwriting syndicates. Each syndicate is made up of one or more investors, called 'Names', which provide capital to the syndicate. Formerly, wealthy individuals were most commonly Names, but today the vast majority of the capital backing Lloyd's syndicates comes from corporations (what is commonly known as 'corporate capital'). The activities of the syndicate are performed by the employees of a 'managing agency'.

9 An 'active underwriter' is the individual with principal authority to accept insurance and reinsurance risk on behalf of the members of a Lloyd's syndicate.

had already been promised by the underwriter and to agree endorsements to policies. Occasionally, he got to do a bit of real underwriting; now I also received this opportunity.

A few months later, I realized that no one was helping Brian Evens calculate the syndicate's reinsurance to close, so I offered to help. I was 22 at the time. I suggested that we kept a file of how we calculated the reinsurance to close. It sounds unbelievable now, but all the calculations had been done on brown paper envelopes, and no records were kept of anything. Helping Brian with the reinsurance to close allowed me to learn more about the business, and by now I was doing some simple underwriting of renewal business. As we were basically a following syndicate, we didn't need to make any big decisions.

In late 1978, Brian decided that the syndicate should begin writing an energy account and a reinsurance account. No one but Brian had a clue about what to do, and he wasn't too sure, either. So, with Brian's blessing, I took it upon myself to learn about energy insurance and reinsurance. I was pretty much self-taught. I read some books, but they weren't all that helpful. What did help was to dissect underwriting slips, which are basically summaries of policies. I began to understand why certain underwriting decisions were made and how policies were priced.

Virtually single-handedly, I developed from the ground up an energy account and a reinsurance account starting with the 1979 underwriting year. For the first time, brokers were seeking me out, half of them energy brokers and half reinsurance brokers. Bizarrely, the brokers liked that mix because it gave the energy brokers fresh faces – the reinsurance brokers – with whom to talk while they were queueing to see me at the box, and vice-versa. Most syndicates had separate reinsurance and energy underwriters, so the brokers would usually stand in a queue with the same familiar faces. At our box, the brokers didn't necessarily meet the same people.

At the time, there were a lot of people my age who had just started as brokers, probably because broking back then paid better than underwriting. I steadily built up a network of brokers of my own age who had been given some authority, and I remain close friends with many of them more than 35 years later. Even though I worked for a syndicate that had always been a following syndicate, I persuaded some of my broker chums that I could lead something for them. I started leading some excess-of-loss reinsurance contracts and eventually began to lead energy business.

That was the time – when I became comfortable underwriting energy and reinsurance business – that I truly decided to make a go of it at Lloyd's and in the insurance business. It had taken me several years to work out how

Lloyd's and the insurance market really came together. There wasn't a book you could buy in those days to explain it, and I couldn't find anyone inside the firm who could explain it to me, either.

It was also at that time that I had worked out for myself that insurance had a true social value. I had not been able to decide whether Lloyd's was an institution that added social value or whether it was just a big gambling casino. The truth of the matter was that it was probably a bit of both.

After a year or so as a true underwriter, the competition noticed, and I began getting some job offers. I remember one offer came from Anthony Bartleet of Murray Lawrence & Partners, one of Lloyd's top managing agencies at the time (Murray Lawrence later became chairman of Lloyd's). Anthony wanted me to become the deputy underwriter of one of the Murray Lawrence syndicates. That job would have paid me £9,000 annually, with a company car and a profit commission that could have been worth another £6,000 per year. That was a lot of money considering that I was making only £5,000 at the time with no car and no profit commission; it was terrible pay.

In those days, if you got a job offer from a rival agency, you waited until your prospective boss spoke with your current boss. I did suggest to Brian Evens that we might want to have a cup of tea together during the afternoon. Then, unannounced, Anthony showed up at our box at 10 a.m. to have a word with Brian. He came back from the conversation looking as black as thunder and said, "Stephen, we had better make that a cup of coffee!"

I explained to Brian that I had been approached by Anthony and all I had done was listen. He asked what I had been offered, and he shook his head when I told him. "This is bloody ridiculous to be offered a deputy job at the age of 25," he remarked and asked for some time to think about it. Eventually, Brian offered me a raise to £8,750 per annum, a car and profit commission "in due course". He also promised that I would someday be made deputy underwriter.

I stayed on, much to my wife Helen's consternation. I believed I had a job to finish.

Over time, I received other offers, including one from Ian Posgate, who at the time was considered by some as the most successful underwriter at Lloyd's; Posgate was nicknamed 'Goldfinger' because of the great returns he had made. However, a lot of people in the market weren't convinced that Posgate was all that some people thought, and history proves that they were correct.

While Posgate offered me my own syndicate, I declined.

It was also about this time that I bought a reinstatement premium protection policy to cover the reinsurance account that I was writing.

I bought it from Richard Outhwaite, who would later become a well-known figure at Lloyd's due to the huge losses incurred by his syndicates. Buying the policy was a true no-brainer for me because it provided nearly full protection for our account. Plus, we were not required to pay reinstatement premiums[10], even though our syndicate was collecting reinstatement premiums on the reinsurance contracts we had written when they had paid out. In other words, as the gross loss on our reinsurance account increased, so did our net profit!

That type of reinsurance arbitrage became an important concept to me, and one I remembered well once I had established my own syndicate.

Life went on for another three or four years. I was still underwriting the reinsurance and energy accounts and was acting as Brian's deputy, although I did not have the formal title and I had not yet received the promised profit commission.

Near the end of 1983, I was finally formally appointed as deputy underwriter, but the salary increase that I received was less than the amount I had received the year before. I was surprised by that because the earnings from the accounts I wrote had more than doubled the syndicate's profits. In addition, another employee had been made a director of Anton Underwriting Agency; I thought it should have been me.

I finally complained to Brian and was offered an ex-gratia bonus of £5,000 and a firm promise that I would be given a profit commission the following year. Now that I had a child, that extra money would come in handy.

However, I was about to refuse what Brian was offering me.

Something else had occurred. Hugh Jago, chairman of Jago Venton Underwriting Agencies Ltd., several months earlier had offered to back me if I ever wanted to start my own syndicate. I had thought a lot about it, and after what had happened over the past several weeks, I decided that "I have to get out of here".

I finally discussed it with Helen a couple of weeks later. It was Sunday lunchtime, and Helen was just getting the meal ready. I remember she was straining the peas; it was that very stressful point of the cooking process at which a cook is trying to get everything on the table at the same time while each dish is still hot. I knew that was a good time to ask Helen something if I wanted an immediate and honest reaction, because she didn't have enough time to give a measured response.

I asked her, "What do you think I should do?"

---

10 A reinstatement premium is for the reinstatement of the full limit of a reinsurance contact that has been reduced or exhausted by loss payments.

To my amazement, she replied, "Look, Stephen, you're going to do it sometime. So, if that's the case, why don't you go ahead and do it now?" I later learned that she had already spoken to three people in the market who knew me well.

So I said, "Okay, are you sure?"

"Yes."

"Then here's the deal. If I do this, I leave for work on Monday morning and I finish on Friday evening. I'll try not to work at weekends, but it will happen sometimes. Don't count on seeing me too much during the week."

I had said that to cover my back, not realizing that was exactly what it would be like for more than 30 years: I worked flat-out during the week and tried as much as I could not to work on weekends. Helen went into it with her eyes open, and ever since she's faithfully backed me all the way. That type of support from your wife is a wonderful thing. I'm lucky, very lucky.

Another major factor in my decision to set up my own syndicate was the fact that Antony Gibbs, the bank that owned Anton Underwriting Agency, had been purchased by HSBC. Under recently enacted amendments to the Lloyd's Act, a holding company could no longer own both a managing agency and a Lloyd's broker, and HSBC owned broker Hartley Gibbs Sage. In other words, HSBC had to divest either the underwriting agency or the broker. HSBC believed that Hartley Gibbs Sage would be more compatible, so Anton was up for sale. I was worried that Anton would be sold to either Merrett Holdings plc or to Sturge Holdings plc, which owned two of the largest Lloyd's managing agencies, and I did not want to work for either.

Hugh Jago and I had tentatively agreed that we would set up a new managing agency that would manage my own syndicate. The original agreement was that I would own 65 per cent and Hugh would own the other 35 per cent.

Brian Evens did his damnedest to persuade me to stay on. Along with another underwriter, he had set up what was known as a baby syndicate, a small Lloyd's syndicate that had a select group of investors and selectively wrote high-margin business. The profits produced by baby syndicates were indeed often huge, and not many years thereafter they were banned. Brian offered me half of his share of the baby syndicate to remain.

"I can't take that," I told him. "You know you're in the last part of your career, and I have just started mine. If you wanted to keep me, you should have spoken to me sooner. I don't want it on my conscience that I'm dissipating your personal wealth. It's very kind of you, but I couldn't live with that."

When I eventually got Brian to accept my resignation, I said to him,

"There are two things I have to ask you. One, would you consider being an independent director of the company, my company? Secondly and independently of that, I would like to offer you 5 per cent of the company as a thank-you for what you've done for me."

He looked at me and said, "You are a funny chap. You spend all this time trying to get away from me, and then you ask me back."

"There is a difference," I said.

"What's that?" Brian asked.

"The difference is that I can now fire you!"

Fortunately, Brain saw the funny side of my remark and accepted the offer.

I kept working for Brian until August 1984, while at the same time beginning to set up my own agency.

After my resignation was accepted, David Robson, who was chairman of Anton Underwriting Agency, said to me, "I want to thank you for all of your work, Stephen. We all think you're doing absolutely the right thing ... and can I come on the syndicate as a member, please?"

* * *

The new company, S.J.O. Catlin Underwriting Agencies Limited, had £25,000 of paid-up capital. Hugh gave me a £25,000 subordinated loan, on which I paid a commercial rate of interest (I managed to pay it off in two years). Even by the standards of the 1980s, the figures were small. My share of the capital was £15,000. I took a cut in salary from £21,000 to £20,000 and I had a £45,000 mortgage, so I was skint.

A number of people wondered at the time why I had included the 'S.J.O.' in the name of the agency. I said, "Why not? That's my name: Stephen John Oakley Catlin." They were correct, however. Within a year or two, I realized that the initials were superfluous, so we dropped them, and over time the agency was formally called Catlin Underwriting Agencies Limited and known simply as Catlin in the marketplace.

I never really thought at the time whether it was a good idea to use my own name or call the company something else, but in those days the active underwriter was king of the business, so nearly every Lloyd's syndicate was named after the founding underwriter: Merrett, Sturge, Kiln, Murray Lawrence, Beazley and Hiscox to name a few. At that time, the brand that people truly recognized was Lloyd's, not necessarily the name of the managing agency or syndicate.

Thirty years on, the role of the active underwriter has changed. He or she is no longer all-powerful, but simply a leading member of a larger team.

As Lloyd's is now dominated by listed companies, both companies primarily based at Lloyd's as well as international companies, each managing agency's brand has increased in importance, although Lloyd's is still probably the most recognizable insurance brand worldwide.

One of the first things I had to do was to line up support from members' agencies[11], which managed the affairs of Lloyd's members or 'Names', the purportedly wealthy individuals who in those days provided capital to Lloyd's syndicates. I was fortunate to have good support. The Fenchurch Members' Agency backed us from the beginning, as did Anton. Dick Outhwaite, who had a good name at Lloyd's during those days, was very helpful, as were many others. It was hard work to entice members' agents to support a new operation, and it was tremendously influential to have senior people in the market say, "You want to back that one."

I offered the job of deputy underwriter (the only other agency employee from the outset) to Rupert Atkin, who I had tried to lure to Anton several years earlier. However, he wasn't hired at the time because he was thought by others to have been too smart for the job.

I spoke to Lloyd's at the end of March about setting up my business and was told in principle to go ahead. I kept in contact as the months passed. However, in September, someone from Lloyd's called me and said, "Sorry, we can't approve you this year. We haven't got the time."

"How can that be?" I asked. "We've been speaking since March!"

"Well, it is what it is, and we haven't got time," the person at the end of the telephone responded. "You'll just have to do something else."

I was absolutely livid. While I could easily have given up at that point, I believed I had been wronged. I had told Rupert that, even if we did not receive permission from Lloyd's, I would pay him until he got another job; I felt I had a moral obligation to him. If that had happened I would have been bankrupt. I had also lined up £6 million of capacity from Names. I thought Lloyd's had behaved unfairly, and I thought to myself, "Sod it. I'm going to stand up and be counted."

Lloyd's came back to me and said, "We've had a think about this. We don't think your agency's board is strong enough, so we want Anthony Bartleet of Murray Lawrence (the same person who tried to hire me five years earlier) to go on the board, and he needs to have 5 per cent of the equity."

Talk about jobs for the boys! I was furious.

I rang up Dick Outhwaite and explained what had transpired.

---

11 A members' agent manages the affairs at Lloyd's of individual Lloyd's Names. One of a members' agent's duties is to advise Names regarding the syndicates to which they should provide capital.

"It's outrageous, Stephen," he said. "Leave it with me." He rang me back later that day and said, "Stephen, I've got it sorted. Maurice Hussey (one of the directors of Dick's agency) will go on the board. He doesn't want a shareholding. We'll sort it out next week."

"You don't understand," I said. "The deadline for the application is tomorrow at 4 o'clock. I need to get all the papers signed by Maurice now. And by the way, have you actually asked Maurice?"

"Don't be so bloody cheeky!" Dick said.

The application was finally approved, but one more hurdle had to be crossed.

Each new Lloyd's business had to appear before a 'Rota' meeting with members of the Council of Lloyd's, the market's top governing body. I had to present a business plan, a detailed piece of work that included spreadsheets that I had done by hand. My business plan included underwriting classes of business with which I had been involved while working for Brian's syndicate: a chunk of energy, a chunk of reinsurance, some blue-water hull, some cargo and some war risk business.

Murray Lawrence was deputy chairman of Lloyd's at that time, and he chaired the meeting. He and other Council of Lloyd's members sat at one side of the table, while I was on the other side, joined by Hugh Jago, several of his partners and Brian Evens. The Council had worked out a set of questions to try to trip me up, and I dropped one real clanger. I was asked, "Have you had any experience of reinsurance to close?" I replied, "I've been doing the Syndicate 264 reinsurance to close since the 1974 accounts."

Of course, as head of the syndicate, Brian was responsible for the reinsurance to close. What I said came out wrong, but Brian, bless his cotton socks, covered for me. "Mr. Chairman, I can confirm that the RITC was my responsibility, but Stephen did understand what was going on," he said.

The syndicate was approved.

Afterwards, I apologized profusely to Brian as I had implied to the Council that Brian, as active underwriter, was only partially involved with the RITC. But Brian was gracious about my gaffe.

A few days later, I received a hand-written letter from Murray Lawrence that said how delighted he was that my syndicate had been approved. "I am sure you understand that we had to go through due process, Stephen. By the way, in the light of your performance at the Rota, could I please have a place on your syndicate?" In other words, the deputy chairman of Lloyd's wanted to be one of the Names who provided my syndicate with capital.

Looking back, those days of uncertainty seemed like a near death experience with almost everything on the line. They changed my attitude, probably made me a better underwriter and certainly honed my capacity to take risk. When I first began to underwrite on behalf of my own syndicate, brokers would often threaten me, saying that if I did not accept a certain bad risk, I wouldn't see any of the good business. However, after what I went through in setting up my business, I did not feel threatened, and I actually found these threats amusing. I thought to myself, "If you think you can frighten me after what I've been through, please think again."

It had been the most extraordinary year: I had joined the club, even though I had not gone to the right school. I was just 30 when the approval came through. Now, it was just Rupert Atkin and me, and we didn't even know each other very well. It was 2.30 p.m. in the afternoon, and we sat down at our box in the Underwriting Room, just a two-seater. In terms of company assets, I had the silver inkwell that Brian had given me as a leaving gift, some thin strips of that pink blotting paper and some out-of-date Lloyd's publications. That was it, aside from our £6 million in premium capacity.

10. Creating Catlin

Working with the good, the bad and sometimes the ugly

Rupert Atkin, my deputy underwriter, and I made a good team. By now, I had significant experience as an energy and reinsurance underwriter, and I led some business. Rupert had worked for Ian Posgate, and he had good contacts in the marine hull war risk market, which was an important class of business in those days. We pretty much shared responsibility for the cargo account. What was most important was that, each night, we would go through everything we had written. Rupert knew what I had written, and I knew what he wrote.

In fact, the first business that Syndicate 1003 underwrote was a piece of junk. It was a construction policy – and I wrote only a very small line. The whole experience was terrifying for a guy who had just turned 30. I would go to the Lloyd's Building each morning, put a smile on my face and force myself to keep it there. As the newest syndicate in the market, we were shown a tremendous amount of rubbish. We turned down at least ten risks for each one that we wrote.

After a week or two I said to Rupert, "I think we need to do something a bit bigger. We've got to say no to a lot of stuff, but we can do one or two big things; it's not going to kill us. I've tied up the reinsurance, so we aren't going to lose money." Around that time, Tony Pickering of Jenner Fenton Slade, who was a very important energy insurance broker, told me something that resonated strongly. He said, "Stephen, you have to make a political move to get noticed."

A short time later, a broker from Sedgwick contacted me to ask whether I would lead a 'corridor layer' – a primary package policy layer that covered nearly all interests – for a major oil company. In those days, Sedgwick was one of the biggest, most powerful brokers at Lloyd's and remained so until it was bought by Marsh in 1998. So, I did it: I led the policy with a 1.5 per cent line, meaning that I had agreed to provide 1.5 per cent of the coverage. I did not know it at the time, but Sedgwick only had a 10 per cent order – they were only supposed to be placing 10 per cent of the entire policy – but they went to see two other well-known Lloyd's underwriters, who each took another 5 per cent, and I think they were finally able to place 25 per cent.

There was a problem, however. During the time that I had temporarily stopped underwriting because I was busy setting up the business, Lloyd's underwriters had decided to stop writing liability coverage on an 'occurrence' policy form and switch to the more restrictive 'claims-made' policy form. I did not know about the switch because I had been out of the market. So, I gave the client much broader coverage than it would have probably obtained elsewhere, although major underwriters still followed my lead.

Tony Pickering rang me up afterwards and said, "When I told you to do something political, I didn't mean with a capital P!" Tony was worried that I would certainly lose money on the policy, but I had managed to buy facultative reinsurance covering the risk and, combined with the syndicate's reinsurance treaties, I knew I could not lose money. In fact, I made some money on it on a net basis. However, the odds of making money on the coverage gross of reinsurance was absolutely zero.

I was lucky something big had come my way early on, and I went for it. Looking back, it was a very ballsy thing to have done

I had to do other things to make sure that I was not bypassed by the big brokers. I would help the smaller brokers where many of my friends worked to win accounts from the larger players, so that the big brokers would have to do some business with me just to keep me in line. I was part of what was then known as 'Ego Alley', along with other members of a new underwriting generation who were just making their names at Lloyd's, including Ian Agnew, Mark Brockbank, Raymond Dumas, John Charman and others. They all had a lot more experience than I had.

We ended up with pretty good support from some of the major brokers. I had built myself a decent network of broker chums by that stage, and they were quite influential in terms of speaking to their organizations. "What do you think about Catlin?" they would ask. They would either hear, "He's a complete twit," or "Actually, he's pretty tough. You don't get much past that guy."

In those days, there were more than 400 syndicates in the Lloyd's Underwriting Room; some of the underwriters were excellent at their jobs, but others were just useless, people who couldn't even add up. Provided you could demonstrate that you had a reason for being there, you were delivering value and you were consistent, you were halfway home.

We wrote about £2.5 million in premium the first year against our £6 million in capacity, and we made about a 15 per cent return on capacity. Our reserves were about £250,000. That seems a long time ago now.

The reinsurance to close in the first year was easy. It was one of the easiest reinsurances to close that I have ever calculated in my life. I had been involved in reinsurance to close for a decade, and with my own business it was even easier than when I was working for Brian Evens' syndicate for two reasons.

First, I had full knowledge of what we had written; I could pretty much recall every single slip that we wrote. When it comes to the reinsurance to close, you need to know where to look, and there weren't any skeletons in our cupboard unlike other syndicates at the time which were positively rattling with them.

Secondly, I had managed to negotiate an all-embracing reinsurance program, so the only real issue was my credit risk, and most of the reinsurance had been written by Lloyd's syndicates, which meant the credit risk was minimal. I was confident that the reinsurance arbitrage I had set up was going to work.

In 1986, our second year of underwriting, we doubled our capacity to £12 million, then we went to £18 million in 1987 and £24 million in 1988, by which time we had about 25 employees. We mostly worked from our box in the Underwriting Room. Jago Venton had a small office in Plantation House, a short walk from Lloyd's, and we also had a tiny, segregated space there.

* * *

One of the main reasons for our success in the early years was that we managed to hire great people, both in terms of business skills and in terms of loyalty to the company.

The first member of staff, apart from Rupert and me, was Lesley Denekamp, who joined us in January 1985. I met Lesley at a New Year's Eve party; she and the host's wife had attended both secondary school and Southampton University together. I recall her job interview, which took place in the Jago Venton office. We had sandwiches and a bottle of wine for lunch! Lesley was young, blonde and bubbly, and she turned heads when she came out of the interview room.

During the interview, Lesley said to me, "Stephen, the one thing I'm concerned about is that I might get bored." I said to her, "Lesley, there are not many things I can promise you, but the one thing I can promise is that you won't be bored."

Persuaded, she said she would do it for three years and started work as a combination personal assistant/underwriting assistant. Lesley's three-year commitment lasted for more than 30 years, with Lesley retiring from the company only after it was acquired by XL in May 2015. Along the way, she did almost every job imaginable.

As soon as Lesley joined, I asked her: "What do you know about typewriters?" She replied, "Not very much." So, I said, "Well, go find out and then buy one." That episode says a lot about the company in its early days. We had been up and running for a couple of months, and we did not even have a typewriter (this is before desktop computers arrived in the underwriting room). We did not have a fax machine for two years, and the box next to ours kindly let us use its photocopier. More importantly, we did not know much about running a business. We certainly needed a typewriter, but we did not have a clue what they were all about.

There still were very few women working in the Underwriting Room in 1985. It is not very politically correct to say this now, but having Lesley work in our box was a great way to attract business. She was – and still is – a lovely and vivacious woman who everyone liked, and brokers buzzed like bees around a honey pot when she was working at the box. I soon found that she was also great at working with members' agents to attract capacity to the syndicate, and I would never again try to meet with a members' agent without her.

To get the support of the members' agents, we would do a group presentation at least once a year, just as a publicly traded company would hold analysts' presentations today. However, the presentations like the ones we held for members' agents generally were not conducted by Lloyd's syndicates during those days. I would speak for an hour or so with slides and then take questions for an hour more.

In addition to these group presentations, Lesley and I would meet individually with every single members' agency at least once a year, giving them 90 minutes of our time on a one-to-one basis. We were as open and transparent as we could be. We stuck to our word and generally delivered what we said we would deliver. An insurer is a capital-intensive business, and you can only get from A to B if you have enough capital.

I believe Lesley and I did a reasonably good job in persuading people that we knew what we were doing. We were able to increase capacity consistently during an era when Names were leaving Lloyd's and many syndicates saw their capacity withdrawn.

At one time there were 69 separate members' agents supporting Syndicate 1003, which was a nightmare to manage. I give a lot of the credit to Lesley. And, it was all good preparation for going public and having to deal with investment analysts.

Lesley carried on being my PA, amongst all her other duties, for a long time. She then officially became members' agency director and was one of the first female directors of a Lloyd's agency. She was managing director of Catlin Underwriting Agencies Limited for a time, and as we expanded, she became chief operating officer of our London operation. She then spent many years leading our human resources team.

* * *

One of the best hires I ever made was in 1987 when Paul Brand – known to most people in the market as simply 'Brando' because there were too many people around called 'Paul' – joined the business. Paul was practically a kid when I hired him, but he rose quickly through the business and directed all underwriting operations at Catlin for many years.

The funny thing is: I almost didn't hire him. Paul was a heavy smoker in 1987 (he quit a long time ago), but back then he smoked about 60 a day. He chain-smoked during his job interviews. "What do you think?" I asked Rupert. "Well yes, I think it's the right choice, but on one condition: we have a no-smoking office," Rupert replied.

Another key hire during the initial years of the business was Andrew Brooks, who at that time worked on the claims side of the business with Rupert. He later joined Martin Reith to form Ascot Underwriting Ltd., and Andrew has been CEO there since 2008.

Soon thereafter, Tim Peters joined us from Alexander Howden Ltd., at the time one of the largest Lloyd's brokers, to manage the financial side of the business. Tim wasn't a chartered accountant, but he turned out to be one of the best syndicate accountants in the marketplace because he learned how Lloyd's works inside out. As Catlin grew, Tim moved over to take charge of reinsurance recoveries – making sure we collected the money that reinsurers owed us – which is a vitally important job.

When I look back, I take pride that my initial hires have subsequently done very well. Rupert Atkin is currently chairman of Talbot Underwriting Limited, after serving as CEO for many years, and has served as deputy chairman of Lloyd's. Paul Brand ran the insurance operations of XL Catlin, a $10 billion business, following the acquisition and now leads its internal innovation team. Andrew Brooks is CEO of Ascot Underwriting, one of the major managing agents at Lloyd's. Lesley Denekamp and Tim Peters each worked for Catlin for 30 years, and Tim now has a high-level role with China Re's Lloyd's syndicate.

* * *

The insurance business – and Lloyd's – was a lot different in those early days, and shady deals and dodgy characters were not in short supply.

I recall stupidly underwriting one policy placed by a shifty broker. It was a complex policy, and the risk insured was something that we would not touch today with a barge pole. It later became clear that the broker did not supply me with all of the relevant information, so I had underpriced the policy by a significant amount. It became even clearer that this policy would probably lose a lot of money for the syndicate.

As the losses began to be reported, the broker told me to pay up. If I didn't, he said he would sue me and put me out of business.

I told him, "Here's the deal. If that's what you want to do, go ahead and do it. You're right that you will most probably bankrupt me. By the way, I will do my level best to bring you down with me. I have nothing to lose because I know you can take me out. However, you probably have something to lose, so you must decide how you want to play this."

One of my good mates in the market told me that I could *not* afford to take this broker on. However, I replied, "You know what, I can't afford not to do it. If I roll over on this one, everyone in the market will remember. If I want to retain my personal integrity and have any kind of respect within the marketplace, I have to do what's right."

We ended up coming to a settlement.

There was a lot of shenanigans going on at Lloyd's during the 1980s. It was sometimes difficult not to follow the undercurrents flowing through the marketplace at the time.

* * *

The Lloyd's market changed greatly during the first five years of Catlin's operations. We were outperforming the market, which probably wasn't that difficult due to the turmoil at Lloyd's during those years *(see Chapter 15)*. There were growing concerns regarding losses from asbestos and pollution from the distant past (being a start-up, we did not have those worries), and there were increasing worries about a run of catastrophe losses, such as 87J, a fierce London/UK windstorm in 1987, the Piper Alpha North Sea rig explosion in 1988 and the Exxon Valdez oil spill in 1989.

By October 1987, I believed it was time for the people working for Catlin – including me – to take control of the agency. Jago Venton still owned 35 per cent of the business. I asked Hugh Jago if he would reduce his shareholding – in return for a decent payback – to 25 per cent, so that I could give some equity to key employees, but he would not budge. While I appreciated that Jago Venton had backed us from the beginning, when we needed support, the team and I were creating the wealth, and I believed that we should own the business. I also realized that if I did not buy out Jago Venton soon, it was going to cost a hell of a lot more later!

So, I decided to give Hugh an ultimatum, which I communicated through his son Chris Jago, who was a friend of mine and who worked for his father as an underwriter. "Chris, here's the deal," I said. "I'm going to buy you out. I'm going to value the company at £1 million. You put in £10,000 and you are being offered £350,000 after 2½ years. Either you take it, or I'm going to start over again."

"You can't do that, Stephen," Chris told me.

"You watch me," I replied. "You've got a week to get back to me, but I'm not joking. I've tried to do this reasonably, but you haven't got the message."

What I did was probably naughty, but at the end of the week Jago Venton had agreed to the buyout. From that point, we were completely separate from Jago Venton, which meant that we had to find our own office, still in Plantation House, and we had to begin acting like real grown-ups. Our first office was only about 900 square feet and had no air conditioning and no view. But, we thought we had really made it. We thought it was just wonderful.

Looking back on it, we were rather like a bunch of kids. In 1987 I was still in my early 30s, and most of the team were younger. We were sitting around the table doing all these things you do in management meetings when you are in your 50s or 60s. And we had an absolute scream. It was a fun time. It was terrifying ... but it was fun.

* * *

Of course, to buy out Jago Venton I had to come up with £350,000, and I didn't have it. I went to Barclays Bank, looking to borrow £250,000 for the company, £50,000 apiece for Rupert Atkin and Paul Brand, secured against their homes, and an unsecured overdraft facility for the company. All of that significantly exceeded the assets of the company at the time, so I made sure that I went into the meeting with everything I would need: I had prepared a spreadsheet, cash-flow analysis and stress test, all by hand.

The meeting that morning lasted an hour and a half, and I managed to answer every question that the bankers fired at me. By 4 p.m. I had a letter on my desk from Barclays, confirming that the bank had agreed with everything I sought.

I succeeded in part because I could answer every single question on the spot. Every time the banker said, "You'll probably have to come back to me on this one," I replied, "No, I can tell you exactly what it is and here's the number." He was dismayed: "How on earth could you remember that?" But that was just me. Part of the answer is that since I had done all of the work by hand, not using a computer as one would today, all of the numbers were fresh in my mind.

This kind of transaction would be unheard of today; there was no credit committee, no collateral. I got the deal done because of my connections in the marketplace and having done all the work myself. Determination, hard work and a bit of the old blarney paid off.

*　*　*

Shortly after the management buyout from Jago Venton, I made a decision that – while not very important some 30 years on – was an indicator that Catlin was not going to be a 'business as usual' company. While we now had employee shareholders, I did not want to pay a dividend because I felt strongly that we should reinvest the money in the business. In addition, since I now owned about 70 per cent of the company, I would essentially be paying most of the money to myself. I would be the only person who would significantly benefit from a dividend.

So, to help pay back the shareholder-employees for all the work they had done for Catlin in the formative years, the company bought a villa in Southern France, between Valbonne and Biot, about ten miles inland of Antibes. As I told Rupert, "We should get a decent return on the investment and the shareholders will get a real benefit." Rupert was a keen skier, so he would have favored a chalet in the mountains. However, I realized that not everyone liked to ski and there would probably be fights over who got to use it, especially during the year-end renewal season which was the company's busiest time of the year. So, we decided on the South of France, where the weather was decent at least two-thirds of the year. It was close enough to London if somebody wanted to drive, and it wasn't too expensive to travel there by air.

The employees loved it, and we were also able to hold broker seminars at the villa, which helped differentiate Catlin from other syndicates. We made sure that the seminars were pretty short, giving the brokers plenty of time to relax and enjoy themselves.

I think we paid 4 million French francs for the villa, which was equivalent to about £400,000. Over nearly 30 years, we used it to incentivize key employees, who would take their families on a holiday at the villa for a very reasonable cost. It was a great investment.

*　*　*

It would be nice to say that Catlin was consistently profitable during its early years thanks to my superb underwriting skills. I don't think I was a bad underwriter, but the reason we were one of the most profitable syndicates at Lloyd's during the second half of the 1980s – a time of fairly momentous upheaval in the marketplace – was that I was a shrewd reinsurance buyer.

One of the benefits of underwriting a reinsurance account is that I learned the reinsurance arbitrage game at an early age. I soon learned that my syndicate, Syndicate 1003, could be virtually guaranteed a net profit after reinsurance, no matter what we wrote and whatever the claims experience, due to the reinsurance program I had put together. All I faced was the credit risk – the risk that reinsurers would not or could not pay – and the fact that I bought the bulk of the reinsurance from Lloyd's syndicates meant that we were protected by the Lloyd's Central Fund if a syndicate could not afford to pay.

While I was still working for Brian Evens, I bought a reinstatement protection policy from Dick Outhwaite's syndicate; it was expensive, but when you looked at the value it provided, the premium was ridiculously cheap. When I went out on my own, I went back to Dick, tongue in cheek, to see if I could get the same deal. I never thought I would be able to duplicate it because Brian's syndicate had many losses on its policy, but Dick wrote essentially the same policy for me on the same basis. I couldn't believe it. While the 1986 year of account was nearly loss-free, 1987 and 1988 were the exact opposite: those were big years for losses. However, due to the reinsurance, we got to the stage where the profit we made on a net basis actually rose as our losses *increased*! We received the benefit of the reinstatement premiums coming in following these losses, but our own reinstatement costs were much, much less because we had bought a reinstatement premium protection policy that covered all of our reinstatement costs excess of a deductible.

I don't claim to be a genius; I was simply applying market knowledge and common sense. I knew, even during the mid-1980s, that some people in the reinsurance market were taking questionable underwriting decisions and that they were going to be eventually driven out of business as a result. I knew in my own mind, without any shadow of a doubt, that the reinsurance market would someday go pop … that it would change radically. I knew that before I started Catlin. At that time, I reckoned it would be another three years or so before the reinsurance market fundamentally changed, largely due to the LMX spiral, ending the reinsurance arbitrage game for good. I thought that would be long enough to get the syndicate established.

As it happened, it actually took six years for the reinsurance market to blow up.

From 1990 onwards, I saw a lot of my peers at Lloyd's go out of business. During the period from 1988 through 1992, Lloyd's syndicates lost nearly £9 billion, an unprecedented amount that nearly led to Lloyd's collapse.

Lloyd's losses 1988-1992 (£m)

1988	510
1989	2,063
1990	2,915
1991	2,048
1992	1,193
Total	**8,729**

Source: Lloyd's Global Results

I am happy to say that Catlin Syndicate 1003 produced a profit in each of these years. The problems that led to these losses are discussed in Chapter 16.

It was during this period that I became truly interested in thinking about the concept of risk, the probability of loss, and loss frequency and severity. I refined my own thought process in terms of how and when risk aggregated and how an underwriter needed to price business correctly to make a gross profit, rather than relying on reinsurance arbitrage.

It was also at this time that I began to really concentrate on what some people would say became my mantra: building a business for the future. When I established Catlin in 1984, my goals at the time were to pay off the mortgage on our house and pay for my children's education. These were sensible goals for a 30-year-old. My original ambition was, over time, to build a syndicate with a capacity of £50 million or so. When I resigned from Brian's syndicate, it had a capacity of about £40 million. Syndicate 1003 got to £40 million within about five years, and we were continuing to grow because members' agents were happy to commit more money to syndicates that made profits, not losses. A lot of syndicates were going down at the time, but Catlin was going up.

I decided I wanted to leave a legacy. I did not want to be seen as someone who went into the market and then left, riding off into the sunset with a big check, leaving employees, policyholders and loyal brokers in the lurch. So I decided my goal would be to build a business for the future.

11. Thriving Amid Crisis

Steering a successful course during stormy times at Lloyd's

Saying you are going to build a business for the future is one thing. Actually building it is quite another!

By 1992 Catlin was a fairly mature business. We had stood the test of time. The company had made a profit each and every year for seven years. I found that rather than simply being an underwriter and a reinsurance buyer, I now had to be a manager and a leader. While I probably wouldn't have used the word at the time, I had become an entrepreneur.

If you look at various definitions of the word 'entrepreneur', you will find that most dictionaries describe the word as a risk-taker. As an underwriter, of course, I was considered a risk-taker, but someone who forms his or her own business is most likely to be taking more personal financial risks than an underwriter may wish to assume. I had pledged my house as collateral when I sought financing to establish Catlin, and I would have been ruined financially if Lloyd's had not approved the application. But an entrepreneur must also take other types of risk, and perhaps the biggest is the responsibility of leading a team. The 25 people who worked for Catlin – it was about 25 back then and one day it would be 2,500 – looked to me for leadership, for support and probably, most importantly, their monthly wages.

Once you've taken the first big risk, the risks that come later are not as daunting. I'd been there, done that and even got the t-shirt. I knew that through grit and determination I could achieve the things I really wanted. However, there was still some weight on my shoulders. While I no longer had to psych myself up every morning to walk into the Underwriting Room at Lloyd's with a smile on my face, I had learned that I still had to be upbeat. I found out that employees watch the boss's mood very carefully, and wearing one's heart on one's sleeve was not a good thing to do. I found out that I could even bring down naturally upbeat people, like Lesley Denekamp and Paul Brand, if I wasn't careful. I admit that I probably did that all too often. Over time, I discovered that employees must believe in you and have confidence in you ... however desperate you're feeling at that moment.

* * *

Catlin's growth to date had been organic. We had increased our premium volume each year on the back of increased capacity from Lloyd's Names through their members' agents. However, during the early 1990s, the Lloyd's market was changing quickly. The LMX reinsurance market – which had supported us during the earliest years – had collapsed. Huge losses from long-tail exposures – such as asbestos and pollution – had created financial problems for many Lloyd's syndicates. We were largely immune from those problems because we only began underwriting from the 1985 year of account. Some of the largest and most famous Lloyd's managing agencies were on the brink.

One of the reasons I resigned from Brian Evens' syndicate and established my own was that I was afraid that Anton Underwriting Agency, which managed Brian's syndicate, would be sold to either Merrett or Sturge, the owners of the two largest agencies at Lloyd's. I did not agree with either agency's management philosophy, so I did not want to work at either place. As it turned out Anton was sold to Merrett, and Merrett found itself in serious trouble by 1992. Some of Merrett's syndicates had produced vast losses, and the Names who supplied Merrett's capital were abandoning what turned out to be a sinking ship. It remains a lesson to us all that when the mighty fall, they can do so suddenly.

As Merrett began to unravel, Lloyd's was desperately trying to find homes for Merrett's various syndicates, even if it were just to run off the business. One of the syndicates was Syndicate 179, then known as the Lark Syndicate and previously known as the Hampton Syndicate. Richard Lark was running what had been the sister syndicate to Brian's at Anton. It was about double the size of Brian's syndicate and made a lot of money, mainly from motor reinsurance and retrocessions.

Our acquisition of Syndicate 179 only took four weeks from beginning to end. We did no due diligence because there wasn't time; the syndicate had an 'open year' (meaning that it could not estimate its liabilities so it had left an annual account open, which meant that we had virtually no reserve risk), and I pretty much knew what the syndicate had written. Even though at the time I owned a controlling interest in Catlin, I sought support from the company's board. The board's response was: "Okay, fine. If you think we should do it, we'll back you." It doesn't happen like that anymore.

Stephen Merrett called me a lot during those four weeks, but I refused to speak to him; I did everything through a third party because I knew that if I got involved with Stephen, I would probably lose out. I paid £1 for the syndicate, along with 50 per cent of the managing agent's fee charged to the Names for two years, as well as 50 per cent of any profit commission we would receive for two years. We paid that consideration only after we had written business, so there was no negative cash flow. In hindsight, it was probably the best deal I have ever made.

As soon as the deal closed, I called a meeting of Syndicate 179's staff in our office. It was about 4.30 p.m. in the afternoon, so we gave them a glass of champagne, which they had never experienced before at Anton. "You're in for a culture shock," I told them. Over the seven years since I had left an Anton-managed syndicate, Syndicate 179 had not moved forward one inch. For example, the syndicate's claims ledger was written in pencil. "Why is that?" I asked. "So we can rub it out," was the answer. This conversation, of course, occurred right at the end of the Dark Ages of Lloyd's.

One of the lines of business written by Syndicate 179 was binding authority business, which was primarily property coverage written through managing general agents on behalf of the syndicate. The account produced a 115 per cent combined ratio, which means that it was losing 15 pence for every £1 of business written. I noted to the account's underwriter that 80 per cent of the business was making money, but that was more than offset by the other 20 per cent.

"Why don't you get rid of that 20 per cent?" I asked the underwriter.

"I can't do that, Stephen," the underwriter replied.

"Why is that?"

"Because if I lost that 20 per cent, I'd lose the other 80."

"OK, let me put it another way," I said. "If you renew any one account of that 20 per cent, you'll lose your job. Do you understand me?"

I could tell that he had never been spoken to in such a manner. To reassure him, I said, "I'm the one who is going to take the risk on the business you lose. But that's how it is going to be."

He didn't renew that 20 per cent of the portfolio. How much business did he lose? One account. The combined ratio tumbled from 115 per cent to 85 per cent in a year, which is extraordinary.

There was an added benefit from the acquisition. The deputy binding authority underwriter, a chap called Gary Mountford, continued to write that class of business for more than 20 years on behalf of Catlin. Gary's account was consistently profitable.

* * *

Our next milestone, and a very significant one at that, came in 1995 when Western General Insurance Company took a controlling interest in Catlin. At that point, I stopped being an owner and became a salaried employee, although I retained a significant equity interest.

Nothing but bad news seemed to come out of Lloyd's during the early 1990s. Paul Brand and I did not know which direction Lloyd's was heading. In fact, we wondered if we should get out of Lloyd's completely until David Rowland, who later became Lloyd's chairman and who I credit as Lloyd's savior, produced with others what was known as the Lloyd's Task Force Report in January 1992. That report, which among other things called for the introduction of corporate capital alongside the existing Names, seemed like a pretty good blueprint for the future. Robert Hiscox, chairman of Hiscox Limited, had made a name for himself at the time by saying (somewhat loudly) that unlimited liability Names were a thing of the past. While we didn't verbalize it in the same way as Robert, Paul and I pretty much shared his views. With hindsight, I think most of us were really surprised at how long it took for unlimited liability Names to disappear, but at that time it was a very controversial issue.

While I owned a controlling interest in Catlin for the first ten years of the company's existence, I had virtually no control over the capital against which we underwrote business; that was supplied by the Names through their members' agents. Once Lloyd's approved the introduction of corporate capital effective January 1, 1994 – over many Names' fierce objections – we decided that Catlin should underwrite using our own capital. Of course, we would have to raise money as the business did not have anything close to the amount we needed.

Having our own capital would allow us, if necessary, to withdraw from Lloyd's and reorganize the business as a traditional insurance carrier. That wasn't to say that we necessarily wanted to leave Lloyd's, but we did need to have the option: the outlook for Lloyd's at that point in time was fairly cloudy.

Having taken that decision, we started talking to investment banks. That was completely uncharted territory for me at the time. I, of course, had dealings with Barclays as our banker, but this seemed like a different league. Brando and I decided to divide our roles: he took over responsibility for underwriting, while I devoted nearly all my time to raising capital, with the help of Paul Swain, who had recently joined Catlin in a senior role.

We spent nearly 18 months looking for capital with the help of Nicholas Lyons, who was then with the investment bank Salomon Brothers, and his partner Marty Dolan. Nick, who later moved to Lehman Brothers, ended up being a member of the Catlin Group board of directors for many years. Nick and Marty introduced us to Western General, along with five other potential capital providers.

I soon learned that raising capital is not for the faint of heart. A deal that appears to be certain one day disappears the next. I recall one instance when we were holding a Catlin management retreat on the Scottish Borders. Suddenly, Nick called to say he had lined up a meeting with a US venture capital fund, but the meeting had to be held as soon as possible. Paul Swain and I left the management retreat in mid-meeting, hustled down to London and caught the Concorde – you could still do it in those days – to New York. We then had to go up to New England for the meeting. And, after all that, nothing came of it.

Because investing in a Lloyd's-related company was something new, we had to spend considerable time explaining Lloyd's structure, how it all actually worked and so on. The would-be capital providers had no fundamental knowledge of how Lloyd's businesses worked, so there was a massive learning curve that had to be completed before we could even get close to talking turkey.

Eventually, Western General became our best option. There were no bitter negotiations; once they realized that investing in Catlin would be a sound move, it was a very friendly transaction.

Western General was owned by one of a number of trusts set up by the wealthy Chicago-based Pritzker family. The Pritzkers' biggest holdings were the Marmon Group, a conglomerate which was later sold to Berkshire Hathaway, and Hyatt Hotels. Western General, which was based in Bermuda, was run by Robert Pritzker, the younger of the two sons of A.N. Pritzker, the family patriarch. While Bob was not a member of the Catlin board, he was involved in the business and attended a couple of board meetings a year. Peter Rackley, who worked for Western General and reported directly to Bob, became chairman of the Catlin board.

It was a great relationship. Bob Pritzker used to say to me, "Stephen, we are not looking for income; we are looking for capital appreciation. Capital is not an issue; return on capital is." Over the seven years that Western General was Catlin's controlling investor, it never asked for a dividend until after our initial public offering. (Catlin paid its first dividend after its IPO in 2004.) Western General's accounts were prepared according to Canadian GAAP (generally accepted accounting principles), so for the year-end we would translate the Catlin accounts from the Lloyd's accounting method to Canadian GAAP; for the half-year, we would just divide by two. Otherwise, they left us pretty much alone.

Western General invested £21 million in November 1995 and a further £8 million the following year, which enabled us to underwrite, with our own capital, nearly 50 per cent of our portfolio within two or three years. We split the business into two syndicates: Syndicate 1003's capital was supplied by the then-traditional Names, while Syndicate 2003 underwrote on behalf of our own capital. Each risk underwritten was divided between the two syndicates proportionally based on the syndicates' capacities in a given year, so no one could accuse us of keeping the good business for ourselves and writing the more risky business on behalf of the Names. That had been a problem at Lloyd's for many years, and we certainly did not want to continue that practice.

Western General supported us for nearly a decade through the IPO in 2004, including the turbulent period following 9/11. We learned a lot from our relationship, and I doubt if we would have been able to raise $500 million in capital following 9/11 without the lessons we received from Western General. Our relationship was based on transparency and accountability; it reflected the values of the Catlin business.

The Western General investment produced another benefit for Catlin apart from simply capital. Western General was incorporated in Bermuda. At the time, Bermuda was evolving from an insurance marketplace that many thought to be a bit suspicious to a market that was attracting both capital and the respect of the industry, first with the establishment of ACE and XL in the mid-1980s and then the formation of several catastrophe reinsurers, including Renaissance Re, following Hurricane Andrew in 1992. While it took some time, we finally received clearance from the UK Inland Revenue to move our group domicile to Bermuda in 1999. Regulation and access to new business opportunities were a greater consideration than tax in our decision to redomicile in Bermuda, although tax was a driver.

Catlin was the first UK-based insurance group to move to Bermuda, but others – including Hiscox – followed years later.

12. Raising Capital

How I learned to love (and sometimes hate) the financial markets

I was at a hotel in Houston on the morning of September 11, 2001. I was with Paul Brand and Doug Howat, who at the time was our senior property and energy underwriter. We were about to hold a strategic planning meeting with the staff of our Houston office, which was established two years earlier.

The first plane hit the North Tower of the World Trade Center before we left the hotel. The second plane crashed into the South Tower as we were driving from the hotel to the office. As no one really knew what was happening at the time, we began the meeting. Then, the third plane crashed into the Pentagon. We gave up on the meeting at that point.

Clearly, the first thing you think about when something like 9/11 occurs is the human element. We knew the loss of life would be huge, and my first concern was to make sure all of our employees were safe. We had several employees traveling in the US who were scheduled to fly that day. Some people ended up in extraordinary places and were grounded for a week, but thankfully everyone was okay. There are too many companies in the insurance industry that were not able to say that.

However, once we knew that all employees were safe and sound, I began thinking about the company's balance sheet. What would a tragedy such as this cost? Would it be big enough to take us out? I can remember having a chat with Brando in the early afternoon. We asked each other what the loss to Catlin would be on a gross basis. We both had the same figure in mind: about $250 million in a worst-case scenario. The next question was regarding the cost to Catlin net of reinsurance. The answer: not more than $50 million in the worst case.

No one could have conceived that depraved terrorists could ever commit such loathsome acts. However, we could take a stab at the numbers because a common 'disaster risk scenario' for the industry at the time was the collision of two Boeing 747s over Lower Manhattan.

We turned out to be not too far off the mark: the gross loss to Catlin from 9/11 turned out to be just $150 million, while the loss net of reinsurance, after reinstatement premiums were included, was $28 million. That magnitude of loss would certainly hurt us financially, but it would not take us out.

Brando and I were pretty much on the money with our initial assessment because we understood the dynamics of our balance sheet, as well as the nature and the aggregation of the policies we had written. That said, however, there was something we absolutely did not contemplate should a disaster such as 9/11 occur.

* * *

Brando, Doug and I ate a sad dinner together that night, got some sleep and then went back to the Houston office at 2 a.m. so we could talk to the team in London when that office opened. None of us were feeling very good, and I must say that working in a Houston office in the middle of a warm September night when the air conditioning was shut off did not make matters better. We spoke with several key employees back in London and made good progress. It was the following day, September 13, when the surprise came. My phone rang.

"Stephen," one of our London underwriters said, "Do you remember the NFL cancellation policy? And do you remember that you agreed that we could write a larger line than we normally would?"

I did.

We had taken the view that it would be impossible for the National Football League to cancel its entire slate of games across the US on a Sunday. As we were underwriting the policy, we considered risks like windstorms or earthquakes, and we couldn't foresee any event that would impact more than four or five games in a given region. So, I allowed the underwriter to write double the normal line that Catlin would take on such a policy because the maximum foreseeable loss, as we saw it, was much lower than the actual indemnity offered under the policy.

When I discussed the problem with my colleagues in Houston after the call, they agreed that the NFL would never cancel its entire Sunday schedule. It would be unheard of. But, lo and behold, all of the games were eventually cancelled by the league. Not one of us had contemplated that a terrorist attack could shut down American football on any given Sunday. We had not priced for such an event, nor had we aggregated for it. The lesson learned was that, when underwriting, you have to always take a step or two back and try to think the unthinkable.

* * *

One of the first things I did on September 11, of course, was to call my wife at home in the UK.

"How are you doing?" Helen asked.

"Fine, how are you?" I replied.

"Fine. Is everybody OK?"

"Yes."

"How is the business?"

"No idea. I think we're okay, but I don't really know yet."

And then Helen said to me, "Stephen, I told you that we started out in a two-up-two-down, and if we had to go back to one again, that's fine by me. Don't worry about it."

That type of support from your wife is amazing. I'm lucky – very, very lucky.

* * *

When one looks back on 9/11, the scale of the human tragedy is still shocking. Nearly 3,000 people in total died. Two insurance brokers, Marsh and Aon, together lost more than 450 employees when the Twin Towers collapsed.

Immediately after 9/11, it was quite clear that the disaster would cause the insurance market worldwide to go through a period of monumental change, probably the most significant I had seen and perhaps will ever see again. Capital began flowing into the industry as never before, particularly to start-up insurance and reinsurance companies in Bermuda.

One banker rang me up several weeks after the disaster and said, "We think you might quite like a billion dollars worth of extra capital."

"Sure!" I said, laughing.

"No, no, no. I am being serious."

So we had a chat, and while that conversation did not go anywhere, it started me thinking about how much additional capital Catlin could utilize efficiently. There's no point in raising additional capital if you can't really use it. After considerable debate among our top executives, we settled at a goal of at least $500 million.

I remember calling Paul Jardine into my office. P.J. had only joined Catlin a few days earlier on October 1, 2001, after serving as chief actuary and commutations director of Equitas (see Chapter 16).

"How do you fancy being part of a billion-dollar capital raise?" I asked. He went white and nearly fell off his chair. A short time later, Paul Brand was seriously injured in a car accident and was away from the office for many months, so P.J.'s support during the capital-raising process was invaluable.

I had to serve not only as CEO, my usual role, but also fill in for Brando as chief underwriting officer. At the same time, I was managing the capital raise, a full-time job in itself.

The actual process was partly driven by private equity funds. P.J. and I must have seen 20 to 25 firms during the process. We drew up a shortlist, but some pulled out and some we didn't like. Eventually, we formed a nucleus, and that is when the real work started. The problem is that private equity investors don't like their competitors very much. In these types of negotiations, there are a whole mass of people and ego issues that have to be delicately handled. The long and short of it is that it was very hard work.

One of the first things we realized was that there was a huge bias in the investment market against Lloyd's-based businesses. There were a lot of questions at the time about the Lloyd's market's ability to withstand the 9/11 losses, and as chairman of the Lloyd's Market Association I was working hard to support Lloyd's reputation among insurance brokers and regulators *(see Chapter 17)*. In addition, the stigma of the Reconstruction and Renewal program and continuing uncertainty around the ultimate success of Equitas helped to drive many potential investors away from Lloyd's businesses.

P.J. and I were working ridiculously hard during this period, often 18 hours a day. Once we got home from work, we would often be on conference calls until midnight. We were lucky if we only worked eight hours a day during the weekend. This lasted for at least six months. We found that dealing with most private equity funds was very different to dealing with Western General, which by then was like family. The private equity investors were so much more aggressive and intrusive.

By June 30, 2002, we were down to six private equity partners, plus Western General, which had agreed to increase its monetary stake in Catlin by another $25 million, even though its ownership stake would be substantially diluted by the capital raise. We wanted to get the deal done that day – frankly, we were tired of the bullshit – so a midnight deadline had been set. P.J. and I had probably been up for the past 24 hours. As we approached midnight, Dan Primer, Catlin's general counsel, called me to say, "This isn't going to happen. They're nowhere near getting the documents together. I think they may just be playing around with us."

I said to P.J., "I'm not doing this. I've worked too hard for too long. I'm not throwing it away, but I'm not going to give it away either."

I told Dan to tell the private equity guys the deal was off. I then went to a hotel near Catlin's London office to catch a couple of hours of sleep. I later found out that P.J. had wandered around the City, London's financial district, in the middle of the night to clear his head.

The next morning, I rang Geoff Bromley, who at the time worked for reinsurance broker Guy Carpenter & Company. I knew that we had to protect our position in case the private equity negotiations failed, so I had negotiated a separate deal with Ajit Jain, who heads Berkshire Hathaway's reinsurance operations. Ajit at the beginning of the year had offered to write a 30 per cent quota-share reinsurance of our entire portfolio. It was not capital per se, but it was nearly as good and would allow us to underwrite more business. I placed an order for 5 per cent, and Ajit gave me an option that expired on 30 June to increase his participation to the full 30 per cent. On 30 June, recognizing that the private equity negotiations were breaking down, I placed an order with Ajit for a further 5 per cent quota share, and now I was asking Geoff to call Ajit to see if the option for the remaining 20 per cent could be extended for another four weeks.

I decided the best thing to do at that point was catch up on sleep, so I went back to bed. When I woke up again, at 1 p.m., the private equity guys wanted to come back to the table, and the deal was done four days later. In the end, we raised $532 million in private equity financing ($482 million of new equity capital and a $50 million term loan facility). Catlin was the only company operating at Lloyd's to receive private equity financing in the wake of 9/11. Billions of dollars were injected into the insurance market over a 12-month period, but the lion's share went to Bermuda start-ups.

The good news was that the capital allowed Catlin to grow. The bad news was I now had to deal with private equity investors. The main interest of most private equity investors is making as much money as possible in the shortest time possible; the welfare of employees, clients or the company itself are secondary concerns. That type of corporate culture is totally contrary with the corporate culture that we at Catlin had tried to nurture over the years.

The period between the private equity raise and our initial public offering in 2004 was probably the most challenging in my life. Twice during a seven-week period, the private equity guys summoned me to meetings in New York on a day's notice to second-guess our management decisions. On both occasions Sir Graham Hearne, who had been appointed the independent chairman of Catlin, came with me. Graham insisted on coming; I didn't ask him, but I am grateful that he did. At the second meeting, I had been listening to moans and groans from our investors non-stop from about 10 in the morning until late in the afternoon. I thought to myself that if the meeting went on for another 30 minutes, I would walk out.

If I had done that, I would have probably lost my job, I would have devalued the value of the company and I would have put a lot of employees' jobs at risk. However, I had come to the conclusion that I had simply had enough. I couldn't be true to myself, and I couldn't be true to my colleagues.

Just then, as I was nearing the breaking point, Graham Hearne blew up and proceeded to destroy the private equity investors' arguments against me one-by-one. It was an incredible performance, and I could have hugged Graham for defending me so well.

When we were alone, heading for the airport, Graham put his hand on my arm and said, "Stephen, I could have done that better."

I looked at him. "What are you talking about?"

Graham had saved the day, and we had come out of the meeting in one piece. However, his reaction was, "I could have done that better." To me it was a really good lesson. If you are prepared to self-appraise, even when you have done well, you will do even better next time.

* * *

While relations were never very good between Catlin management and some of the private equity investors, ill feelings were exacerbated when we had to explain that we needed to strengthen prior-year casualty reserves significantly. This, unfortunately, occurred just after the deal had been finalized.

As I explained in Chapter 5, accurately estimating reserves is not the easiest thing in the world. The fact was that the entire insurance industry had underestimated the cost of US liability claims during the late 1990s. In my opinion, actuaries at the time were looking in arrears when setting casualty reserves, rather than looking at current circumstances, such as the evolution of case law in the US and the increase in awards by US juries. The actuarial profession learned from this episode, and I don't think it will ever happen again.

Still, back in November 2002, I had to tell the investors that we had a black hole. I knew that they would be thinking I had covered this up during our negotiations, but it was something that we had only recently learned. I knew that other companies would be reporting similar levels of reserve strengthening in due course, but I couldn't wait for public support. I had to come clean.

"We found a problem," I told the investors who at that time were also our board members. "It's not a Catlin issue, it's not a Lloyd's issue and it's not a London market issue. It's a global issue, and everyone is going to feel it."

Their reaction was something along the lines of, "Fine. If that's the case, why are you the only company saying it?" It all got fairly accusatory.

They finally backed off a bit, but the next several months were painful.

Finally, Maurice R. (Hank) Greenberg, who at that time was still chairman and CEO of American International Group, reported that AIG was significantly strengthening its reserves; moreover, he used basically the same language in his February 2003 announcement that I had used before my board in November 2002. Some of the private equity guys even had the grace and decency to call me and say, "Okay, that is exactly what you said would happen."

Still, it was not a great situation, and the reserve strengthening meant that Catlin reported a loss for both 2001 and 2002.

*   *   *

The new capital allowed us to do something that I had wanted to do for several years: buy out the Names who provided capital to Syndicate 1003, the original Catlin syndicate.

For the past eight years, we had been underwriting at Lloyd's through what is known as a 'split stamp'. A percentage of each policy was underwritten on behalf of Syndicate 1003, which was supported by traditional Lloyd's Names, while the remainder was written on behalf of Syndicate 2003, which was backed by Catlin's own capital. Over the years, the capacity of Syndicate 1003 had decreased as Names resigned from Lloyd's, while the capacity of 2003 increased as we reinvested profits back into the business.

Buying out Names is difficult. First, they usually want to stay on, especially if they are backing a profitable syndicate. The Names on Syndicate 1003 had made good returns over time, so why would they want to give that up? Secondly, we had to do a deal with many different parties, not just one.

However, buying out the Names was the right thing to do. As Names were free to switch the syndicates in which they invested each year, they weren't really investing in an ongoing business, which in my opinion was one of the fundamental flaws of the 'Old Lloyd's'. At the same time, under the rule of agency, a managing agent such as Catlin had a clear duty of care to look after the best interests of its capital providers, in this case the Names. So, there was a fundamental conflict of interest. Did we build a business for the future, which was my ambition, or did we do everything possible to maximize profits each year, which was possibly in the best interest of the Names?

In 2002, there were many more individual Names at Lloyd's than today, but there were also many more syndicates that were seeking capital from Names. In other words, Names had far more choice. They could find capacity from other syndicates, probably for much less than the amount we reimbursed them for their Catlin capacity.

Trying to get the private equity investors to understand this type of transaction was quite difficult. It was way outside their experience, and the negotiations were at times 'nip and tuck'. But we finally got there. From 2003 onwards, Catlin only underwrote business on behalf of its own capital. While the Names buyout is now largely forgotten, it was actually a major turning point in Catlin's development.

* * *

The one good thing about private equity investors is that they want to head for the exit as soon as possible, while still making as much money as they possibly can. We knew that time was short, and that we had two options: we could sell out to another investor, or we could go public. We didn't particularly want to sell to another party, although there was always the possibility of the proverbial 'offer you can't refuse'.

We began thinking about an initial public offering just days after the private equity raise was completed. There was a lot to do. It was clear we had to beef up the Catlin team. Within the space of a month in early 2003, we hired a chief financial officer, a chief risk officer and a head of communications, who could deal with media relations and help us communicate with the outside world more effectively. Over the next year, we continued to beef up our management team in preparation for an IPO.

One problem with going public is that there is very little written about it. If you were like many of the people at Catlin, who had spent most of their lives working for private companies, it was a bit tricky figuring out how an IPO really works and what it involves.

While we worked on the IPO for more than a year, the real activity was condensed into a three-month period. We had meeting after meeting with the advisors working with us on the IPO, who told us what we could and couldn't say and who rewrote our story to meet the expectations of investors. The whole thing was capped off by a two-week 'roadshow' in March 2004 during which a handful of us – including Brando, P.J. and Chris Stooke, who had joined Catlin as CFO a year earlier – traveled to various financial centers to hold half-hour meetings from morning to night with potential investors. Once the day's meetings were finished, we'd move on to the next city, catch some sleep if possible and start again early the next morning.

As IPO day approached, however, conditions in the investment markets began to deteriorate. A terrorist attack on the commuter train system in Madrid in March 2004 had shaken investor confidence. After all our work,

I was frightened that the IPO would not get off the ground, and I wondered whether it should be postponed.

One good thing that came out of the IPO – other than separating ourselves from the private equity investors – was the relationship I formed with one of our advisors, David Mayhew of Cazenove (later J.P. Morgan Cazenove).

Early on the day before the flotation, David telephoned me and asked, "Could we have breakfast tomorrow morning?"

"I've got my first meeting at 8 a.m." I said.

"That's fine," David coolly replied. "I'll see you at 7 o'clock in my office."

I took our recently hired head of investor relations, William Spurgin, with me to the meeting.

David said, "Stephen, I just wanted to tell you something."

"What's that, David?" I asked.

"It's fragile."

"How fragile?"

"Stephen, it's fragile."

What he was saying was that there was a real possibility, maybe even a probability, that the transaction wouldn't get done. And failing to do an IPO leaves a stigma – always.

I said to David, "I really appreciate your telling me that so I know where I am."

Then, I said to William, "You are not to comment about this conversation to anybody else at Catlin until after the close of play today under any circumstances. If you're asked the question, we learned a lot from David, okay? And by the way, we're going to go into these last meetings as if we have got the deal done. We're going in there with absolute confidence."

At midday, the IPO was 75 per cent subscribed, which would have been a failure. But by 4 p.m., we were two-and-a-half times oversubscribed. Catlin was now a publicly traded company, and we had raised nearly $200 million in additional capital.

Raising capital is a bit like herding cats. If the market thinks that something isn't going to work, it holds back. If the market believes that something is going to work, it wants to be part of it and will put money on the table. Depending on its level of conviction, the market will put more or less money on the table. In fact, investors will often put up more than they actually want to invest because, if a deal is oversubscribed, they are sure to be signed down.

* * *

In late 2006, we had to raise more capital to replace the temporary financing we put in place to acquire Wellington Underwriting plc *(see Chapter 14)*. Catlin's prospects had never been stronger.

I remember going to a meeting with our advisors, along with Chris Stooke and other members of the Catlin finance team. The advisors suggested that we attempt a Tier 1 and Tier 2 capital raise, seeking up to $300 million of Tier 1 debt in the US and $300 million in Tier 2 debt in Europe. They suggested that the issue take place in the spring, just after we released our year-end 2006 results.

"Why would we want to wait that long?" I asked. "Why wouldn't we want to do it now?"

"Well, normally companies do these after the year-end results," the advisors said.

I explained that the world and his wife had already been through our books because of the due diligence processes relating to the Wellington acquisition. Why couldn't we try to accomplish the debt raise on the back of that?

"Well, Stephen, that's not normally how it happens," I was told.

"I didn't ask what normally happens. My question was, 'Why can't we?'"

There was a lot of "umms" and "ahhs" from across the table. I persisted and asked the advisors to do some research and then tell me whether we could complete the transaction in short order, rather than waiting several months.

Two days later, the advisors came back to me. "Actually, Stephen, you're absolutely right. We can do it on the back of those numbers."

"Fine, let's go and do it," I said. "If we go in now, nobody else will be in the market. Everybody else will be waiting for the year-end numbers."

So, in the middle of January, Chris Stooke and I went to New York with the intention of raising $300 million in Tier 1 preferred debt. The book runners would be Lehman Brothers and J.P. Morgan Chase (this was nearly two years before Lehman Brothers collapsed). We were in luck because it appeared there were all kinds of investors with wads of cash in their back pockets, not knowing what to do with it as there were no transactions happening. After the first half-day of meetings, which was a Monday, I said to the banks, "I think we could do the whole deal here in New York," referring to both the Tier 1 debt and the $300 million in Tier 2 debt that we were planning to raise later in Europe. "We're getting a very good reception."

On Tuesday night, we had a dinner with the advisors and the two traders who would lead the debt raise. An advisor told me before I met the traders, "Make sure you give them a hard time. Don't let them get away with anything. Be firm."

So, I met the traders, who were resisting the notion of placing the entire amount at one time. I decided to go for it. "Look chaps," I said, "let me make one or two things clear to you. If we try to raise $300 million and it fails, that's my fault and my responsibility. If we try to raise $600 million and fail, that is also my fault and my responsibility. So the decision is mine, not yours. I've taken the decision that I want to raise the entire $600 million now, so that is what I want you to do."

There was a bit of teeth-sucking so, looking directly at the traders, I added, "By the way, the word 'wimp' comes to mind."

We hoped to close the transaction on Wednesday, so that morning I rang up both traders' offices and asked, "Could I please speak to Mr Wimp?" Word of my teasing flew around their offices, and the traders were given such a ribbing they just could not believe it.

I sat on the edge of the trading floor to watch the transaction take place. By around 2 p.m. we were oversubscribed to the tune of $5.8 billion. We had gone out to raise $300 million, but we had actually raised $600 million and had subscriptions for $5.8 billion! The preferred shares paid a yield of 7.25 per cent per annum at a time when the risk-free rate was about 5 per cent. The issue was completely unsecured, and we had the cash in our bank account within five working days.

I remember going back home and saying to Helen, "There's something awfully wrong here because we should not be able to go out and in two and a half days raise $600 million unsecured at 2.25 per cent above the base rate. It's unheard of."

The market collapsed two months later. If we had waited, as was originally suggested to me, we probably wouldn't have got the debt issue home. Sometimes it is all about timing – and some luck – and then making sure that you maximize on the luck that you have.

* * *

Two years later, we did something slightly different. Catlin was still expanding, and we needed yet more capital. There was a huge debate as to how much we should seek to raise, this time through a rights issue of Catlin common shares: should we raise $200 million or $500 million? This capital raise was taking place following the near-collapse of American International Group at the height of the financial crisis, and we wanted to capitalize on the opportunities that were being offered to AIG's competitors such as Catlin. However, I worried about the timing and how the investment market would react because the rights issue would have to be quite heavily discounted.

The board discussions went round and round, but there was no consensus. Finally, Sir Graham Hearne said, "Stephen, you have to decide ultimately."

In my view, more capital is better than less capital. I thought $300 million was about the right number because we could utilize that amount straight away, but I was still wavering. The rights issue would take place the following Monday, coinciding with the announcement of Catlin's 2008 financial results.

One of the advisors working on the rights issue telephoned Graham on the Friday before the rights issue was scheduled. "I don't normally do this, but I wanted to tell you that I really think Stephen should do this transaction. I know he is wavering, and I understand that, but he has always been on the front foot. I think he should stay there."

Graham called me immediately and told me about his conversation with the advisor. I was in Cologne, meeting with our European management team.

"What do you think, Stephen?" Graham asked.

"I'm still worried it won't get off the ground," I said. "I am worried about the reaction if that happens, so frankly I am minded not to do it."

After a further conversation between Graham and the advisor on Saturday, Graham again called me to say that the advisor suggested that I call him on Sunday evening to speak with him directly, which I did. The advisor spent about an hour convincing me to go ahead with the rights issue the next morning. I finally agreed.

We raised $289 million on the Monday morning that we announced our 2008 financial results. It was not a bad morning's work.

The very next day, it was announced that HSBC was attempting to raise $19 billion – an extraordinary amount of money, even for HSBC. That deal got done, and the market then shut down. What the advisor had been telling me, without saying it, is that we had to get our deal done then and there, because there wasn't a chance in hell that we would be able to raise $300 million after HSBC raised $25 billion. Several of our competitors, which were considering raising capital at roughly the same time, were shut out of the market.

* * *

Raising capital is not my idea of a good time. It's damned hard work. Perhaps the toughest part is learning how to communicate your messages so that a potential investor understands them. It's relatively straightforward to communicate your messages in your own words, but translating those messages into language that an investor will understand is a whole new ball game. I learned how to do that through experience, essentially by making my own mistakes.

I also learned that if you tell an investor what he or she wants to hear, you're practically allowing the investor to run the business for you. So, you must maintain a balance between being firm and determined regarding what you want to achieve, while at the same time listening to the investor's concerns and explaining any issues in language the investor can comprehend.

After working closely with bankers and other advisors during these capital raises, I also discovered that as a client you really must learn to understand the bankers' language; they won't try to learn yours.

Bankers are primarily remunerated by a success fee, which makes sense because it forces them to work hard to achieve the ultimate goal. However, I've observed on more than one occasion that the nearer a transaction moves toward completion, the more bankers start thinking about their own rewards and less about you, the client. There are many critical decisions that must be made near the end of the process. However, the client can find itself on its own because the advisors may have actually stopped giving impartial advice.

For example, say a bank will earn a $25 million fee on a $500 million transaction, of which $20 million represents a success fee. Once the bank has completed the bulk of its work, it will already have banked the success fee. At that point, the advisor may encourage the client to complete the transaction, even if it may not be in the client's best interest. The bigger the fee, the bigger this issue can become.

* * *

Looking back, Catlin's ability to raise capital when we needed it was defining. In most cases, a bank will lend you lots of money when you are flush, but it won't lend you a cent when you really need it.

If you can raise capital at a time when a lot of people have not or cannot, you're ahead of the game. Having spent 18 months working on the Western General capital raise during the 1990s, we then spent nine months working on the private equity raise, which was more detailed and more tortuous, partly because of the anti-Lloyd's stigma at the time. If I had wanted to do a start-up, I might have raised the same amount of money in six weeks.

When I look at Catlin post-9/11 – when we raised $500 million through the private equity raise, another $200 million at the time of the IPO two years later, then $600 million in Tier 1 preferred debt and finally nearly $300 million through the 2009 rights issue – we were able to grow rapidly because we could raise capital when competitors could not necessarily do so. From 2003 to 2005, we grew the top line by a factor of three, and we grew the bottom line by a factor of six. I'd love to say that was because we were really good underwriters, but the truth of the matter is that we had something that many competitors didn't have: surplus capital. We paid a price to raise it, but doing so allowed us to grow the business organically in a hard market, which is exactly when you want to do it.

13. Going Global

The insurance business was changing,
so Catlin had to change, too

The problems that arose at Lloyd's during the 1990s certainly sent a chill down the spine of many a Lloyd's underwriter, including me.

While the Reconstruction and Renewal program was a success and Lloyd's was put back on its feet, it did cause concerns for the future. Could some other unforeseen event, or series of events, topple Lloyd's? If Lloyd's failed, would there be a London market? Would there always be London brokers to produce business? I began to wonder whether Catlin should diversify outside our London base, just in case history repeated itself.

As the 1990s progressed, I had formed a fundamental belief that day-to-day risks would increasingly be insured on a local basis by local underwriters. Insurance and even reinsurance markets would increasingly form on a regional basis. Smaller to medium-sized business would be written in those markets, leaving only the big-ticket, difficult-to-write business to be written in the London wholesale market, of which Lloyd's was the center.

I also began to believe that underwriting a portfolio composed solely of large insurance and reinsurance business was not necessarily the best strategy. Such a portfolio was inherently volatile. If Catlin continued down that route, we would always be left wondering whether we had sufficient capital and how we could replenish our capital after the inevitable major loss.

Branching out from the London market would make us less reliant on Lloyd's, give us access to business that I believed would increasingly be placed locally and diversify the portfolio away from an over-reliance on 'big-ticket' insurance and reinsurance business.

Little did I know, as those ideas coalesced, that within 15 years Catlin would go from one office in London to 55 offices in 25 countries around the world *(see Appendix 2)*. And, that doesn't include the handful of offices, particularly in the UK, which we closed over the years.

* * *

It took me quite some time to persuade Paul Brand that it was a good idea to expand globally. Brando certainly didn't come running to the altar. It took a lot of debate, but eventually Brando and I agreed that we would dip our toe into the water and begin diversifying on a gradual basis.

We started the process in 1999 and immediately got it wrong.

We began diversifying in two areas: the US and Asia. In the US, we purchased a Houston-based coverholder that also operated a small office in New Orleans. Buying an existing business meant that we automatically had a team of employees, cash flow and a portfolio of business. Unfortunately, we had no idea what we had actually bought. In Asia, we started from scratch. We were the first syndicate to establish an operation in Singapore under the Lloyd's Asia license, and we opened what was essentially a back office in Kuala Lumpur, Malaysia. So, in Asia, we thought we knew exactly what we were getting, but we had no employees, no cash flow and no business.

Neither operation proved to be successful at the outset. We slowly realized that we needed people with different talents to run the businesses. While both the US management team we had acquired and the Asian management team we had put in place had successful insurance backgrounds, they didn't necessarily have the skill sets to grow the businesses.

I recall Brando coming up to me one day and saying, "Stephen, do you know we have completely screwed up on both of these operations? Do you think we ought to get the hell out of there and go back to our previous existence?"

I replied that we shouldn't necessarily throw away some valuable lessons we had learned.

So, we basically started over, chalking up two years and a bit of lost money to experience. We tried to remember what we had learned the hard way and did things differently the second time around.

First, we made sure that we hired people overseas using the same criteria we used in London. We found people we liked and who we believed had the same values and ambitions that we had nurtured in London. In some cases, we transferred employees overseas from London, but we generally preferred to hire local people to represent Catlin in local markets.

Secondly, we took a much more hands-on approach. When we first expanded to the US and Asia, I did not visit the new offices very often, but I soon learned that leading from the front – as I had been doing in London for 15 years – was just as essential, if not more so, if you are opening overseas branch offices. People who have known me over the past 15 years realize that I spent most of my time traveling; I was usually living out of a suitcase. But in 1999, I was pretty firmly rooted in London. That changed when we began going global.

* * *

While we began building our international network of offices through both acquisition (in the US) and a start-up operation (in Asia), we quickly learned that the latter route was in keeping with Catlin's corporate ethos. Usually, when opening a new office, the deciding factor was the people we could hire in a particular location, not the location itself. In other words, we emphasized hiring the right people, those who shared our beliefs and ideals and who would easily embrace the Catlin culture. We didn't simply stick pins in a map, as some of Catlin's critics insinuated.

One of the problems with growing organically is that it can be a slow process. It usually takes several years for an office to produce sufficient business to offset the initial expense, and capital markets generally do not like organic growth because it takes too long to produce a payback. A long-term diversification strategy was not compatible with Catlin's private equity ownership from late 2002 until early 2004 as it did not suit most of our investors' short-term strategy. That was another good reason to seek an initial public offering.

However, we still faced similar problems after we went public. Some investment analysts complained that we were spending too much money – and not producing sufficient short-term profits – by building our international network of offices, which later developed into six distinct underwriting hubs: London, US, Bermuda, Europe, Asia-Pacific and Canada. To some extent they were right. Had we not spent so much money on producing organic growth from scratch, we might have produced earnings on par with the most profitable of our competitors. However, we wouldn't have been building a business for the future, especially as I saw it.

Back in 2002, a friend who happened to be the CEO of one of our competitors asked me, "Stephen, what on earth are you doing expanding in Asia and America? You would make much more money if you just stayed here in London."

"You know what? Today you're right, I agree with you," I replied. "But that doesn't mean to say it will be right for tomorrow."

A decade later, I met with him and one of his top executives. Separately, they both said something along the lines of: "Now we can see why you did what you did, and we rather wished we had done it ourselves." One of them even said, "I was a seller of your stock back then. Now, I'm a buyer."

I recall a trip that I made with Benji Meuli, who had succeeded Chris Stooke as Catlin's chief financial officer in 2009, to visit a fund manager based in Iowa. My explanation of our international diversification strategy – opening offices based on the quality of the people we were able to hire rather than sticking pins in a map – came as something of a revelation to the investor, which acquired a reasonably sizable shareholding shortly after our meeting.

While other London-based insurers have diversified geographically, others have not done so on a large scale. Perhaps they did not share our vision or didn't have the tenacity to endure an extended period of expense overhang. However, if you look at the XL/Catlin business combination *(see Chapter 14)*, the deal at a stroke made XL's relatively modest UK business relevant; it made Catlin's growing US business much more relevant; and it helped make the merged company a considerably stronger player in Europe, Asia and Latin America. The business combination probably saved both companies five years of work to achieve the same relevance if Catlin and XL had remained independent.

That demonstrates the importance of scale in today's insurance industry, unless you intend to be a truly niche player. To be successful as a specialty insurer and reinsurer, I believe that a company must have sufficient scale and should have a global presence.

* * *

One of the earliest steps we took in building Catlin's global infrastructure – and reducing our ultimate reliance on Lloyd's – was the establishment in 2002 of what came to be known as Catlin Bermuda.

Catlin already had a relationship with Bermuda because we had re-domiciled the holding company in Bermuda in 1999. At the same time, we established what is known as a 'shell' reinsurance company in Bermuda. Catlin Insurance Company Ltd. was capitalized at only $1 million and dormant, but it could be activated quickly whenever we had sufficient capital and ambition to do so. However, 1999 was not the appropriate time because we did not have excess capital and the insurance and reinsurance market conditions were truly horrendous.

The time became right after the private equity capital raise in 2002, when prices were rising across nearly all classes of business in the aftermath of 9/11. We contributed another $99 million in capital to the Bermuda company and received Class 4 status from the Bermuda regulator; in a matter of weeks, Catlin Bermuda was up and running, writing reinsurance business in a strong underwriting environment. Catlin Bermuda went on to become a significant player in the Bermuda market.

The timing of Catlin Bermuda's formation became even more fortuitous three years later, in 2005, following Hurricane Katrina. The hurricane, which devastated New Orleans, remains the most costly windstorm in history in terms of insured damage. By then, Catlin Bermuda was well-established and was able to substantially increase its premium volume at very good margins.

The development of Catlin Bermuda also reinforced our strategy of hiring the right people to manage international operations. We originally sent a small team of London employees, led by Paul Swain, to Bermuda as we didn't have the time to hire locals. However, a couple of months later, we managed to hire Graham Pewter as CEO of Catlin Bermuda, which was a massive stroke of fortune. Graham moved from London to Bermuda in the early 1980s and quickly became woven into the fabric of the local business community. Before joining Catlin, Graham was CEO of Commercial Risk Partners, a Bermuda-based reinsurer that was originally owned by French reinsurer SCOR and Western General, although SCOR later acquired 100 per cent ownership. SCOR closed Commercial Risk shortly before we activated Catlin Bermuda, and Graham found himself without a job. As they say, timing is everything.

Graham, who embraced the Catlin values as much as anyone in the company, remained CEO of Catlin Bermuda until he retired in 2015.

What was also significant about Catlin Bermuda is that it represented a separate legal entity from our Lloyd's operation. The offices that we had previously opened in the US and Asia operated as coverholders of our Lloyd's syndicates. Now, Catlin's eggs were no longer solely in the Lloyd's basket. In addition, taking advantage of the capital and financial efficiency that the Bermuda market offers led to the bulk of Catlin's capital being held by Catlin Bermuda. Our other legal entities largely operated as subsidiaries of Catlin Bermuda, which provided the group with capital efficiency that was far superior to that of many of our competitors.

As our international strategy continued to develop, Catlin would later form insurance/reinsurance companies in the UK, US, Switzerland and Singapore. Most of our offices in Europe, Asia, Australia, Canada and Latin America continued to operate as coverholders of our Lloyd's syndicate, because Lloyd's international licenses allowed Catlin subsidiaries to operate in many countries without establishing a local insurance carrier.

* * *

Although the US was the location of one of our first offices outside London, we did not have much success initially operating domestically there. We were underwriting a large amount of American wholesale business through our operations at Lloyd's, but that's not the same as operating on the ground in the US.

There aren't many British companies that have successfully set up business in the US, both in the insurance industry and in the entire financial services sector. One of the biggest challenges is communication. Brits and Americans both speak English, but that doesn't mean they speak the same language. In meetings between people who speak English as a second language, they listen very carefully and speak very deliberately, making sure they choose the correct words. If you listen to Americans and Brits speak to each other, they just assume they are both speaking the same language. They don't listen carefully, and they don't recognize the differences in idioms and meanings, which can be substantial. I think all Brits and Americans who do business together should read the book *Amglish: Two Nations Divided by a Common Language* by Mike Powell.

In fact, language and cultural differences can exist within America's borders. I remember a meeting of the Catlin board of directors, in which we were discussing a potential deal with a company based in Texas. One of our directors, who was an American from the Northeast, quipped: "You do realize they're not American, don't you?" I think he actually meant what he said.

After our initial experience in the US with the Houston office, I learned that operating in America successfully would be hard work. During the period 2000 to 2005, we had our hands full with the IPO, the formation of Catlin Bermuda and the establishment of offices in Asia, Europe and Canada. Over time, I realized that to operate a successful US operation required a strong American CEO who shared the Catlin values and who recognized the differences that exist between Brits and Americans. Such a person was difficult to find.

I must have interviewed 20 people during the course of a year, assisted by Ken Goldstein, an American who was a long-time confidant and a former Catlin board member. The board and my fellow executives were becoming impatient: what was taking so long? I told them, "I can suggest some very good people who I've met, but they aren't going to fit with the culture."

Then I was introduced to Richard Banas. Within five minutes of meeting Rich, I looked at Ken Goldstein, he looked at me and we knew that we had finally found the right person to run Catlin's US operations. Rich had held executive positions at several major US insurers and was running a large division at XL when we met. He knew the US insurance market inside out.

The great thing about Rich is that he did not promise miracles overnight. From the outset, he worked tirelessly but carefully, making many great hires and building a business organically, just as we wanted. His job was made a bit easier when we acquired Wellington Underwriting plc in 2006 *(see Chapter 14)*. While Wellington was best known for its Lloyd's syndicate, it had built a small but successful reinsurance underwriting business in the States, which Rich was able to use as a springboard for growth. He immediately identified the portions of the Wellington US business that weren't very good and acted accordingly. He then went about building a US business for the future.

While it wasn't a walk in the park by any means, Catlin US grew in less than a decade to become a $1.5 billion business under the leadership of Rich, who is now retired, and subsequently Andrew McMellin, a long-time Catlin underwriting executive who succeeded Rich as CEO.

The lesson we learned is that it is easy to set up a business almost anywhere in the world. Due to its nature, it's relatively easy to underwrite reinsurance business successfully, even if you are new to a region. However, creating a profitable primary insurance business from scratch is hard work, no matter where you establish an operation. It takes time. You have to build a reputation. You must also prove that you can offer stability and continuity to brokers and clients. The first five years of operations are tough, but maybe that's a good thing; otherwise everybody else would do it.

* * *

Please don't think that everything Catlin touched turned to gold; I have to admit to a big mistake.

Shortly after we opened our first branch offices in Asia and the US, we decided to establish an office in Glasgow, Scotland. That office never really worked out, and the operation turned out to be a minor headache.

We persisted, however, in expanding our presence in the UK. Around the time of the IPO, we decided to establish a network of offices around the country to write small to medium-size risks, business with which Catlin had little previous experience. At one point, we had six or seven UK underwriting offices, but they never made much money. As we continued to expand globally, the UK offices became a bit of an afterthought.

After a decade of trying to make the UK offices successful, we finally gave up and closed most of them. Then a funny thing happened. We ended up keeping a lot of the good business that had been written by these offices; we were able to do it from London. These clients liked dealing with Catlin no matter where their policies were written. While I never, ever, got pleasure from putting employees out of a job, closing these UK branch offices was a good decision.

* * *

A big challenge we faced was breaking into the Chinese marketplace. We had some success, but like the US it was going to be a long process, and our Chinese operations were still not fully mature by the time Catlin was acquired by XL.

It was Paul Swain, who joined Catlin as CEO of our London operation back in the 1990s, who got me interested in China. Paul worked for the UK Foreign Office in Asia for several years. He had learned to speak Mandarin and understood the region far better than most people, including me.

So more than 20 years ago, I traveled to China with Paul. I did it to placate him, but I never regretted it. We went to Beijing, of course, but we also visited Changchun in Jilin Province in northeast China. China then was nothing like it is today. Even in Beijing, there were donkeys and carts everywhere. The hotels were low-grade. There were few highways and the traffic was appalling with the roads filled with tiny Chinese cars. I spent most of my time explaining what the word 'insurance' meant, but I did not get much of a reaction. Nobody really understood why anyone would purchase such a thing.

Then Paul got Catlin involved with the Lloyd's China study group, and he was really the person who put what is now Lloyd's China on the map. I don't think Lloyd's China would have happened without Paul. He had a much stronger vision than I regarding the opportunity China would present to insurers. He made it crystal clear, however, that anyone looking to enter the Chinese market had to take a ten-year view.

I kept returning to China because I was fascinated by it. I would visit the major Chinese insurers at the time, including PICC (People's Insurance Company of China), CPIC (China Pacific Insurance Company) and Ping An Insurance Company. When I first met with executives from PICC, I don't think they'd heard of the concept of aggregating exposures. PICC is a very different company now than when I first went there 20 years ago.

Guided by Paul Swain, we eventually opened an office in Shanghai in 2007, which was part of Lloyd's China. We focused on reinsurance business because the agency system in China, much like Japan, makes it nearly impossible for a Western company to enter the primary insurance market.

My next step, in mid-2011, was to take the Catlin board on a trip to China so they could see first-hand what opportunities China could offer to Catlin. Some of the directors had questioned whether we should operate in China in the first place and were hesitant to go, but they all eventually made the trip.

I can remember speaking to one of the directors when we arrived in Shanghai. When he saw the Pudong skyline, the director said to me, "Stephen, I had no idea of the magnitude of the place."

Later in the week, another director said, "Stephen, I had no idea how much you knew about China." I explained that the company had paid for me to visit China quite a few times, so it was a good thing that I had learned something.

By the end of the week, the directors were all saying, "Stephen, we all think you're doing absolutely the right thing in China. But, are we going quickly enough?" I replied that, yes, we were moving ahead at the right pace, keeping in mind all the difficulties inherent in operating a Chinese subsidiary.

While the board made the obligatory trip to the Great Wall of China (I still have never seen it), I took the opportunity to meet with the management of China Re (Group) Corporation in Beijing. I had an inkling there could be an opportunity for doing something with China Re, the state-owned reinsurer. It turned out that China Re wanted to write quota share reinsurance of some companies' portfolios, and Catlin was on the list. That didn't really interest me. However, I did hear a rumor that China Re was interested in getting involved as a capital provider at Lloyd's. Now that *did* interest me.

As part of the Wellington acquisition, Catlin had established two special purpose syndicates for the Lloyd's Names who had provided capital to the Wellington syndicate *(see Chapter 14)*. Could China Re possibly be interested in establishing an SPS that would write whole-account reinsurance of Catlin Syndicate 2003? The advantage of an SPS over traditional quota share reinsurance is that there is a credit risk associated with a quota share, but there's significantly less credit risk associated with an SPS.

After an hour-long pitch to Li Peiyu, China Re's chairman at the time, during which I explained the concept of an SPS, he told me what I said was interesting ... but could I possibly go through it again? I thought he meant at a different time, but he actually wanted me to go through my presentation once more, then and there. I did so, more slowly. Closing, I told him that he must also realize that a time issue was involved. If China Re wanted to establish the SPS for the 2012 underwriting year, the necessary funds had to be deposited at Lloyd's by November 30, 2011.

Chairman Li explained that China Re usually did not move that quickly, but I reminded him that Catlin had other companies that were interested in establishing a similar SPS. If China Re wanted to wait a year, I could not guarantee that we would need its involvement.

The $50 million necessary to establish the SPS was with Lloyd's by mid-November. That represented relatively breakneck speed for this kind of deal, let alone a deal with a company owned by the Chinese government. As part of our agreement, China Re and Catlin agreed to work together to learn more about each other's respective markets. A group of China Re employees was seconded to work at Catlin in London, and some of our employees worked at China Re in Beijing. That was an invaluable benefit for both parties because it provided insight into our respective markets that we could not obtain as outsiders.

China Re's long-term ambition was to establish a traditional Lloyd's syndicate, not simply an SPS, that could reinsure both Chinese risks as well as underwrite traditional London market business. Catlin helped China Re work with Lloyd's to make the syndicate a reality, although – at Lloyd's insistence – Catlin had to agree to manage the syndicate on behalf of China Re for the first several years of its existence. China Re Syndicate 2088 ('eight' being a lucky number in China) commenced operations in January 2015 with Matthew Sage, a long-time Catlin employee, serving as the syndicate's active underwriter, and Tim Peters – the same Tim Peters who joined Catlin in its early days – as syndicate manager, responsible for non-underwriting operations.

The China Re syndicate represented the first true investment by a Chinese company in the Lloyd's market, satisfying a goal set by Lloyd's several years earlier.

*   *   *

If I could do it all over again, would I 'go global'?

The answer must be a firm 'yes'. I think most of the big mistakes were made right at the beginning of the process. Although we had some other setbacks along the way – usually because we did not hire the right type of person for a certain job – overall, the international expansion was successful and ultimately profitable. In 2014, Catlin's last full year of trading as an independent company, 54 per cent of gross premiums written was produced by our non-London operations. In addition, 47 per cent of Catlin's underwriting profits in 2014 was contributed by offices outside the UK. It's hard to argue that Catlin would have done better if it had concentrated solely on its London wholesale business.

When we began to expand internationally, I thought that it was going to take us 10 to 15 years to finish the job. I was wrong; our European and Asia/Pacific hubs were not fully mature when Catlin was acquired by XL in 2015. If we'd had another five or six years, we would have got there, which means that our international expansion would have been a 20-year project.

In retrospect, international expansion certainly hurt Catlin's share price over the years because our return on equity was lower than it would have been had we not invested in the future. In addition, our global structure meant that Catlin did not fit into the same box as the other publicly traded

Lloyd's underwriters. The investment market doesn't like companies that don't fit in the same box as their peers and, as I said earlier, they do not like companies whose strategies are largely based on organic growth, particularly offshore and in the US.

14. Acquiring and Being Acquired

One deal made Catlin a major player;
another ended the story

The capital that Catlin raised during the years immediately following 9/11, plus our growing international footprint, put Catlin in a much better position than some of our London peers. We had raised about $700 million in capital in less than two years, and we no longer had to run our business solely as an annual venture because we were no longer tied to capital supplied by individual Lloyd's Names.

No Lloyd's-based underwriter, other than Catlin, was able to raise a substantial amount of capital during the 18 months following 9/11, largely because of the lingering doubts regarding the stability of Lloyd's *(see Chapter 17)*. So, there was now a real difference between Catlin and competitors such as Wellington and Hiscox, two much older and well-respected brands at Lloyd's.

In 2001, we were about half the size of those two businesses in terms of premium volume; two years later, we had caught up. The reason was not necessarily because we were great underwriters (although I would like to think we were), but because we were able to attract new capital. I had learned that you cannot progress in the insurance business unless you can raise capital.

Following the IPO, Catlin continued to grow in a robust insurance/reinsurance market in the wake of the 9/11 tragedy. However, the hard market did not last for very long, and by 2005 we chose to decrease our gross premiums written by 3 per cent, keeping our focus on bottom-line profit rather than top-line growth.

Premium rates increased sharply later in 2005 after Hurricane Katrina smashed through New Orleans in August. Katrina was followed later that autumn by Hurricanes Rita and Wilma, both of which also made landfall in the US. Combined, the three windstorms caused more than $100 billion in insured damage, an unprecedented total at the time.

The losses certainly had an impact on Catlin's 2005 results. Our net exposure to these three historic storms, net of reinstatement premiums, amounted to nearly $400 million, substantially greater than our 9/11 losses (although it must be remembered that our 2005 gross premium volume was more than three times our 2001 volume). Still, we managed to make nearly $28 million in profit before tax, thanks to a good underwriting performance in other portions of our portfolio and a robust reinsurance program.

*   *   *

Others were not so fortunate, especially Wellington Underwriting plc, one of the most venerable managing agencies at Lloyd's. Simply put, Wellington had got its aggregates wrong, and its 2005 hurricane losses blew through its reinsurance program. In other words, Wellington ran out of reinsurance when other underwriters – including Catlin – did not.

Wellington had a bigger problem in the eyes of investors. It could not accurately estimate its share of the hurricane losses, and it was forced to issue a series of profit warnings throughout the autumn of 2005. Shockingly, it issued a sharply increased hurricane loss estimate a little more than a week after an earlier announcement.

In my experience, a company is probably in trouble with investors if it must issue a profit warning. If a company must issue two profit warnings within a week, then it is really hurting. To be frankly honest, the investment community was really concerned about Wellington.

I started talking to Preben Prebensen, Wellington's CEO, about the possibility of a Catlin-Wellington transaction. Preben had headed Wellington for less than two years; he was a former J.P. Morgan banker, and this was his first hands-on experience in the insurance industry. We were able to discuss constructively the benefits of combining the two companies.

Acquiring Wellington had several potential advantages for Catlin. It certainly would mark a step-change in terms of our scale. At the time Wellington's premium volume was nearly as large as Catlin's, and Wellington had established a network of US offices. By acquiring Wellington, we would no longer be the owners of a medium-sized Lloyd's syndicate but rather a true multinational insurer that owned the largest syndicate at Lloyd's and underwrote $2.7 billion in gross premiums.

Lloyd's itself really wanted Catlin to acquire Wellington since, because of the profit warnings and the loss estimates being so wrong, it had become a problem case for the market. Keeping in mind all the misfortunes of the past 20 years, Lloyd's did not want Wellington to collapse, and the market's leadership was concerned that Wellington could represent yet another hit to the Lloyd's Central Fund.

We did the deal very quickly. I agreed a price with Preben on September 21, 2006, the offer was publicly announced on October 30, and the deal was closed on December 18. The whole transaction – from start to finish – took just four months, which might have set a record for the acquisition of a UK publicly held company. However, we had to act quickly. The deal had to be completed by the end of the year if we wanted to combine Catlin's and Wellington's Lloyd's syndicates for the 2007 underwriting year, and we also wanted to conclude the acquisition quickly because we did not want any chance of a rival bid.

Something did nearly catch us out, though. Wellington had a fairly well-developed network of US reinsurance underwriting offices, whose holding company was domiciled in Delaware, and we couldn't complete the acquisition without regulatory approval from the Delaware authorities. The Delaware Insurance Department promised a 90-day turnaround regarding a decision, but we only had about a month to go before the end of the year. Fortunately, we managed to get the process accelerated so that the necessary approval was granted in about 15 days. The whole acquisition could have collapsed if Delaware had waited until after the New Year to give us its blessing.

Another issue that could have sunk the acquisition was a familiar subject to us at Catlin: Lloyd's Names. While Catlin had bought out the remaining individual Names on our syndicates back in 2002, about one-third of Wellington's Syndicate 2020's capacity was supplied by individual Names. After working so hard to buy out the Names four years earlier, we did not want to find ourselves back in the same position. However, buying out the Wellington Names was easier said than done, and we finally had to offer them the option of participating for three years on special purpose syndicates that would write quota-share reinsurance of Syndicate 2003, into which Wellington Syndicate 2020 would be merged.

It was a big price to pay, but it was worth it, partly because we were able to use the same type of mechanism five years later when China Re decided that it would reinsure Syndicate 2003 (see Chapter 12). Paul Swain, who by that time had retired from Catlin, came back and used his considerable expertise to help us negotiate a deal with the Names and their members' agents.

Catlin's acquisition of Wellington was completed on December 18, 2006, at a cost of $1.18 billion, composed of cash amounting to $347 million and 86.1 million new Catlin shares.

Nearly everybody thought it was a risky transaction. The almost universal reaction from the get-go was either, "They're going to fall flat on their face," or "There's a real risk that they will, but I hope they don't." By the time we got to the end of 2007, it was clear to the marketplace that the acquisition had been successful, and there was a remarkable turnaround in people's sentiments. People were now saying, "Blimey! Well done! Good on you!"

Once the acquisition was a done deal, we still faced two major challenges. We had to retain as much of the business previously underwritten by Catlin and Wellington as we could, and we had to integrate the two businesses successfully.

The former was easier than we had thought. Paul Brand and I agreed that I would ring up the CEOs of all the major brokers, while he would speak to the individual brokers' team leaders at the coalface. I was painting the big picture ("This is where we are going"), while he was focusing on the operational side. What we essentially told them was, "We are here for the future; this is a long-term deal; we are here to look after your clients. And for the avoidance of doubt, 2 plus 2 equals 4; it doesn't equal 3½." In other words, we wanted to continue to write the same line sizes previously written individually by Catlin and Wellington.

I think we had one or two tussles with brokers regarding line sizes during the first four or five days, but the concept was quickly accepted. It was almost a given that when a broker came to Catlin to renew business, Catlin would write a line that would equal the combination of the former Catlin line and Wellington line.

Brando and I had pessimistically planned for a 30 per cent loss of business. In my heart of hearts, I thought it would be 15 per cent. The reality was that we lost virtually no business, other than some poor accounts that we wanted to discard in any case.

* * *

The integration of the two companies was another thing altogether, even though we weren't under any illusions that it was going to be easy. There would be systems issues, regulatory issues and, of course, people issues. The Wellington transaction more or less doubled the size of Catlin overnight, so for a start, we suddenly had two of nearly everything.

A number of years previously, the then-Catlin management team had participated in a short mergers and acquisitions course at Templeton College at the University of Oxford. Sir David Rowland, the former chairman of Lloyd's, was then the president of Templeton College and was very keen on upping professional standards in the marketplace. Somehow or other, David found out that we were on the course, and he was at the door when we turned up. He took off his jacket and put it on the floor to make a 'red carpet' for me to walk over – which I didn't do!

We came out of the course with a blueprint for what we should do if we ever embarked on another merger or acquisition. I have never forgotten what I learned from the course.

More than two-thirds of M&As in the UK and the US *decrease* shareholder value after a three- or four-year period. We looked at case studies to determine why these transactions were not successful and found that there were two clear reasons. One was that the acquiring company paid too much or, in the case of insurance companies, the acquired company was under-reserved. The second reason was that the two companies were integrated too slowly. Unless 75 per cent of the integration was completed within the first 12 months and the other 25 per cent during the next 12 months, the acquisition was not very successful.

An example in our industry was Royal Sun Alliance, now known as RSA Insurance Group plc. That transaction was announced in May 2006, and to this day you can still find Royal people in one corner of the office and Sun Alliance people in the other. Shareholder value has decreased in real terms over a 20-year period. The companies had a combined market capitalization of about £6 billion at the time of the merger; it was only about £5.5 billion in November 2016.

Remembering how easy it is to slip up when acquiring another company, I told my colleagues that once the Wellington deal closed, I wanted to get 75 per cent of the integration done within the first six months. "That means making some quick decisions. If we get 80 per cent of them right, we're going to win. We have some difficult decisions to take, but if we don't take them, our expenses will be out of control, the management will be out of control and the direction will be out of control," I told them. "We're inevitably going to make some mistakes, so let's accept that and not hold back on making a decision for fear of making the wrong decision."

Luckily, our first big integration decision turned out to be a huge success. At the time we made the offer to Wellington, it just so happened that a large space on the ground floor of the London Underwriting Centre – the building in which Catlin's London office was then located – was available. It had been occupied by Employers Reinsurance Corp., which had been recently acquired by Swiss Re. The space would make a perfect underwriting floor for the merged Catlin-Wellington underwriting teams. I had gone to the absolute maximum of my spending capability as CEO – without going to the board for approval – to secure this space, even though the Wellington transaction had not yet been finalized.

We closed the Wellington acquisition at 5.45 p.m. on Monday, December 18, 2006. On Tuesday morning, both the Catlin and Wellington underwriters showed up for work at the new underwriting floor. Each underwriter had a

Peter Jordan/Alamy Stock Photo

Ros Drinkwater/Alamy Stock Photo

ARLIS/Alamy Stock Photo

Three catastrophes contributed to Lloyd's massive losses from 1988–1992, (clockwise from top left): the Piper Alpha rig explosion, a devastating UK windstorm and the Exxon Valdez oil spill; the 9/11 tragedy also raised questions about Lloyd's survival.

DPA Picture Alliance/Alamy Stock Photo

i

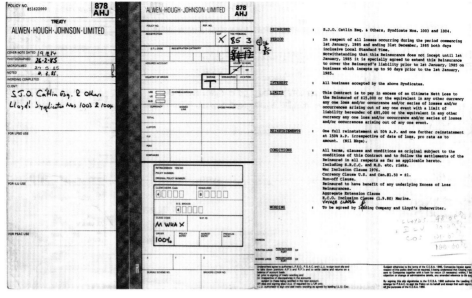

Lloyd's

Lloyd's

Lloyd's

(Above)
Stephen Catlin began work at Lloyd's in the Underwriting Room of the 1958 building.

(Top and above right)
David Rowland was Lloyd's chairman during the Reconstruction and Renewal program,
while Sax Riley also introduced market reforms during his tenure as chairman.

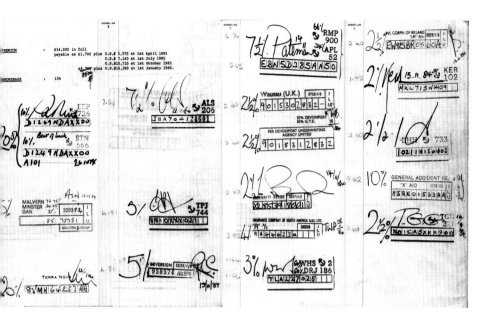

(Above)
The placing slip for the reinsurance program covering Catlin Syndicate 1003 for the 1985 year of account.

(Below)
The original Equitas board of directors; Stephen Catlin stands at the center of the back row.

(Above clockwise from top left)
Catlin's first office was located in Plantation House in the City of London;
Catlin's underwriting floor shortly after the Wellington acquisition; Catlin
moved into a new London office at 20 Gracechurch Street in 2011.

(Opposite)
Stephen Catlin and Wellington CEO Preben Prebensen; the Catlin Group
Executive Committee in early 2011: Paul Brand, Benji Meuli, Stephen Catlin,
Paul Jardine, Richard Banas, Jo Mier and Andrew McMellin. Adrian Spieler
later joined the GEC.

(Opposite)
The Catlin Arctic Survey
from 2009-2011 helped
build the Catlin brand;
Stephen Catlin, left,
and Paul Brand, right,
led a group of broker
executives on an expedition
near Svalbard.

(Above)
The Catlin Seaview Survey
continued Catlin's
commitment to
environmental research.

(Left)
Stephen Catlin with the
BBC's David Attenborough
at COP 21 in Paris in 2015.

Stephen Catlin through the years
(clockwise from top left):

c. 1972
c. 1982
c. 2000
c. 2015

desk, a brand new ergonomic chair, a PC connected to both the Catlin and Wellington systems, and a telephone that actually worked! We grouped the underwriters by the classes of business they wrote, so a Catlin underwriter and a Wellington underwriter, who one day before were fierce rivals, were now sitting side-by-side, getting to know each other as colleagues. I went down to the new underwriting floor at 10 a.m., and the atmosphere was amazing. Everyone was drinking coffee from a dedicated coffee bar, shaking hands, and having a laugh and a joke. By midday, they were working together, underwriting renewals. That morning really set the scene for the next six months

Big credit goes to the Catlin facilities team, headed by Myles Ruffy. Myles and his team had come to me saying, "What do you want to achieve? What is your goal? What are the timeframes? What have we got to play with?" They did a remarkable job against an extremely tight deadline.

On the personnel front, we established a small group – four Catlin people and four Wellington people – who made the decisions regarding employees who were to be retained and those who were to be let go. We worked on the basis that the best man or woman for the job won. It wasn't a question of one Catlin, one Wellington; it was a question of who was best suited to remain.

We parted company with Wellington's aviation underwriting team soon after the acquisition was finalized. We had said to them, "You join the party or you leave the party," and they didn't want to join. Paul Brand came to me and said, "I don't think I can win this one." I knew that Brando was correct, and they were out of the door very quickly.

That sent a message through the entire organization – "These guys mean business!" – and a lot of people's attitudes suddenly changed. About a third of the Wellington employees were still working at Catlin nearly a decade later. We lost a lot of the back-office employees because they had been with Wellington for many years and found it difficult to get used to the Catlin corporate culture. But, after a year, you couldn't find an ex-Wellington employee at Catlin. If you asked someone who they worked for, they did not say, "I used to work for Wellington." They said, "I work for Catlin." In their hearts, they had become part of Catlin.

We divided day-to-day operations and responsibilities into six separate functions. Paul Brand took responsibility for underwriting, and others were responsible for claims, finance and actuarial, operations, IT, etc. The people dealing with back-office functions, such as IT, had the most difficult job to do. Back office integration proved to be tougher than the client-facing operations. I suspect it was a question of style as much as anything. The front-end style you can deal with; it is more transparent. The back-end style isn't so transparent.

By May 2007 – five months after the acquisition had been finalized – we had completed about 85 per cent of the integration, but it did take the next 19 months to do the last bit: systems integration. Wellington had a mass of legacy systems and integrating those was a painful, time-consuming process. The complexities were greater than we had thought.

After the event, I was deemed to be a hero by the Catlin board, but there is absolutely no doubt I would have been called a failure if the transaction had fallen over. I might not have kept my job. But I was convinced that we could get there. I was determined to do it, so I was prepared to take the risk. However, I must stress that the positive outcome of the transaction was truly a team effort. Without the strength of the team, the outcome could have been very different.

* * *

I worked on the integration nearly non-stop for six months, so I did virtually no traveling or networking. It was only after I got back on the road that I realized that, due to the Wellington acquisition and the added scale it provided, people were looking at Catlin very differently than before.

My first overseas trip was to Australia. When I had traveled there previously, I was usually asked by clients and brokers, "I see you're still around. How are things going?" That was usually the end of it. However, by mid-2007, their attitudes had changed dramatically. The reaction was more like, "Stephen, gosh, you've been doing some fantastic things! How can we do business together?" There was a step-change from cynicism to the realization that Catlin was a business that was going forward, partly driven by the fact that we were a much bigger, and in their view, more stable company. They started thinking, "We had better take notice of what Catlin is doing because if we don't, we may lose out."

If I compare the Western General transaction, the private equity raise, the IPO and the acquisition of Wellington, the Wellington deal was the most difficult to execute by a country mile. There were far more moving pieces, added uncertainty and far more people-related issues. A greater number of employees had to be involved in the process, and that was a significant management challenge. Of all the things that I am proud of in terms of management achievement, the Wellington acquisition is where we at Catlin demonstrated what we could do as a team. While that transaction took place a decade ago, it stands out as one of the handful of insurance company acquisitions that have truly worked and have significantly increased shareholder value.

Was it luck? Partly. But primarily, it was hard work and team effort.

* * *

Not too long after we bought Wellington, the financial markets began to melt down.

The main impact that the global financial crisis had on Catlin was to reduce investment return. During 2007, we were forced to take a $75 million charge for fixed income investments in our portfolio related to the subprime mortgage market, although the company still reported a very healthy $544 million in profit before tax. However, Catlin made a $46 million loss on a pretax basis in 2008 largely due to $115 million in fixed income investment losses, most of which were unrealized. In other words, we suffered paper losses, not actual losses. These investment losses reversed themselves in 2009 when asset values rebounded, and we reported a record $603 million in profit before tax.

What the financial crisis really accomplished, from an insurance industry perspective, was to demonstrate quite clearly the different dynamics of insurers' balance sheets compared with banks'. For years, insurers had been pretty much lumped together with banks, which was quite wrong because the dynamics of insurers' and banks' balance sheets are so very different. As I noted previously, a banker's perspective on downside risk to capital is not the same as an insurer's. The insurer's daily job is to assume and manage risk, and we charge for this. Banks, on the other hand, try to trade with the least amount of risk possible on their balance sheets.

Interestingly, if you look back now with the benefit of hindsight, the only companies in the insurance industry that were severely impacted by the financial crisis were insurers whose activities had strayed from traditional insurance operations: AIG, Swiss Re and XL. All three companies took a financial pounding because of those activities, but fortunately all three companies have rebounded.

One good thing that came out of the financial crisis, as far as Catlin was concerned, was that Benji Meuli joined us, initially as interim chief investment officer and then as chief financial officer. Benji had been CIO of Swiss Re prior to the financial crisis. He had spent several years tidying up the asset side of the Swiss Re balance sheet to get rid of what he believed was inappropriate risk. As quickly as Benji was de-risking the asset portfolio, Swiss Re was taking on similar risks on the liability side of the balance sheet by writing products like credit default swaps that weren't really insurance. Benji eventually left, and Swiss Re was in the headlines as a potential casualty of the financial crisis due to the losses it sustained from these products. A multi-billion-dollar investment from Warren Buffett's Berkshire Hathaway helped Swiss Re steady the ship.

Benji's appointment as Catlin's CFO solidified our top management team, or what we called the Group Executive Committee. I, of course, was a member as were Benji, Paul Brand and Paul Jardine. Rich Banas was also a member, both in his role as head of Catlin US and because of his overall insurance expertise and wisdom. Andrew McMellin, a Catlin underwriting executive, joined the committee in 2009 when he was appointed as Paul Brand's deputy; Andrew later succeeded Rich as CEO of Catlin US.

Two others joined the committee in the years before Catlin was acquired by XL. Adrian Spieler, who had worked with Benji at Swiss Re, joined Catlin in 2012 as chief administrative officer, responsible for all of our IT and back office operations. Adrian was only with Catlin for three years before it was acquired, but he accomplished great things during that time. Jo Mier, who had served as my chief of staff for several years, was appointed to the committee in 2013, reflecting the important role that she played across Catlin. Jo had joined Catlin more than ten years earlier, serving as an underwriter, an operations director and as head of IT.

* * *

Catlin continued to grow and prosper. Between 2008 and 2014 gross premiums written nearly doubled. All of that growth was organic and the company was consistently profitable. It's worth remembering that 2011 was the second worst year for natural catastrophes in history, trailing only 2005 (the year of Hurricane Katrina). Instead of one colossal catastrophe, there were a series of major events around the world: the Japanese earthquake/tsunami, two New Zealand earthquakes, a record series of tornadoes in the US and flooding in Thailand that was largely unforeseen by insurance models. However, thanks to our reinsurance strategy, largely directed by Paul Brand, Catlin recorded profit before tax of $71 million, while many of our competitors reported losses for the year.

Our non-London operations – which we had only begun to establish 15 years earlier – had matured rapidly. In 2014, Catlin's last full year of operations, 54 per cent of our gross premiums written and 47 per cent of our underwriting profits were produced by the five underwriting hubs outside of London: US, Bermuda, Europe, Asia-Pacific and Canada. Our international strategy was at last beginning to pay off.

However, there were also dark clouds appearing on the horizon. Catlin's shares traded at a lower multiple than some of our UK peers – particularly Amlin plc and Hiscox Ltd – because, in my opinion, analysts and many investors still did not fully understand the potential earnings power of Catlin's six-hub international infrastructure. Our model was perhaps too complex to be comprehended easily by the market.

In addition, it was clear that the commercial property/casualty insurance market was heading towards yet another down cycle. Rates were already falling for most forms of property coverage – despite the near-record insured catastrophe losses of 2011 – and pressure was building on rates for casualty and specialty classes of business.

The cost of compliance, the cost of regulation and just the general cost of doing business were going up, and as a consequence our expense ratio was rising. The truth of the matter was our expense ratio was too high, and I couldn't see any means of changing that trend in the near term, especially as the market was softening. The only real way of lowering the expense ratio was to increase our top line, which we could have done by 50 to 100 per cent over the medium term. However, aggressively increasing volume in a falling market doesn't make much sense to me.

Finally, it was becoming clear to me that size was what increasingly mattered to insurance brokers. Although Catlin's gross premium volume had grown by nearly 1,300 per cent between 2001 and 2014, the question remained: was Catlin truly large enough to compete if the marketplace contracted?

* * *

I had known Mike McGavick, CEO of XL, for a number of years. Mike joined XL in 2008, in the midst of the financial crisis and at a time that the company's existence was seriously in doubt because of huge losses stemming from an affiliate that wrote financial guarantee insurance. Mike did a great job of turning XL around, as he had previously done in his role as CEO of Safeco Corp, a Seattle-based insurer.

Mike and I found ourselves attending an insurance regulatory conference in Brussels in the spring of 2013 and found time for a chat. I asked him what he thought would happen in the marketplace.

"It's going to consolidate," Mike said.

"When?" I asked.

"Two to five years," Mike replied. "Out of interest, what do you think?

"Actually, I would have answered those same two questions identically," I said.

We looked at each other, and Mike asked, "When are you going back to London?" We agreed that we would fly to London together and continue our conversation on the plane.

We had a much more detailed discussion about the future of the marketplace on the flight to London, and we found ourselves pretty much in complete agreement. I then asked him if there was any merit in having a further conversation. Mike's jaw dropped, and he asked me what I meant.

"Is there any merit in talking about bringing the two businesses together?" I asked.

"Well," Mike replied, "I've got a list, Stephen, but you're not on it."

I looked at him in the eye and asked, "Why is that? Are we *that* bad?"

"No," he responded. "I never thought you would actually contemplate such a thing."

"On that narrow issue, you're wrong," I told Mike. "I would contemplate such a conversation because I have a duty of care to our shareholders, our employees and our counterparties. We're a public company."

Mike made it clear that any combination would have to be an acquisition of Catlin by XL, a significantly larger company in terms of premium volume, employees and market capitalization. Mike also made it clear that the XL board of directors would want Mike to continue to be the CEO of the combined company. I said I understood that, and so we began an 18-month-long process that ended in XL making an offer to acquire Catlin.

Mike and I talked to each other, on average, once every two or three months for at least a year until negotiations began in earnest. We spent quite a long time discussing social issues, strategic issues, business issues and business ethos in an effort to make certain that we were coming from the same position. We reached the conclusion that no one thinks identically to another person, but that we were pretty close.

Mike and I had been talking one-to-one for about a year when we decided in June 2014 to meet at Mike's house in Idaho, each with one of our closest colleagues: Catlin's Paul Brand and Peter Porrino, who at the time was XL's chief financial officer.

During these discussions, Pete worried that the two companies could lose as much as 15 per cent of their combined business if an acquisition took place. I told Pete that we would not lose that much, explaining that I had modeled that Catlin would lose 30 per cent of the combined business when Catlin acquired Wellington, but we ended up losing virtually nothing. I didn't think XL and Catlin would lose nothing, but I didn't think we would lose 15 per cent.

Pete asked, "What do you really think we will lose?

"Not more than 5 per cent," I said.

"I'm going to mark it down as 10 per cent," he responded.

"You're the buyer, so you do whatever you want. But you asked me my view, and I told you."

As with the Wellington acquisition, XL lost very little business after it acquired Catlin. It was more than nothing, but it was less than 1 per cent, which frankly is just a rounding error.

We got through that meeting in Idaho with both sets of parties thinking that it would be an extremely difficult transaction to do. There were lots of complexities. But if we could make it work, the reward at the end of the tunnel should be substantial. So, without really discussing it, we took about three months as a cooling-off period. Neither Mike nor I talked about what we were doing at this point; I think we instinctively knew what each other was doing.

Come September, I had come to the conclusion that an XL-Catlin combination was the most attractive transaction available to Catlin, with regards to both our shareholders and our employees. Mike similarly indicated the attractiveness of an XL-Catlin transaction to XL. I reminded Mike that if we were going to move our conversations forward and include more people from each company as well as outside advisors, the clock would start ticking and a leak was probable, if not inevitable.

A month later, we held a meeting in a law firm's offices in New York, where we took over an entire floor. There were about 20 people from both sides at the meeting, broken into ten or so smaller sub-meetings. The feeling I had was that the people were actually engaged, enjoying the meeting and even having a bit of laugh. There didn't seem to be a 'them and us' mentality. Later in the evening, we held a dinner, and you would have never guessed that everyone had been talking all day about a major transaction. The mood was jovial. That gave us the confidence to take things forward because no one had found anything that caused extreme concern as to why we couldn't – or shouldn't – continue with the discussions.

The combination appeared to be sensible. XL was a major player in the US, and although Catlin was growing in the States, we weren't all that big, so that was a good match. Catlin had owned and managed the largest Lloyd's syndicate for seven years running, while XL's operations in London were below critical mass. So, that also seemed like a good fit. At a stroke, you were building a really powerful London business and an equally powerful US business. Then, when you examined Europe and Asia-Pacific, both companies were probably beneath critical mass. Bringing the two companies together would probably save both parties at least five years' work. And, by combining,

XL Catlin would probably be big enough that the combined company should be able to control its destiny in an increasingly consolidating marketplace.

You could debate whether Catlin alone would have been large enough to be relevant in a contracting marketplace and you could even argue over whether XL would have been relevant – but there was no question that XL Catlin would become a major player if the acquisition went ahead.

* * *

All of the discussions between Catlin and XL were strictly confidential ... that is until the *Financial Times* got wind of the talks in the middle of December 2014.

I was in Beijing, boarding a plane that was scheduled to arrive in Singapore the following morning, when I got an *FT* news alert on my iPhone. I read the alert and thought, "Oh shit!" before turning my phone off because the plane was ready to take off. I had a whisky and then went to sleep. I slept quite well actually, which was just as well because I didn't get much rest for the next 48 hours.

After I landed in Singapore, I turned my phone on and saw a slew of texts, emails and voicemails. I was scheduled to conduct a 'town hall' meeting with our Singapore employees as soon as I arrived at the office from the airport. "What am I going to say?" I thought to myself. "What can I say?" My freedom to say much was pretty restricted due to the legalities regarding the potential acquisition of a publicly held company, but equally I couldn't speak to employees and say nothing. I ended up saying something along the lines of, "You probably have read some articles in the press. I'm not at liberty to talk much about this, but I can confirm that we will act in the best interests of our shareholders and our employees."

However, life soon got pretty frantic. For the next two days, my last call of the day took place at about 2:30 a.m. in the morning and my first call of the next day was at 4 a.m. I was literally getting only about an hour and half's sleep. I was in absolutely the worst time zone to speak to America and to the UK. It seemed like a complete disaster that the news had leaked, but as is often the case, it all worked out for the best. We had prepared ourselves well for such an eventuality, so we could quickly issue a holding press release. We went into an operational mode rather than a panic mode.

As it was the middle of the year-end renewal season, this kind of a leak could have been disastrous for both Catlin and XL, but it wasn't. Neither company lost any significant business due to the transaction, even though the deal was still up in the air. That gave us a strong indication that brokers supported the proposed transaction and thought it was strategically sensible. Catlin's share price, of course, rocketed upward toward the proposed price quoted in the *FT* article, but XL's share price did not suffer. The reactions from insurance brokers and investors gave both companies' boards of directors some comfort that the deal would be acceptable to the marketplace.

*　　*　　*

Of course, it wasn't up to me to decide whether Catlin should sell itself to XL. That was the Catlin board's duty.

Something I learned was that it is quite different speaking as the CEO to a board of directors as an acquiree, as compared with an acquiror. I'd never been an acquiree in my life, so it was *de facto* a new experience for me. When I proposed an acquisition, as with the Wellington deal, I basically laid out a plan, set out parameters as to what I thought we might have to pay and the board, for the most part, bought into it. "Go and do the best job you can and we'll support you," was pretty much the board's response.

However, when your company is being acquired, it is an entirely different type of negotiating experience. The board placed a heightened scrutiny on me during the process of negotiations. Although I was doing the negotiations with XL, the Catlin board retained the ultimate decision as to whether to sell the company. John Barton, who had succeeded Sir Graham Hearne as Catlin's chairman several years earlier, did a great job leading the board during the months leading up to the transaction.

I believe, in the end, it was a fair price for the transaction: 388 pence in cash and 0.130 XL ordinary shares for each Catlin common share, or the equivalent of 715.3 pence per share based on the closing price of XL ordinary shares on January 8, 2015, the day before the transaction was formally announced. In other words, XL paid about $4.1 billion. Catlin shareholders received a 22.9 per cent premium compared with Catlin's share price the day before the offer announcement was published, including a special dividend.

The acquisition was overwhelmingly approved by Catlin's shareholders. However, it was something else that convinced Mike and me that the purchase price was probably a fair one.

After the acquisition was finally announced, Mike and I did an investor road show in London. One of the firms we visited was an American fund manager with a UK affiliate. We were in London with a video link to the firm's US headquarters. About halfway through the meeting, one of the UK analysts asked me whether I thought the price was fair. Before I could open my mouth, one of the US guys said across the video feed, "No, XL paid far too much." A lengthy debate then ensued among the fund's UK and American analysts as to whether the price was reasonable, with the US guys – who followed XL – saying XL overpaid, while the UK guys maintained that Catlin had been undervalued.

I said to Mike afterwards, "If ever either one of us want validation that we got the price right, that was it."

* * *

Mike and I held a conference call with all analysts shortly after we announced XL's official bid. As Mike was the CEO of the acquiring company, he fielded most of the questions, but at one point in the call, I was asked for my views. I said, "If you thought that consolidation was about to occur in your industry, why wouldn't you get on the front foot, be proactive and choose your partner? Otherwise, your partner will probably be chosen for you."

I came up with that line on the spur of the moment. After the conference call was finished, Mike told me what I said had been great and that I should repeat it whenever we were asked for rationales for the acquisition. Predictably, I couldn't remember what I had said; we had to get a transcript of the conference call to find out my exact words.

That spontaneous reaction became a mantra over the next several months, and I think it still holds true today. Other mergers and acquisitions have since taken place in the industry. Some were very well thought through, and others weren't. Some of the deals have worked out well, and some haven't.

* * *

Many people have asked me why I would want to sell the company I had founded. However, at the same time, they also remarked that the XL-Catlin combination made enormous strategic sense. Nobody has told me to my face that selling Catlin was the wrong thing to do. Many people have commended me for being prepared to relinquish being a CEO to accomplish something that benefitted Catlin's shareholders. Not many CEOs would do that, they said.

I don't know whether that's true or false. I do know, though, that a CEO's duty of care is first and foremost to the shareholders, then to the company's employees and its counterparties. It isn't appropriate for a CEO to put self-interest ahead of those duties.

So, to answer a question I have often been asked, I didn't really find agreeing to the acquisition a difficult decision to make. I believe it was the right thing to have done.

* * *

We announced XL's official offer to acquire Catlin on January 9, 2015, and we completed the acquisition on May 1. The nearly four months between these two milestones were filled with integration planning. I could not stress clearly enough, based on our experience with Wellington, that it was paramount that we integrate the two companies' operations as quickly and seamlessly as possibly. I think we did a pretty good job, but as time passes I am sure that areas will be identified where we could have done better.

On Catlin's last day as an independent company, I was in Bermuda, where Catlin was domiciled, to attend the final meetings associated with the change of control. That morning, I worked by phone with Catlin's head of corporate affairs, Jim Burcke, in London to draft a final message to the 2,500 Catlin employees worldwide. Jim had worked at Catlin since 2003 and had helped me write most of my speeches and presentations.

The message was titled simply, "Thank You":

Dear Fellow Catlin Employees,

As most of you know, my goal since I established Catlin more than 30 years ago has been to build a business for the future.

Over the years, Catlin has grown from a very small Lloyd's underwriting agency to a global insurer and reinsurer, writing $6 billion in gross premiums annually. More importantly, we have earned the respect of brokers and clients alike for our underwriting expertise and our superior service, particularly our claims service.

We have passed many milestones during the past 30 years: establishing our first offices outside of London in the late 1990s and the subsequent evolution of our global network; the formation of our various underwriting platforms; a series of important capital-raising initiatives, including our IPO in 2004; and of course the Wellington acquisition in 2006. I am deeply grateful for your hard work and your contributions to Catlin over the years that have allowed us to prosper and grow.

Today, we reach another milestone: the completion of XL's offer to acquire Catlin. I must admit that today I have mixed emotions. Catlin, the company that we have together worked so hard to build, will no longer exist as an independent entity. Many changes, some perhaps unsettling, lay in wait. Most sadly, we will be forced to say goodbye over the coming months to some of our colleagues, as this is unfortunately an inevitable element of modern business restructurings.

However, my thoughts then return to my original goal: to build a business for the future. In today's insurance/reinsurance environment, the combination of Catlin with XL makes perfect sense. Brushing aside sentimentality, combining our two businesses will result in a stronger company in terms of people, knowledge, infrastructure and finances, giving us an increased ability to seize on opportunities as they emerge. While Catlin could have continued to succeed as an independent company, I firmly believe that joining with XL serves the best interests of our shareholders, clients, brokers and, not least, the vast majority of our employees.

The acquisition of Catlin by XL is yet another important milestone in the Catlin Story. Together, XL Catlin immediately becomes one of the world's most important specialty insurers and reinsurers. We now have a solid, enlarged base from which we can do great things. In other words, we are still building a business for the future.

So, please join with me today in raising a toast to Catlin and to what we have accomplished as a team since the group was established in 1984. Then, let's all have another (seems natural): to XL Catlin and to the bright future ahead.

Yours sincerely,
Stephen

*   *   *

Friends have asked me if I was emotional on that last day of Catlin's existence. I wasn't just emotional; I was *extremely* emotional. I had thought the whole thing through rationally after all, but finally recognizing that the company that I had established was no longer independent was emotionally draining.

I think it really hit me the hardest the next morning. We had sent out the email to the employees late in the afternoon of April 30, and the next morning I made the mistake of switching on my iPad to look at emails before I had even got out of bed. I can remember explicitly that I had received 47 emails in response to my message to employees (many more arrived later).

All expressed employees' views and emotions about what they thought they were leaving behind. It opened the floodgates, and I was literally in tears; I was absolutely beside myself.

Reading the first two or three emails was great in the sense that it felt good to receive so much support from employees. By the time I got to the 47th message, I had to spend a couple of hours to pull myself together so I could go to work. I was in such a state that I simply couldn't go straight into the office as I normally would.

Am I ashamed of that? No, I'm not. Did I see it coming? No, I didn't. I thought I had my emotions in control, but I was mistaken. I guess it's a credit to the whole Catlin team that their messages provoked such raw, intense emotions. Their emails spoke volumes about what people thought about the business and the leadership we had provided. People who know me have heard me often say that all I've ever been is a team leader. What makes a good business is good *people*; one person does not make a good business.

To this day, some former Catlin employees still hanker for the old days, but that's foolish. One cannot turn back the clock. In business, you either move forward or you move backwards. You either sink or you swim, and I am proud that XL Catlin is swimming ahead nicely.

Part III
Lloyd's and the London Market

15. THE BAD OLD DAYS

Lloyd's on occasion sailed close to the edge

Lloyd's of London has sometimes resembled the mythical phoenix, with its propensity to self-combust only to rise again anew. The marketplace did just that in the late 1980s and early 1990s, and came close to repeating it after the tragedy that was 9/11.

There have been several books written about Lloyd's troubles in the 1980s and 1990s, some good and some not quite so good. If you want to find out more regarding Lloyd's problems during this era, I would recommend reading *On the Brink: How a Crisis Transformed Lloyd's of London*, written by Andrew Duguid, who was a Lloyd's executive during the period, and *Ultimate Risk*, a now out-of-print analysis of Lloyd's problems by Adam Raphael, an award-winning journalist and a former Lloyd's Name.

I don't intend to rewrite history here, nor provide a detailed account of Lloyd's problems and the subsequent Reconstruction and Renewal (R&R) program. However, I would like to share some observations of what it was like to work at Lloyd's before it truly cleaned up its act. My viewpoint is that of an underwriter active in the market at the time, not as a Lloyd's official or a Name who had lost his or her fortune, although I was a Name during much of this period.

* * *

When I turned up at Lloyd's on my first day of work in 1973, I was nervous as hell because I had no real idea what I was walking into. On the one hand, it was a bit like a bunch of public school[12] boys having a bit of fun. It was as if I was joining a City club. On the other hand, there clearly was some work going on, but I had no real idea what it was about.

In those days there was no concept of an employee orientation or induction program. "There you are. Fill in that ledger. Get on with it, boy,"

---

12 In the United Kingdom, the term 'public school' refers to what Americans and other nationalities would define as a 'private' school; that is, a privately funded school with selective entry that charges tuition fees.

was pretty much all I was told. I could quickly recognize that the processes we were using were rooted in the Dark Ages and, in retrospect, the 'process' still hasn't changed in many ways. Overall, the standards were very sloppy.

What I didn't recognize in my early days is that Lloyd's, together with the rest of the London market, was – and still is – the most fantastic wholesale insurance marketplace in the world. Only at Lloyd's can a broker, on behalf of his client, syndicate an insurance policy among many different underwriters using the exact same policy wording. Claims adjustment works in a similar way. When a policyholder purchases coverage outside of the London market, it probably won't be possible to obtain a common policy wording from a group of different insurers, and there will probably be inconsistencies among these insurers with regards to claims handling.

* * *

I remarked earlier that, when I first joined Lloyd's, I was not sure if it was the most famous insurance marketplace in the world or a gambling casino. At the time, both observations would have been correct.

For many years, until they were banned in the 1980s, there was active trading in policies that were labeled as 'PPI', which stands for 'policy proof of interest'. They weren't really insurance policies; they were wagers cleverly disguised as insurance. Under Section 4 of the Marine Insurance Act 1906, a policyholder must have an 'insurable interest' in the risk covered by the policy for the coverage to be valid. Under the concept of a PPI, the mere fact that the policy was purchased allegedly proved that the policyholder had a proof of interest in the policy. In other words, the insurable interest was the policy itself. Pretty clever, huh?

This led to all types of wagers disguised as legitimate insurance. There were 'tonners', which were simply policies that stated how much global shipping tonnage would be lost during a particular year. If that amount was reached or exceeded, the policy would pay out. A 'chinaman' was based on the same principle but in reverse: if the stated amount of tonnage lost was not reached, the policy paid out. If you think about it, these types of policies were not much different to bets on a football or soccer match in which the wager is tied to the number of goals scored.

'Overdues' were another example of these types of policies. Overdues were essentially a bet on whether or not a ship would reach port following an incident.

The syndicate on which I worked participated in these 'gambling' policies, which had been a part of Lloyd's for many years, but I refused to get involved. I didn't want to be part of it; I didn't even want to enter the details of these types of policies into the syndicate's ledger. However, as the years passed and I learned more about the true value of insurance – never mind the tonners – I realized that the job I was doing did have a social value, even if most people wouldn't recognize it.

* * *

Another thing that became apparent to me – not that anyone would ever confuse me with Einstein – was that a very large number of the people working within the Lloyd's marketplace were cerebrally challenged. It certainly wasn't a hotbed of intellect in those days. Once I realized that the competition in general wasn't that great, I thought to myself, "Maybe I can just get on here. Maybe I can get away with this."

During the 1970s, very few of the men – there weren't very many women – working at Lloyd's were university graduates. It seemed that if a person went to a public school and did not go to university, enter the army or become a cleric, he probably ended up at Lloyd's. Some were the sons of leading underwriters and brokers; you met guys whose grandfathers had worked at Lloyd's. Then, beginning in the late 1960s and early '70s, you had a bunch of East End traders which began to enter the market, who were basically 'barrow boys'[13]. Some of them were very bright and very good at their jobs, but you had to watch some of them quite closely because they weren't necessarily high on morals.

In fact, I quickly learned there was some questionable behavior in both underwriting and broking at Lloyd's in those days. Some people ran their Lloyd's businesses for very selfish personal gain, with no apparent moral compass as to what was right and wrong. They did not have their policyholders' best interests in the forefront, and likewise they really didn't give a lot of thought about the Names who supplied their syndicates' capital. After a couple of years, I decided I would never work for certain underwriters, either because I thought they were incompetent, morally questionable or, in some cases, downright dishonest.

Being a leading Lloyd's underwriter in those days meant that you practically had a God-given right to see business. Nearly all big-ticket risks came to Lloyd's. However, underwriting big-ticket business wasn't the deliberate process it is today. In those days, an underwriter was expected

---

13 Barrow boy, in its original meaning, refers to street traders who sold fruit and vegetables from a handcart.

to make an underwriting decision on the spot at his box, no matter how complex the risk was. While an underwriter could occasionally think about a placement overnight, that was not the norm. Nowadays, no one would dream of an underwriter quoting a rate on the spot for a complex risk.

Access to information in those days was tricky. An underwriter was never certain if the broker knew information concerning a risk that he wasn't disclosing, and you never quite knew exactly what the client had told the broker. The duty of care to represent the risk properly was often not clearly recognized, and things were often done rather too quickly when there should have been a far more considered effort to understand the risk and model it.

The energy insurance market, where I began working after several years at Lloyd's, was particularly sloppy. There was a lot of money in the energy business in the early 1980s, and insurers could make a lot of money underwriting energy insurance. As a consequence, standards were often not as high as they could have been. As the energy insurance market became more and more competitive, it became increasingly difficult for insurers to make money. As a result, underwriters became more careful about what they did and how they did it. Energy underwriters, among others, were at the forefront of the effort to obtain more information about the risks they were insuring.

* * *

Looking back, three issues caused the problems that led to the nearly £9 billion in Lloyd's market losses between 1988 and 1992. Among them they almost precipitated Lloyd's collapse. First, there were asbestos claims. Secondly, there were seepage and pollution claims. (Those two were somewhat related.) Finally, we had the LMX (London Market Excess of Loss) reinsurance spiral, which had a completely different dynamic compared with the first two issues.

The asbestos and pollution problems were created, in my opinion, by the US court system. When it was clear that many Americans would die due to exposure to asbestos, the companies that produced and sold asbestos products went to court during the 1970s and '80s to argue that they were entitled to the widest possible interpretation of their liability insurance policies, some of which had been written decades earlier. And the courts obliged. US courts basically rewrote the coverage and intent of insurance policies dating back to the 1940s or before. The same thing essentially happened with seepage and pollution claims.

Insurers maintained that they never intended to cover asbestos injuries, nor did they intend to cover non-sudden – i.e. gradual – seepage or pollution.

Therefore, they had not priced their policies to include such exposures. Unfortunately, a great number of these policies had been underwritten by Lloyd's syndicates and other London market insurers.

Although it was clear from the early 1980s, if not earlier, that asbestos and subsequently pollution losses would be sizable, no one could adequately comprehend the magnitude of the problem. As more information became available, it became clear that many Lloyd's syndicates were grossly under-reserved, which dealt the Names who belonged to these syndicates a double-whammy: huge losses and open years of account. If a Name was a member of a syndicate that could not close its account for a particular underwriting year, normally because the losses could not be accurately estimated to calculate a reinsurance-to-close premium, he or she was barred from resigning from Lloyd's. By the time the Reconstruction and Renewal program was approved in 1996, there were tens of thousands of Names who wanted to resign from Lloyd's but who couldn't.

Both the asbestos and pollution claims were what is known as long-tail claims. It's difficult to comprehend if one does not work in the insurance industry, but it can take many years for some liability claims to be filed and then settled. For example, as at March 31, 2015, it was estimated that Equitas, the vehicle set up to handle Lloyd's old liabilities, still faced nearly £5 billion in claims, discounted for the time value of money, even though all of the policies in question had been underwritten prior to 1993.

The asbestos and pollution issues, while extremely complex, are relatively easy to explain. Underwriters had to pay huge losses that they never intended to insure many years after the policies were originally underwritten. The LMX spiral is more difficult for a layperson to understand, however.

As explained in Chapter 6, nearly all insurers purchase reinsurance. It's the prudent thing to do. An insurer must be careful, however. If an insurer purchases too much reinsurance and has a relatively loss-free year, the insurer has essentially ceded too much profit to its reinsurers. However, if an insurer buys too little protection and catastrophe strikes, the insurer could potentially become insolvent.

Of course, a reinsurer must make the same decisions when it comes to buying retrocessional coverage which, as explained earlier, is essentially the reinsurance of reinsurance. At Lloyd's, the retrocessional market became a spiral. While Lloyd's syndicates bought protection from reinsurers all over the world, they bought the bulk of their retrocessional protection from other Lloyd's syndicates.

Excess-of-loss reinsurance became a big money-maker during the 1970s and early 1980s. The relatively few syndicates at Lloyd's that specialized in writing London market excess-of-loss reinsurance made big profits. Names were eager to join these syndicates due to their profit potential. More syndicates began writing LMX accounts, but all too often they proved to be not very good LMX underwriters. As capacity increased, rates decreased and contract terms widened. Thus, insurers were tempted to buy more and more cheap reinsurance.

We at Catlin were quick to take advantage of this favorable reinsurance market in the early days of our syndicate, using reinsurance arbitrage as a significant portion of the syndicate's capital base. However, we also knew that this type of reinsurance market would someday cease to exist. I originally expected this marketplace to last for three years after the syndicate was established in 1984; it actually lasted for six.

The spiral occurred because Lloyd's syndicates fell into the habit of selling reinsurance to the same syndicates from which they bought protection. So, when a major loss occurred, Syndicate A sought payment from Syndicate B, while at the same time Syndicate B sought payment from Syndicate A. Syndicate C bought and sold protection to both Syndicates A and B. You get the point.

Exacerbating the problem was the limited number of syndicates that sold high-layer retrocessional coverage. Again, 'retro' protection was cheap and easy to buy, but the market dynamics meant that – rather than spreading risk as reinsurance is intended to do – the LMX market actually concentrated risk among the handful of syndicates that specialized in writing retro coverage.

This unreal environment lasted as long as it did because relatively few catastrophes occurred in the early and mid-1980s. As the decade progressed, however, insurers' fortunes changed. First, there was the October 1987 UK windstorm – 87J in insurers' parlance – which caused $3.1 billion in insured losses, a huge amount at the time. This was followed by the Piper Alpha drilling rig explosion in 1988, which cost the market $1.4 billion and for many years was the largest man-made loss in insurance history. The next year, the Exxon Valdez oil tanker ran aground off Alaska, creating a huge oil spill. Later in 1989, Hurricane Hugo caused nearly $10 billion in insured damage in the southeastern US, the most costly hurricane at the time. Another severe windstorm that hit the UK and Europe in 1990 added another $2 billion in losses.

Due to the nature of the reinsurance spiral, it took years to quantify reinsurers' losses, but they were huge. While many Lloyd's syndicates were impacted, a few syndicates – like those managed by the Gooda Walker and Feltrim managing agencies – suffered losses that exceeded 500 per cent of their capacity.

Interestingly, the spiral was not a new phenomenon. Reinsurance claims had been spiralling in the Lloyd's market for years, just not to the same extent as in the late '80s and early '90s. One of the first claims I entered when I started working at Lloyd's in 1973 was from Hurricane Betsy ... which occurred in 1965!

Some Names who were already hard-hit by the asbestos and pollution losses were all but wiped out by the LMX spiral.

* * *

The perfect storm created by a growing number of asbestos and pollution claims and the LMX spiral meant that Lloyd's capital base was eroding, and there was real fear that Lloyd's would not be able to pay valid claims in full. Prior to the introduction of corporate capital in 1994, the capital backing Lloyd's syndicates was solely supplied by individual Lloyd's Names, who in those days had unlimited liability for losses produced by their syndicates. In other words, a Name could be liable for losses on his or her syndicates far beyond the amount of money he or she had invested; theoretically, he or she was liable without limit for any or all liabilities incurred by a syndicate. As the losses skyrocketed, so did the ill-feelings of many Names, who wanted to resign as members of Lloyd's but could not because of open years.

I became a Name after working at Lloyd's for six years. I joined in 1979, putting up £9,000 which allowed me to write £40,000 in capacity according to the rules at the time. I probably shouldn't have been allowed to become a Name as I was earning less than £15,000 a year. My father, who had moved to the US, obtained an unsecured letter of credit on my behalf from his bank in America. I paid for the cost of the LoC, and I cleared it as soon as I could. However, there was a chance I could have gone bust being a Name. I knew that, but I did not have much to lose in those days.

I remained an individual, unlimited liability Name until 1997, following the implementation of the R&R program and the introduction of corporate capital. As I had a knowledge of which syndicates were well-managed and which I thought were a catastrophe waiting to happen, I never had open years. In fact, I made money each year that I was a Name, even during the loss-riddled years from 1988 to 1992. It helped that my own syndicate did not make a loss during that period.

When I stopped being an individual Name, I obviously could no longer provide capital to Catlin Syndicate 1003, which was the syndicate we managed on behalf of individual Names. At the time I resigned as a Name,

I think I wrote a £100,000 line on the syndicate. By that time, Catlin had established Syndicate 2003, which was backed by our own corporate capital and wrote a parallel line on each policy written by Syndicate 1003.

One of the Names who belonged to Syndicate 1003 told me that I should no longer be allowed to underwrite because, since I was no longer an individual Name, I had no carried interest in the syndicate. However, through my shareholding in Catlin, I accounted for about £2.5 million in Syndicate 2003's capacity. I told the Name, "If you think I don't care about that, then you don't know me!"

* * *

It was often tough being associated with Lloyd's during the 1990s because so many people had lost so much money. I remember when Helen and I were selling our house. Helen went next door to tell our neighbor, who was a retired corporate executive. When she said we were moving, the man burst into tears.

"What's the matter?" Helen asked.

"Well, we may have to sell our house, too," he replied.

"Why?"

"Because I've lost all this money at Lloyd's."

Once a year, I would go around to his house at his invitation and have a look at the list of syndicates he was backing. I would tell him all the syndicates that I thought were good and remain silent on the ones that weren't so good. He wasn't actually asking my opinion; he was looking for affirmation for a decision that he'd already taken with his members' agent. This went on for three or four years. I knew that he would probably lose a lot of money, but that he wasn't in danger of being bankrupted.

In those days, I wouldn't let friends – or my neighbor – join Syndicate 1003 in case things went wrong. In today's market, where people invest in Lloyd's indirectly by holding stock in companies trading in the market, this type of control is not available.

Names became increasingly bitter as the 1990s progressed, and I stopped going to neighborhood cocktail parties at Christmas time. Why? One year, I had gone to a party at a house down the road. One of the guests asked what I did for a living. When I said I was a Lloyd's underwriter, she shouted at the top of her voice, "You are another one of those lying, cheating bastards!"

* * *

Of course, as we all know now, the Reconstruction and Renewal program was a success, allowing Lloyd's to get back on its feet and individual Names to cap their losses. The keystone of R&R was the formation of Equitas, the company (probably more appropriately called a 'bad bank') that reinsured all of Lloyd's pre-1993 liabilities. Equitas meant that Lloyd's got rid of the asbestos and pollution claims and the spiral losses, allowing it to trade on with a relatively clean slate. In addition, Names were allowed to resign from Lloyd's because their open years had been effectively closed.

There were many instances during the R&R process when I thought that Lloyd's probably wouldn't make it. I was most frightened one day in 1993 when David Rowland, who had recently become chairman of Lloyd's, called a meeting in his office with a group of underwriters. The way David worked in those crisis-filled days was that the head waiter[14] at Lloyd's would ring up to say there would be a meeting in the chairman's office at a certain time. He would then put the phone down. It wasn't, "Can you please attend?" You were expected to be there no matter what else you had planned.

It just so happened that it was parents' day at my daughter's school in Surrey, and my wife was determined that, for once, I would attend. I had to call Helen and explain that I was called to a meeting with the chairman that I couldn't miss. I would drive to the school as quickly as I could afterwards.

During the meeting – and this was at a time when practically everything at Lloyd's was going wrong – David told us that it had been discovered that Lloyd's had somehow misled the New York Insurance Department regarding the size of the Lloyd's American Trust Fund, a highly regulated pot of money from which US claims are paid. Lloyd's had somehow told the regulators that it was four times larger than it actually was. The New York regulator, which administered the fund, could have forced Lloyd's to close there and then. I knew by then that things were bad at Lloyd's, but I was shocked by the degree of mismanagement during previous years.

It was a classic example of how David Rowland worked. He dropped a bombshell – and there were many in those days – and people around the room would gasp for breath, trying to work out how something like that could have possibly happened and what should be done next.

David went around the room, seeking advice. After everyone had spoken, he said, "Gentlemen, thank you for your contributions," and adjourned the meeting (I am ashamed to say there were no women present). David didn't offer a response to any of the comments that were made; he just listened.

---

14 Uniformed support staff at Lloyd's are called 'waiters', who derive their title from the market's origins in Edward Lloyd's 17th-century coffee house.

Then he got on a plane, went to New York and somehow rescued Lloyd's from what looked like an impossible situation.

What was very clever on David's part is that he chose the people he spoke to carefully, and in less than an hour he got 110 per cent support from everyone in the room, rather than just ideas on about how best to proceed. David was always the consummate broker. I am convinced he was the best person to have guided Lloyd's through that particular era. There are not many people who could have made that trip to the New York Insurance Department and carry the day.

If you were to pick one person who contributed the most to the salvation of Lloyd's during that period, it would be David Rowland.

After the meeting, I drove down to my daughter's school. While in the car, I came to a decision that surprised me. Previously, I had thought I would never start another business again. I was so angry about what was happening at Lloyd's and the ineptitude in the marketplace. But that day, I resolved – no matter what eventually happened – to set up another business outside of Lloyd's if I had to, and I would make it work. An angered determination had risen inside me following that meeting.

16. Equitas

Serving on the board of 'Lloyd's lifeboat' taught me many lessons

For more than two years, the Lloyd's market looked towards Equitas, a company that had not even been formed, as its salvation. Equitas was designed to reinsure and run off[15] all of the business underwritten by Lloyd's syndicates prior to 1993. That meant that all of the asbestos, pollution and LMX losses would be rolled into a new company. Oh yes, the Lloyd's market would have to contribute a premium that would, hopefully, be sufficient to pay for all these claims when they finally came due.

In October 1993, Lloyd's commenced what turned out to be a colossal project to examine each open syndicate year of account prior to 1993 and estimate the liabilities arising. It took nearly three years to calculate the amount needed to fund Equitas and to win regulatory approval to establish the company. The so-called Equitas project was the greatest actuarial exercise ever performed at the time. There were several points along the way where it appeared the project would be doomed, both due to litigation by disgruntled Names and to the fact that the numbers were simply too complex with a wide range of possible outcomes.

However, a settlement was eventually reached and approved by the Names, who had been ultimately on the hook for all the outstanding liabilities. Around £3.2 billion in contributions was received from a variety of parties, including the Corporation of Lloyd's, the Names, managing and members' agents, brokers, syndicate auditors, and insurers that wrote errors and omissions insurance for managing and members' agents. In addition, reserves were transferred to Equitas from each syndicate whose liabilities were to be reinsured, and Equitas also assumed each syndicate's reinsurance program.

Equitas commenced operations in September 1996 funded with a premium of £11.2 billion. Including reinsurance recoverables, it began business with assets of nearly £16 billion, making it the largest start-up company in history. Once established, Equitas acted independently of

---

15 Insurance or reinsurance coverage that is said to be in 'run off' is coverage that is no longer actively underwritten. While no underwriting is required, the insurer or reinsurer – or an agent – is still responsible for settling claims arising on the policies and collecting reinsurance recoveries.

Lloyd's, with its own management team and board of directors. The only formal link between Lloyd's and Equitas was that Lloyd's was entitled to appoint one person to the Equitas board.

There was always the risk that Equitas could eventually run out of money and be declared insolvent. If that happened, Lloyd's future would again be in doubt. A lot was riding on the success of Equitas for everyone connected with Lloyd's: Names, underwriters, brokers and policyholders.

As a footnote in history, Catlin posted its first annual loss ever because of Equitas. Even though Syndicate 1003 had been consistently profitable during Lloyd's time of turmoil and we had no open years, Lloyd's required us to strengthen our reserves for the 1992 year of account before those liabilities were mandatorily transferred to Equitas. It was my fault for not hiring an in-house actuary rather than allowing Lloyd's to calculate our liabilities. However, our reserves proved to be more than adequate without the strengthening.

*　*　*

I had never expected to become intimately involved with Equitas. Frankly, it hadn't crossed my mind until David Rowland, in his inimitable style, rang me at the Catlin box at Lloyd's at 11.30 a.m. one morning in the summer of 1996.

"Stephen," he said, "I want you to become the Lloyd's-appointed independent director of Equitas."

"Why are you asking me?" I responded. "There are plenty of people who've probably got a lot more experience than I have.

David was blunt. "I think you should do it," he said. "I need to know quickly."

I explained that I would have to receive approval from Catlin's own board of directors.

"Fine," he said, "I'll ring you back in 24 hours."

I was slightly concerned that I was being stitched up. On the other hand, I thought – and my colleagues at Catlin agreed – that taking a seat on the Equitas board could raise the profile of the company.

Right on the dot the next day, the telephone rang. It was, of course, David again. I said that I would accept the appointment, but I asked him why he wanted me for the job. I didn't really understand it.

David said, "Stephen, every now and again you need to go one rung further up the ladder, and this is your time. I think you should do it."

I had one other issue. As I had not participated in the project that

140

was calculating the premium that Equitas would be paid in exchange for assuming the liabilities, I did not want to join the board until after Equitas was officially formed. As I explained to David, "I am not going to be liable for something I've had no part in and don't understand at this stage. If you're prepared for me to join on the day after Equitas is formed, as opposed to ahead of time, then I'll do it."

He accepted my point and, several months later, I was duly appointed to the board of Equitas.

I'll never know why David selected me to serve on the Equitas board. I think he possibly saw the advantage of appointing someone who was essentially baggage-free of the Lloyd's establishment as well as some of the practices that got Lloyd's in trouble in the first place.

I was 42 when I joined the Equitas board and was the youngest director by many years. Looking back, David Rowland took a big risk. He didn't really know me. He knew of me and he knew of my reputation, but he did not know me.

* * *

To this day, I vividly remember the first Equitas board meeting in September 1996. I had attended many Catlin board meetings, but they were pretty friendly affairs, first with the Jago Venton crew and others, then with mainly my fellow employees and, most recently, with Western General's participation. I had never been to a meeting like this.

There were members of the Equitas management team, who were highly experienced insurance professionals. Then there were other independent directors, all of whom had at least ten years on me and were part of the great and the good of the British business establishment. Finally, there were two Names, representing the seven-member trust that actually owned Equitas on behalf of all the 34,000 individual Names. The Names were given ownership of Equitas, through the trust, because individual Names could conceivably have been held liable if Equitas were unable to pay valid claims in full.

I decided that I would just sit there, listen and say nothing. I wanted to simply work out what was going on. The numbers were so big – tens of billions of pounds – that the only way I could get my mind round the quantum was to drop six zeros off all the figures. Nowadays, I am used to those kind of numbers, but I wasn't back then; Catlin at the time wrote less than £100 million in annual premium volume.

So, I sat, watched and listened. About halfway through the meeting, one of the trustee directors got up and handed a letter to his fellow directors, only giving a copy to the chairman last. I was experienced enough at attending board meetings to know that this was interesting protocol.

The letter was on the subject of the Exxon Valdez oil spill, which at the time appeared to be one of the largest single claims issues that Equitas would face. The chairman in the early days of Equitas' existence had paid a visit to the chairman of Exxon and, on his own, negotiated a full and final settlement of all Exxon Valdez-related claims.

The trustee director, who had been one of the major Names' representatives during the R&R process, was trying desperately to stop that transaction from happening. He and his fellow trustees thought the proposed settlement was far too large.

My instinct told me that the claims could have been settled for significantly less, possibly more than $100 million less. However, if Equitas reneged on the agreement, there inevitably would have been a lawsuit, and we would have potentially been looking at a downside risk of at least $1 billion. I knew enough about the Equitas balance sheet – no matter how many zeros – that the company could not afford to take that kind of hit, especially in its early days.

I suddenly realized that I was the only independent director – as opposed to a member of the Equitas management team – who had any knowledge of the background to the Exxon Valdez oil spill and resulting claims. I quickly took some notes and then spoke for 20 minutes, explaining how the loss occurred, the problems that existed within the marketplace and where that all left us. I stressed to my fellow directors the need to be pragmatic.

On the back of my off-the-cuff presentation, the independent directors supported the chairman and the settlement went through, despite the trustee directors' opposition. Equitas did not publicly disclose the amount of the settlement; as Equitas was not a publicly owned company, there was no legal requirement to do so. However, Exxon later announced that it had been paid $480 million by Equitas.

To this day, I am convinced that we did the right thing, even if we paid too much, because Equitas obtained certainty. That was something in short supply in those early days of the company.

However, the episode did raise fundamental questions of corporate governance, and I had sympathy with the trustees for raising those issues, although I didn't have as much sympathy as to the way the trustee director approached the board.

I then made the fatal error of believing that, because the board listened to me regarding the Exxon Valdez claims, the directors would listen to me all the time. We were meeting as a board once every month in those days, and after a few meetings I realized that I had been out of order and I'd do well to keep my mouth shut. I then only spoke when asked for my opinion. That was a big lesson regarding how one should behave in a board meeting.

Once I stopped talking so much, my level of influence among my fellow directors rose incredibly.

* * *

Equitas was a fascinating journey. The management team executed its strategy very well. Equitas didn't necessarily have the best employees in the marketplace; frankly, a lot of them came from failed syndicates. Michael Crall, Equitas' original CEO, did an excellent job, as did Jane Barker, who was finance director for many years and who later became CEO. I believe that David Newbigging, Equitas' first chairman, was probably the correct person to get the company started, although David wasn't necessarily the right person to take it forward. David put his heart and soul into making sure that Equitas got off the ground, but he had a hard time deferring to management on operational issues. David stepped down after a couple of years, and a search began for a new chairman.

For some reason, I had been appointed to the nominations committee of the Equitas board. Sir Bryan Nicholson, a City grandee and a wise man, chaired the committee. I called Bryan to say that I was not sure I really belonged on the committee as I didn't know the runners and riders in the City of London, from whom the new chairman would be selected. Bryan refused to hear me out; he said he wanted me as a member of the committee because I was baggage-free.

Eventually, Hugh Stevenson, the former chairman of Mercury Asset Management, was appointed as Equitas' chairman, and Hugh did a magnificent job, first in turning around how the board behaved and ultimately in helping to negotiate the reinsurance deal that Equitas made with Ajit Jain and Berkshire Hathaway.

Soon after Equitas was established, it was the nominations committee's job to search for a claims director. I think I was one of the last of the committee members to accept Scott Moser as a candidate, largely because Scott's a lawyer by training and had never worked in commerce; I had a distrust of lawyers playing an active role in a commercial environment. Six months after Scott joined Equitas, I admitted to him that I had been wrong and was delighted with the progress he had already made. Of course, Scott went on to do a great job at Equitas. He succeeded Mike Crall as CEO when Mike retired, and it was Scott who headed the negotiations with Berkshire Hathaway.

Scott had this famous phrase which I've since borrowed: "If you can't change the person, change the person." It's a really simple concept. You either join the party or you leave the party, and Scott was rock solid on that point. One of the problems that Equitas inherited from Lloyd's was a flawed claims adjusting culture. Before Equitas, there was little uniform strategy for managing contentious claims, such as asbestos and pollution claims. Lloyd's syndicates were spending hundreds of millions of dollars per year in legal fees, with a woefully small amount of management and coordination. Equitas changed all that. The company even banned the lavish Christmas gifts that lawyers sent to syndicate claims managers in order to curry favor. When we at Catlin adopted a code of conduct for our employees, it was largely based on the Equitas code.

Equitas had to deal with some quite difficult issues. Management's strategy was to settle liabilities as quickly as possible; it believed, as I do, that a disputed claim is likely to become more costly if it is left to 'mature'. However, management also knew that individual settlements were rarely stand-alone; there was often a domino effect arising from nearly every settlement that was made. Management also knew that the more settlements that Equitas made, the deeper the discount that could be negotiated in the future because claimants realized that Equitas' pot of money was finite.

One of Equitas' greatest successes was meeting its stated goal of reducing its operating expenses by 15 per cent year on year. The idea was that as the liabilities on its balance sheet wound down, so should its expenses. One of the ways that Equitas met this goal each year was by downsizing the workforce, but employee morale remained high. As time passed, Equitas gained a superb reputation, and working at Equitas looked good on an employee's résumé. People knew that if they performed well at Equitas, they wouldn't have a problem finding their next jobs.

* * *

As well as being a member of the nominations committee, I was also a member of the Equitas claims and commutations committee, which was also chaired by Sir Bryan Nicholson. As I was the only non-executive director that had experience in the Lloyd's market at the coalface, I probably belonged on that committee far more than on the nominations committee. As the business of Equitas was focused on paying claims and commuting reinsurance policies, the committee's meetings were fairly lively.

I learned a lot from Bryan about how to behave as a board member. Bryan had this innate ability to ask a question in a supportive but totally unambiguous manner, leaving management with no choice but to answer the question he asked. They couldn't take affront at the way he had asked it, and they couldn't avoid an answer because the question was very carefully constructed. He made very good use of the English language. While Bryan knew relatively little about insurance, he chaired those meetings really well.

On one occasion, we were considering a complex negotiation that was guaranteed to impact future deals, that domino effect to which I referred earlier. We were not much looking at that particular claim, but looking at the starting point for a chain of other claims settlements. Paul Jardine, who at the time was Equitas' chief actuary and commutations director and who would later join Catlin as one of my most trusted executives, had asked for authority to settle the claim for $30 million.

By that stage, I knew how to keep my mouth shut until it was time to speak, and I also knew that Bryan would eventually ask me for my thoughts. I explained the potential domino effect and concluded that negotiating a settlement sooner rather than later was paramount. If it happened to cost a bit more money, so be it. Bryan asked me how much more, and I replied "anything up to $50 million".

At that, Paul banged his fist on the table, shouting, "I only asked for 30; I don't want 50. Just give me a limit of 30!"

Wouldn't you know that Paul settled the dispute for $27 million. I had suggested a higher limit because I was looking at the issue from a bigger-picture point of view, but Paul believed that a higher limit would have weakened his negotiating position.

Looking back, remembering how Bryan Nicholson conducted what could have become a difficult meeting was truly inspirational.

*   *   *

As the Lloyd's nominated director, I was concerned about the conflict of interest between myself as a trader in the ongoing marketplace versus being a board member of a run-off company. My job was to represent Lloyd's interests in making certain that Equitas delivered. If it hadn't, Lloyd's survival was still at risk.

One issue that was discussed when Equitas was formed was whether it would be pressured by Lloyd's underwriters to make larger settlements to help the ongoing market retain business. However, only once was I criticized by someone in the marketplace who thought Equitas should offer a larger settlement to a particular policyholder. The underwriter wanted to make sure that his client was looked after "properly".

I replied that Equitas had a duty to look after the interests of all stakeholders, including the Names. However, I continued, no one would object if his syndicate offered to make an additional contribution to the proposed settlement to help maintain such an important relationship.

I never heard from him again.

* * *

I stepped down from the Equitas board in January 2002 because I had been nominated as one of the initial members of the Lloyd's Franchise Board, which was to be formed later that year. I deemed that being a member of both the Equitas board and the Franchise Board to be a serious conflict of interest. In addition, I had been a member of the Equitas board for nearly six years, and that was probably long enough. It was time someone else did the job.

I persuaded my friend Ian Agnew to take over from me, and he probably made greater contributions than I did. I am satisfied that Ian and I properly looked after the marketplace's interests, which was a major duty of the Lloyd's appointed director.

As almost everyone knows, Equitas turned out to be a complete success. In March 2007, a little more than a decade after it was established, Equitas finalized a whole-account reinsurance transaction with Berkshire Hathaway that pretty much completed the R&R program. The reinsurance allowed the individual Names to achieve what they considered to be 'finality': they were legally protected from being sued should Equitas not be able to pay claims arising from polices underwritten by Lloyd's syndicates.

I am extremely proud to have contributed in a very small way to Equitas' ultimate success.

17. Lloyd's in the 21st Century

'Reconstruction and Renewal' did not mean Lloyd's challenges were over

The Reconstruction and Renewal program and the success of Equitas saved Lloyd's from the grave problems that arose during the 1980s and early 1990s. The introduction of corporate capital gave Lloyd's syndicates a firmer foundation on which to trade. Changes in market practices began to pull Lloyd's into the modern era.

However, all these actions did not necessarily rescue Lloyd's from peril. Lloyd's had dodged several bullets, but it was still in the firing line.

* * *

While Sir David Rowland certainly deserves all the credit he has been given as the person who did the most to save Lloyd's during its darkest days, in my opinion David made one mistake: he stayed on as chairman of Lloyd's for too long after the R&R program was approved. It is difficult to criticize David, but the momentum did not keep pace after September 1996, when Equitas was formally established, to the end of 1997, when David retired. It was unfortunate that not much changed during the term of his successor, Max Taylor, a former Aon executive who served as Lloyd's chairman from 1998 until the end of 2000.

I had decided that I should play a more active role in Lloyd's affairs outside of leading Catlin. I had already been invited to join the Equitas board, and several years later I decided to become more involved with the trade associations that represented the various sectors of the Lloyd's marketplace.

There were a whole bunch of Lloyd's trade groups at that time. Historically, the Lloyd's market had been divided into four sectors: marine, non-marine, aviation and motor. Those divisions had begun to break down over the years, and many managing agencies had consolidated the syndicates they had established in each sector into what was known as 'composite' syndicates. While Catlin Syndicates 1003 and 2003 were established as marine syndicates, they had over time become composite syndicates.

Even though the barriers between the different sectors of the market had largely broken down by the late 1990s, each sector still clung to its own trade association. The oldest, the Lloyd's Underwriters Association, represented the interests of the marine syndicates at Lloyd's, and the non-marine, aviation and motor syndicates all had their own associations. In addition, the members' agents were represented by another association. In the aftermath of R&R, yet another association – the Lloyd's Market Association – was formed to represent the interests of those managing agents that were backed by corporate capital. Robert Hiscox, who spearheaded the introduction of corporate capital at Lloyd's in the early 1990s, was the founder of the LMA.

As I looked at it, the duplication among the different trade associations represented a grotesquely inefficient way of discussing issues within the marketplace. Each association had its own secretariat, so there was certainly a duplication of costs. Even worse, the Corporation of Lloyd's, the administrative body that runs the marketplace, used the duplication among these associations to divide and rule. Lloyd's would request feedback from each association; 80 per cent of the answers would be similar, but 20 per cent would focus on each association's parochial interests.

This was an important issue. There had always been some tension between the Corporation of Lloyd's and the market practitioners. It was all about how the market really operated and about people's personal sensitivities. When everything was going well, nobody cared too much; when things weren't going well, they cared a lot. Of course, that meant tensions were created at exactly the worst time.

The individual market sectors were not particularly collegiate. The marine market, the so-called 'mariners', always believed that they were the forefathers of the Lloyd's marketplace (as Lloyd's began as a market insuring shipping risks) and thus deserved a special status. The marine market largely thought the non-marine underwriters were sort of 'Johnny-come-latelies'. The non-marine market believed the marine market was a bunch of public schoolboys who didn't have a clue what they were talking about. The aviation market thought it was special because aviation underwriters wrote what they considered to be an innovative product. The motor market, which was never that big, regarded itself as being the *crème de la crème* of the UK motor insurance industry.

None of these rivalries was really in the best interest of the market.

When I first suggested that the trade associations should band together, representatives of each one said something along the lines of, "Good idea, Stephen, we get that." And then nothing happened. I learned that working with trade associations was not the same as running a corporate board, where you sit at the table with the management team, debate an issue, come to a consensus and everyone moves on in the same direction. When talking to the different associations, we would sit around a table, debate an issue, propose a way forward ... and five minutes later someone around the table would propose something different, probably benefitting his or her interests. It became an iterative process, and quite often we would have ten meetings on the same subject before we finally reached a consensus that stuck.

For 18 months, I spent roughly a day per week working with the trade associations to bring them together. It was a significant distraction from my duties at Catlin, but we finally got there. The new organization, established in early 2001, kept the Lloyd's Market Association name but also included the Lloyd's Underwriters Association, the Lloyd's Underwriters Non-Marine Association, the Lloyd's Aviation Underwriters Association and Lloyd's Underwriting Agents' Association. For my sins, I was elected the first chairman of the merged associations.

The fact that the LMA was re-established about six months before 9/11 was fortuitous.

* * *

As I noted in Chapter 12, I happened to be in Houston on the tragic day of Tuesday September 11, 2001. All air travel in the US was immediately grounded, and I was not able to return to London until late that week. The first thing the following Monday morning, I received a telephone call from Nick Prettejohn, who had been the CEO of Lloyd's since 1999. Nick simply said, "Help!" which was not something he was prone to do. He was calling me in my role as chairman of the LMA.

We met later that day. It was clear that certain sectors of the insurance industry – as well as others – were worried that Lloyd's did not have the financial wherewithal to withstand the claims that would result from the 9/11 attacks. Lloyd's, like other major insurers and reinsurers around the world, would eventually need to release an estimate of how much the claims from 9/11 would cost.

My advice to Nick was simply, "Don't do it too quickly and make certain it's robust."

"How do I do that?" Nick asked.

I replied, "Why don't you let me and several others sign confidentiality letters, and we'll go through all the syndicates' returns, one by one. We'll try to provide you with a view of which ones look right and which ones do not."

"That's a good idea," Nick said, and we quickly got started.

The process took several weeks, and in the meantime, several big insurers and reinsurers had quickly released initial estimates of their share of the 9/11 losses. I was supported by several people, especially Rob Childs, who is now chairman of Hiscox Ltd.

About 90 per cent of the syndicate returns looked fine to us, but about 10 per cent did not. We thought that some of the latter group had underestimated their losses by as much as 50 per cent, and we suggested adjustments. Unbelievably, we were absolutely correct regarding the syndicates whose returns were erroneous, and we had nearly a 100 per cent success ratio regarding the adjustments we had suggested.

Lloyd's was criticized for not coming out with an estimate as early as some of its competitors, but it took quite some time to go through the returns from more than 50 managing agencies. But, in hindsight, we made absolutely the correct decision to proceed slowly. While competitors came out with their 9/11 estimates much more quickly than Lloyd's, they often had to be subsequently increased, sometimes several times and by large factors. Lloyd's, which had a larger share of 9/11 losses than any of its competitors, never had to revise its estimate significantly.

When I stepped down from my tenure as chairman of the LMA in 2003, Bronek Masojada, the CEO of Hiscox, stood up and gave a vote of thanks. Bronek said, "I want to thank Stephen Catlin on behalf of the market for all the hard work he's put into the trade association. Many, many people have talked about bringing the trade associations together, but nobody had actually done it. Stephen didn't talk about it, he did it, and the market should be indebted to him for that effort."

That meant a lot to me because I know Bronek well, and he's not known for praising others unless they truly deserve it.

* * *

The LMA allowed the market to speak with one voice and helped unify the interests of the Corporation of Lloyd's and market practitioners. This was particularly important in 2001. As chairman of the LMA, I went to New York shortly after 9/11, accompanied by Rob Childs and several others, to visit the headquarters of Marsh, which at that time was the undisputed largest insurance brokerage in the world. Marsh's management had serious questions about the future of Lloyd's in the aftermath of 9/11 – they didn't think we had enough money to pay all the claims – and their leaders were not interested in talking to Nick Prettejohn or other Corporation of Lloyd's officials. They wanted to talk to the people who had underwritten the policies.

While that trip to New York has received little publicity, it was crucial to Lloyd's livelihood. We walked into a hostile environment; there wasn't much sympathy for Lloyd's position from many Americans in the market. One must recall that Americans in general, and particularly New Yorkers, were deeply affected by 9/11, which exacerbated their worries about Lloyd's solvency. The insurance brokerage sector was particularly affected because both Marsh and Aon lost so many employees when the Twin Towers collapsed. As Londoners, people working at Lloyd's were accustomed to IRA terror attacks and bombings, but something like 9/11 has been quite unfathomable in America.

After two days of tough talks, we managed to turn around Marsh's thinking. Rob, the others and I had already begun to review the Lloyd's syndicate returns. At this point, we did not have much in the way of hard data, but we were reasonably convinced that 90 per cent of all Lloyd's syndicates would be okay. There may have been the possibility of a hit on the Lloyd's Central Fund, but it wouldn't be a big hit. We had to be careful, though. I couldn't say that Lloyd's would be in good shape if I did not actually believe it. If I were wrong, my career would have been finished as I would have misled the largest broker.

If Marsh had decided to stop placing business with Lloyd's syndicates so soon after 9/11, when the global insurance industry was in a state of turmoil, it could have tipped Lloyd's over the edge. Looking back on it now, I probably didn't realize at the time just how important that trip actually was. We kept it really quiet; hardly anyone knew about it. Marsh's two biggest competitors, Aon and Willis, didn't know about it at the time because our fear was that Aon and Willis would also begin to show concern if they knew how worried Marsh was.

* * *

As I noted earlier, there were lots of issues at Lloyd's that required action following R&R, but not a lot happened immediately. In some ways, I think many people in the market acted as though R&R had provided Lloyd's with a 'get out of jail free' card and it was impossible for them to perceive that they could wind up in the clink again.

At the beginning of 2001, Saxon Riley became chairman of Lloyd's, and things began moving ahead. Sax, the former chairman of broker Sedgwick, which had been acquired by Marsh several years earlier, was a completely different kettle of fish from previous Lloyd's chairmen. He was a tough Yorkshireman, and he probably did not care if you liked him. Actually,

I liked Sax a lot. I had a lot of respect for him and for what he accomplished in a short time. It was so sad that he died in 2003, shortly after he stepped down as chairman.

As soon as he took office, Sax formed a strategy council – formally called the Chairman's Strategy Group – of which I was a member. By 2001, I was not only chairman of the LMA, but I had also joined the Council of Lloyd's and now I was also a member of the Chairman's Strategy Group. The group met for a half-day once a fortnight for an entire year; it was a major time commitment, but it was worth it. There were some robust conversations, but more importantly – unlike many other Lloyd's committees over the years – we actually accomplished something that turned out to be very important. To quote from the group's final report, issued in January 2002:

"The objective of the proposals is to transform Lloyd's into a modern, transparent and profitable marketplace, attractive to capital providers and policyholders as a place to do business. Lloyd's should be the trading platform of choice for specialist insurance and reinsurance business."

The most important proposal was the creation of a 'franchise' system at Lloyd's, which called for the Corporation of Lloyd's to be a 'franchisor', creating a competitive but stable marketplace where independent businesses could trade. The marketplace would be governed by a 'Franchise Board', and a franchise performance director would be given strong powers to set rules by which syndicates had to comply. For example, syndicates would have to submit detailed annual business plans to the franchise performance director for approval and also submit more substantial quarterly returns than in the past.

Another recommendation by the Chairman's Strategy Group was the elimination of three-year accounting, whereby Lloyd's syndicates would keep their books open for 24 months after the close of an underwriting year. Instead, Lloyd's would operate under an annual accounting system, the same as nearly every other company in the world. In addition, we recommended that no further unlimited liability Names be allowed to join the market.

The proposals generated some heated debate regarding the future of Lloyd's, and individual Names were dead-set against many of our proposals. However, the package of proposals, with some minor amendments, were overwhelmingly approved by the market in September 2002, allowing the Franchise Board to begin its work on January 1, 2003.

I was privileged to be one of the original members of the Franchise Board, even though that meant I had to give up my seat on the Council of Lloyd's. I served as a board member for three years before stepping down at the beginning of 2006. I saw first-hand how the establishment of the Franchise Board changed the way Lloyd's was managed. For the first time in the 30 years I had worked in the market, syndicates and managing agencies were being held to tough standards similar to those that competitors outside Lloyd's faced. The fact that Lloyd's – after being confronted with two near-death experiences in less than a decade – has traded without any huge blemish for nearly 15 years, in my view, is largely due to the actions of the Franchise Board and directorate supporting it.

I think because he passed away suddenly, so soon after he retired as chairman, Sax Riley never got the recognition – or anything close to it – for what he accomplished. What Sax did, in my view, was almost as significant as what David Rowland achieved. David's tireless efforts helped provide Lloyd's with the opportunity to trade into the future, but Sax nurtured the system that allows Lloyd's to be successful today.

* * *

When I first began working at Lloyd's back in 1973, I think it's right to say that Lloyd's was probably the largest – and certainly the most respected – insurance marketplace in the world. Lloyd's syndicates in the aggregate were bigger than AIG, Munich Re and Swiss Re. Lloyd's was the epicenter of the world's reinsurance market and perhaps the only place where you could put together enough capacity to write a truly large insurance risk.

Today, Lloyd's is no longer in that position, and Lloyd's will increasingly have to fight to maintain its relevance. I don't think that's necessarily a bad thing. I have long believed that, over time, fewer and fewer insurance premiums will leave their native shores. Hence, that's an important part of the reason Lloyd's is no longer as important as it once was, and that's why I decided that Catlin had to expand internationally from its base at Lloyd's and put down roots in other markets.

Please do not take that to mean that I do not think Lloyd's is important. The London market, particularly Lloyd's, remains one of the world's major reinsurance marketplaces. In addition, Lloyd's remains the only wholesale insurance market where you can effectively syndicate risk among many underwriters and retain a uniform policy wording. No other marketplace has been able to replicate that. During the 1980s, insurance exchanges sprang up in New York, Chicago and Miami, all of which aimed to challenge Lloyd's. All three were unsuccessful.

While the processes used at Lloyd's clearly need to be modernized as a matter of urgency, Lloyd's and the London market still have advantages that no other market can replicate. The face-to-face trading capability that is still found at Lloyd's is just one example.

I don't think one can ignore the fact that Aon chose to move its head office to London from Chicago several years ago. There are a number of reasons why Aon made this decision, but it would not have done so unless it thought that London – and Lloyd's – would remain a vital insurance marketplace for years to come.

Lloyd's will never have the pre-eminence that it had 40 years ago, and I don't think realistically, whatever Lloyd's had done, it would have kept that position in the light of the increasing growth of regional insurance/reinsurance markets. However, it's much easier for those markets to underwrite small to medium-sized business than the larger accounts. Many policyholders and their brokers still rely on Lloyd's underwriters to lead their business.

*   *   *

One interesting change that has occurred at Lloyd's over the years is related to brand. During the 1970s and 1980s, most people would say that a policy had been written at Lloyd's as opposed to Merrett, Wellington, Sturge or any of the other major managing agents of the day. Back then, syndicates and their managing agencies – including the fledgling Catlin agency – simply did not have a well-developed brand. Most did not have their own company spokesmen; if reporters wanted to know something about a syndicate or managing agency, they called the Lloyd's press office.

If an agency or syndicate had any sort of brand in those days, it was linked to the active underwriter. The most famous underwriters of the day – people like Stephen Merrett and Ian Posgate – were truly regarded as kings. It was a bit like the skipper of a vessel or the pilot of an airplane: whatever the captain says, goes. We have seen in any number of industries that such a system does not really work today. What is needed is strong leadership rather than complete autocracy.

The power of the individual underwriter at Lloyd's isn't the same today. Having said that, the power of the brands of the individual businesses trading at Lloyd's has increased immeasurably. What is now different is that, in most cases, a Lloyd's business is accountable to its shareholders and strictly regulated by the Franchise Board. There was much less accountability at Lloyd's in the old days.

I can still remember reading a non-marine syndicate's annual report to its individual Names shortly after I joined the market. I can still quote that underwriter's report in full: "We've had another satisfactory underwriting year." That was it.

I don't think that would be acceptable today!

PART IV
IMPORTANT ISSUES

18. Corporate Leadership

Every business needs a decisive but collegiate leader

Any company that hopes to succeed – whether in insurance or any other industry – must have good leadership. But, what exactly makes a good leader?

From my perspective, the traits that a good leader needs vary greatly, largely based on a person's individual personality. However, there are certain qualities that I think any good leader should possess.

First, a leader has to be decisive. When the chips are down and a tough decision must be made, a leader must be able to make that decision, even if it is a difficult, unpopular one.

On the other hand, a leader also needs to be collaborative. Perhaps just as important as anything, a leader must be able to listen to the people surrounding him or her and digest what they are saying. After listening, true leaders are prepared to revise their own personal views predicated on what other people have said; all too often, others will see the situation from a different perspective. A good leader will listen to their advice and observations.

Those who have worked for me have heard me say a thousand times that, to be successful in business, you need to have a vision of what you want to be and where you want to go. You then need to turn that vision into a strategy so that you can reach your goals. Finally, you must execute against that strategy. A leader can establish the vision, but I am not sure that anyone on their own can actually devise the strategy, much less execute against it. A leader can only accomplish all of this when he or she is backed by a team of quality people who are willing to follow the leadership.

In other words, leaders cannot act in isolation. If they try to do so, they probably aren't real leaders.

I strongly believe in leading from the front. Employees, counterparties and investors closely watch the leader. They see how the leader behaves and then decide whether they buy into what the leader is doing. If they do, they are more likely to emulate the leader's behavior. That puts a huge responsibility on a leader to behave appropriately.

Leading from the front means setting the tone. I learned a long time ago that if you have a bounce in your step, that if you can build a bit of excitement around yourself, the people around you will act in much the same way. If, however, you're down in the dumps, thinking and acting negatively, it has the exact same effect on employees.

Well-run companies have values or commitments that everyone is expected to follow. This especially applies to the leader. A significant part of leadership is actively exhibiting the organization's values, each and every day. In other words, a leader must walk the walk and talk the talk. If the leader lives by these values, there's a pretty good chance that people following the leader will try to do the same thing.

No one is perfect, and leaders certainly aren't. By the nature of their positions, leaders are quite often under enormous amounts of stress. In situations in which anxiety levels are rising, a good leader knows how to manage the situation, both personally and by helping to manage the stress of those around him or her. A good leader will act confidently, no matter how great the stress levels; a poor leader will show his or her frustration and/or insecurity. In addition, a nervous leader will be less likely to deliver a measured response than a confident one.

Are the essential elements of leadership different in business as compared with politics, sport or even everyday life? I really do not think so. Leadership is leadership, whether you're running a company with thousands of employees or whether you're simply a mother or father trying to set a good example for your family. The similarity is that leaders are watched all the time, no matter whether the followers are 8 years old or 80.

Some of my biggest regrets in life relate to times when I have led badly, which usually means that I behaved poorly in a certain situation or that I have been unnecessarily unkind to someone.

One of the toughest but essential elements of leadership is having the ability to deliver difficult messages. It's really easy to say to somebody, "Well done, good show, good on you." It's a lot more difficult to say, "You made a mistake," or "Maybe you could have done that differently," particularly when that person is angry or emotionally upset.

My first boss, Brian Evens, had a very clever way of delivering difficult messages. Brian realized that if there had been an emotional situation, he wouldn't say anything negatively until the emotions had died down. So, when I made a mistake that created a problem for the business, Brian might not say anything to me for several weeks. I would be thinking, "Perhaps I got away with that," and then – just when I had forgotten about the incident – he would look me straight in the eye and point out my error. By that time, the whole situation had probably cooled down.

I learned a lot about leadership from Brian. He had great people skills. Brian would take me to one side and say, "You know you are right, and I know you are right. So, for goodness sake, stop telling the brokers you are right." I would know I had done something wrong, and nothing else was said at the time. Two weeks later, he would mention it in passing and make me feel like a complete heel, but by that stage tempers had cooled. I knew that there was a lot I could learn from Brian regarding how to manage people and how to deal with stressful, difficult situations. I remain very grateful to him for that.

Brian taught me another important lesson about leadership: choose your fights. You don't have to fight about everything you disagree with. Fight when it matters, and when you do fight, make certain you can win. Don't go into a fight without an absolute intent on winning. If you can't win, don't fight; instead, attempt to find the most sensible compromise. You cannot push water up a hill with your bare hands.

* * *

Leaders must be brave. A leader has to have the courage to make decisions that are counter-intuitive, that sometimes go in a different direction from the rest of the pack. That's when leadership really becomes tough. Very few people are really comfortable with going against the flow, but that's what a true leader sometimes must do.

There are times when, if you think the pack's going in the wrong direction, you need to put your hand up and say, "I'm not sure that's the right way to go. Maybe we should go in a different direction." Having the confidence to make what seems like a brave decision isn't predicated on your own visions if you're working as part of a team; often the entire team will share the view that the business must make a tough decision. However, sometimes a leader is on his or her own, and it takes courage to stand by a decision when lots of people are questioning it.

Being a leader means occasionally being very lonely because you're out on a limb, doing things that many others would not do. That's why I think the best leaders lead from the front. A leader should never ask somebody to do something that he or she wouldn't be prepared to do – ever.

* * *

One of the true signs of a leader is the ability to own up to a mistake. If you mess up, you have to bite the bullet and just admit it. While some people believe that offering an apology is a sign of weakness, I actually believe it's a sign of strength and have always done so. Saying sorry is sometimes a very hard thing to do.

A great weakness in a leader, to my mind, is when they won't admit when they're wrong. The bottom line is that people learn the most from the mistakes they make, not by the things that they get right. To learn from a mistake, a leader must take ownership of the mistake, first and foremost. To be an effective leader, you must communicate to those around you that you have made an error, you've learned from it and the actions you plan to take to make sure the mistake doesn't happen again.

If I didn't admit to my mistakes, how could I expect my employees to do the same?

Sir Graham Hearne, who was chairman of Catlin from 2003 until 2012, actively and publicly conducted what could best be called self-assessment. Graham was in his seventies when he retired from the board, but he never stopped trying to improve. He did not do this silently; he would put his hand up and say publicly, "I've got that wrong," or perhaps, "Maybe I could have done that better." Graham, who had been chairman and chief executive of Enterprise Oil and a brilliant business leader, believed that mistakes weren't necessarily about doing something fundamentally wrong, but rather not doing something as well as you could have done it.

That's a tough standard, but one that true leaders should probably recognize.

Sometimes a leader will get the correct result, but later learns that, in fact, if they had done something differently, a better – or at least less painful – outcome may have resulted. In these cases, again, a leader should discuss what happened with those around him. As a leader, you cannot afford to miss a trick.

* * *

A bit of knowledge about human psychology is another prerequisite for successful leadership. What makes people tick? Why do they react? If you are dealing with a difficult people-related issue – for example, if you are negotiating with somebody – the best thing you can do before you open your mouth is take off your own shoes, get into the other person's shoes and try to work out how they are feeling in the moment. Where are their pressure points? If you understand where their pressure points are, you can then work out how to get from A to B. You're missing a trick if you just say something without thinking about how the other person is going to react.

Of course, people sometimes react in strange ways that are not always predictable. However, I believe that you can narrow the uncertainty by trying to understand what the other person is feeling – and why.

* * *

When asked about the people I consider to be good leaders, I often think of politicians who acted from their convictions rather than simply to please the population. For example, I admire Ronald Reagan, Margaret Thatcher, Winston Churchill and Mikhail Gorbachev, not because I necessarily agree with all their views or actions, but because they were convinced that the actions they took were correct, at least at the time. You can argue whether what they did was right or wrong, but you cannot argue about the strength of their conviction. Nowadays, such 'conviction' political leaders seem to be few and far between.

In the insurance industry, I certainly admire Sir David Rowland. Some people would point out that David was not liked by everyone, and some criticized the sale of Stewart Wrightson, of which David was chairman, to Willis Faber in 1987. However, David's performance as chairman of Lloyd's – at a time when the market was close to a near-death experience – was quite extraordinary.

I think back to that occasion when he called several of us to his office and told us that Lloyd's had misled the New York Insurance Department regarding the size of the Lloyd's American Trust Fund. That problem, which I noted in detail in Chapter 15, in itself could have sunk Lloyd's for good. David told the meeting what the issues were, put his hands up, did a mea culpa, asked for advice, made no comment, thought about it, worked out his strategy, and then went across the Atlantic and somehow carried the day. How he brokered his way through that one, I'll never know.

Patrick Ryan, who built Aon, is another great insurance industry leader. His skill was to build an organization largely through acquisitions, which I know first-hand is a very tough strategy to get right. A couple of his acquisitions probably were not as good as he would have wanted, but when you look at the number of deals that Pat made, it's certain he was not going to get each and every one correct. Then, after retiring from Aon, Pat started over again, and Ryan Specialty Group has done very well since he formed it in 2010.

I also greatly admire Brian Duperreault, who was a senior AIG executive, then took ACE to the next level, and later became chairman and CEO of Marsh when it ran into trouble. Now, he's back running AIG as CEO. One of Brian's greatest qualities, which he demonstrated both with ACE and with Marsh, is knowing when he'd done his job and when to hand over. Most people acknowledge that Evan Greenberg has done a magnificent job at ACE, now Chubb, predicated on the foundation that Brian built, in the same way as Dan Glaser's doing a damn good job at Marsh, again predicated on the foundation that Brian built.

He is not well-known in the insurance industry, but another business leader I really admire is Sir Bryan Nicholson, with whom I served on the Equitas board. Bryan has been one of the most respected business leaders in the UK. He served as president of the Confederation of British Industry (better known as the CBI) and also served as chairman of organizations ranging from the Post Office to BUPA to Cookson Group plc.

The reason why I respect Bryan so much is his unnerving ability as a non-executive director to ask a totally unambiguous question supportively, putting management in the situation where they had to answer his question, whether they liked it or not. They couldn't react argumentatively because he hadn't been argumentative in the first place. It was very difficult to give him an unmeasured response because he had asked a measured question. He encouraged an openness in response that was inclusive in a way that I hadn't seen before.

I've always tried to emulate Bryan because he demonstrated an extremely effective form of management. If you rile somebody, generally speaking they will fight back and you probably won't get the whole truth. Bryan's questions were put in a way that you had to answer them truthfully.

*   *   *

I have become somewhat famous (others may say infamous) as an insurance industry entrepreneur. While I suppose I am indeed an entrepreneur, the whole thing got blown a bit out of proportion when I won the UK Entrepreneur of the Year Award in 2011 from Ernst & Young.

However, winning that award forced me into thinking what exactly the word 'entrepreneur' means and how that label actually applied to me. I hadn't really thought of myself as an entrepreneur, which is defined by Oxford as *"a person who sets up a business or businesses, taking on financial risks in the hope of profit"*. Now that I think about it, I guess I tick the boxes.

In my case, what I think qualifies me to be considered as an entrepreneur is the ability to take financial risks. I may not have truly realized what I was doing when I set up Catlin. If I had, I may not have been brave enough to actually do it. However, when you finally realize that you have put everything you have ever earned on the block, it is a life-defining moment. Not a lot of people are prepared to take that kind of risk, and I'm not saying they should.

However, once you've taken the first big risk, risks thereafter are not as daunting. I have realized that, through grit and resolve, you can achieve most things if you're really determined to do so.

Now that I have studied entrepreneurism a little, I know there are serial entrepreneurs. That's not me: I am more of a long-term entrepreneur. A lot of people who have done multiple start-ups would consider themselves to be entrepreneurs. Their success rate is probably about one in five, roughly speaking. But those serial-type entrepreneurs probably do not stay with a business for more than five or 10 years. They can't segue from the creation of an idea to actually managing the consequences of the idea.

There are indeed many entrepreneurs who cannot make the transition from being the founder, the risk taker, to being a leader who can take on the responsibility of managing a successful business and a team of people over the long term. To my way of thinking, the real entrepreneurs are those who actually build a business for the future over a substantial period of time and leave a legacy. To me, that's what business and entrepreneurism is really about.

I've never admired people who keep changing jobs. All through my career I have seen people who move to a different job every two or three years, and my observation is that those people didn't really achieve as much as they could in the long run. They often didn't learn over time, and they didn't build relationships over time.

For the most part, insurance is not an entrepreneurial business, although I can think of a few true insurance entrepreneurs. I mentioned Pat Ryan, of course, who is one. I think Robert Hiscox could certainly be considered as an entrepreneur; Robert has certainly left a legacy. The late Andrew Beazley was an entrepreneur, and he also left a legacy. Both Robert's and Andrew's companies, Hiscox Ltd. and Beazley plc, may have to fight for an opportunity to move ahead in today's consolidating insurance marketplace, but Robert and Andrew put them in a good position to do so.

If you look around outside of the UK to Bermuda, I think you would have to say that Constantine Iordanou is absolutely an entrepreneur. Dinos, as he's known, has created a fantastic business at Arch Capital Group, which he has continued to grow organically. And you know, he did it from scratch. Dinos doesn't get the accolades he should receive at the moment, but I am sure he will get them in time.

* * *

A business is not a charity. You are not doing it for a single employee or even a group of them. You're doing it to serve your clients and to make money for your investors. However, it's great to build a business where people can succeed. Again, it's up to the leader to make sure that employees do succeed, because if they do not, the business is likely to fail. So nurturing employees is almost a by-product of the desire to make a business prosper and grow.

As the leader of a business, one of the things that makes me most proud is watching people who thought they had a five-foot-high ceiling suddenly discover that the ceiling is actually ten feet. And, when they get to ten feet, they realize that the ceiling is yet another ten feet away. I love watching people realize over time that they can achieve a lot more than they originally had thought. What's even better is knowing that they are stretching themselves; no one is doing it for them.

I'm a great believer in the carrot and the stick approach. Indeed, I probably wouldn't achieve very much without knowing that a reward awaits. I need to be told when I get something wrong, and I also need to be told when I do something well. But I still need to be told that I can do better as well.

During my adolescence, I naively thought the world owed me a living and everything would eventually come my way. Then, I suddenly realized that's not how the world works. A person must get off his or her backside, do some hard work, and then see what he or she can achieve. I think most people can achieve a lot more than they think they are able to achieve. And, I think most people want to do the right thing.

Most of us – myself included – respond to recognition, something as simple as "well done" or "good job". Most people respond negatively to being told off. People tend to respond positively if you say "good job" or "well done" and then follow up with, "Maybe with hindsight you could have done that a different way," or, "Have you thought about doing it differently the next time?" There is always more than one way of cooking an egg, and that applies in business. A leader constantly reminds his employees that they need to consider alternatives.

* * *

In conclusion, I think it's important for people to know that most business leaders aren't simply a bunch of 'shits'. Good business leaders care and nurture people. They realize that you don't achieve much in life without making mistakes. In fact, mistakes often define a leader, provided that he or she learns from them.

If you are going to achieve beyond simply being a bog-standard salaried employee, I believe you have to take risk, even if you are not a so-called entrepreneur. A leader must be prepared to think about quantifying and understanding the downside from those risks, but still have the courage to take them when necessary.

19. CORPORATE CULTURE

It isn't just the bottom line that makes a company successful

There were many reasons for Catlin's success as a company, but arguably the biggest factor was what we called the 'Catlin Culture'. Our corporate culture made people want to join the company, it made existing employees want to stay and it helped us get the best out of our people.

What were its ingredients?

Under the culture that we tried to nurture at Catlin, employees knew what was expected of them. Employees knew how we expected them to act and behave. But, we made it clear that it wasn't just the employees who had responsibilities. Management had the duty to be supportive and inclusive. We encouraged staff to think about doing things differently. We allowed employees to take risks, albeit within carefully monitored parameters.

In short, we encouraged employees to think and act as if they were owners of the company. Once Catlin went public, we made sure that as many employees as possible received Catlin shares as part of their compensation package.

Employees bought into our style of corporate culture in a big way.

* * *

The Catlin Culture developed from the fact that we began as a very small company – just two of us – and we were a fairly small firm for the first 15 years of our history. I was able to address everyone in the company by their name.

We had a fairly free and easy culture when I first started the business. It was just the way it happened. During the first few years of our existence, I didn't try to design a certain type of culture. However, I did insist on a few things. I hated it when a receptionist or secretary answered the telephone by simply saying, "Hello." I wanted them to pick up the 'phone and say, "Good morning, Catlin Underwriting Agencies." Once you have established these little things, the culture gets a life of its own.

As the company grew, I realized that our culture had become part of the Catlin value proposition. This doesn't just happen; you have to build it carefully. You must make sure that the culture permeates the organization.

As I noted in the previous chapter, if management does not live the culture each day, neither will the employees. The leader also must make sure that what works at the top of an organization also works at the bottom.

*   *   *

Shortly before Catlin acquired Wellington, we brought in an outside consultant. I don't really like to use consultants, but every now and again they can accomplish things that you can't do yourself. We wanted to know whether the culture we felt we had at the top was filtering down through the organization. I wanted to find out whether the next layers of management felt and acted in the same way as the senior management team.

The consultant interviewed 50 of the approximately 250 employees at that time regarding the business, the brand and the culture. After he had studied the results, I met with the consultant.

"Stephen," he said, "It is very, very rare – in fact for me it's a first – to come into a business and find that everyone is on the same page. You should be proud of that."

I am sure that I must have beamed on hearing that.

"But," he said (and, of course, it is the 'but' that you are paying to hear), "When I asked people about the brand and the culture, they each spent about a half-hour explaining it to me. They all did it in a different way. What they said amounts to the same thing at the end, but it is a tortuous process. Why don't you find just a handful of words that describes what the company stands for?"

It was a good idea, and I thought it was something that we could do easily. So, once a month for two hours at a time, eight members of the management team met and attempted to describe the Catlin Culture. It took us six months!

What was so difficult? All of us essentially shared the same core values and all believed in the same cultural issues, but everybody had their own slightly different slant on it. No one could agree on the right words. We had huge debates.

Finally, after six months, we ended up with five words to describe Catlin's values, and we used those five words until the day the business was sold:

- Transparency;
- Accountability;
- Teamwork;
- Integrity; and
- Dignity.

The last value was perhaps the most important, but required a bit of explanation. By dignity, we meant that our culture expected employees to deal with people with dignity up the line, across the line and down the line, both internally and externally.

We waited a year or two to test whether those five words described the culture as accurately as possible. Once we were confident that they had done the job, we rolled out the five values not just to our employees, but to our brokers, clients and other counterparties. We made sure that Catlin's annual report focused on the five values because, in essence, these values summed up Catlin: who we were, what we did and how we acted. When we interviewed prospective employees, we tried to make sure that the values they described to us matched our own values. And, when appraising employees' performance each year, we looked at how their behaviors and actions stacked up against the five core values.

Some companies pay lip service to their core values. At Catlin, we really lived them, and I am extremely proud of that.

Shortly before she left the company after 30 years of service, Lesley Denekamp – who was, incidentally, Catlin employee No. 3 – noted: "Everybody bangs on about the Catlin Culture and the Catlin values and wonders if they have changed over the years. And really they haven't. The values that we have are the values that Stephen espoused right from the beginning. Even though we didn't refer to them as values as such – they were things that were unspoken – they were very important to us: teamwork, accountability and transparency. We have always been a very supportive, very inclusive place to work. It is part of our attraction. It is part of our DNA."

If that consultant had returned to the company in 2014, I am fairly certain that Catlin employees would have described the culture using those five words or something pretty close. That consultant's suggestion was probably one of the best pieces of outside advice I have ever received.

* * *

Transparency means being open and honest. But at Catlin, it also referred to our offices. I am a huge advocate of open-plan offices. I tried to limit private offices to only those executives who truly need them, and even then, all private offices had to have glass walls and doors. That was not because I thought managers should see what the employees were up to, but rather so the employees could see what management was doing!

Open-plan offices, to my thinking, get people out of their silos. They foster communications and teamwork. They build camaraderie.

Of course, not everyone agreed with me. When we first opened the offices in Houston and Singapore in 1999, the local management resisted the notion of open-plan offices. "We don't do that," they said. The team in London who were helping to set up the offices told me that I would have to go to each location to sort it out.

So, I did. And the conversations in both Houston and Singapore both went something along these lines.

"Okay, you know why I am here," I began.

"Yes, Stephen," they said. "The thing is, Stephen, you just don't understand."

"I probably don't. Why don't you help me?"

"The thing is, this is a cultural issue."

"I completely agree with you. It is called the Catlin Culture. You either join the party or you leave the party."

"What do you mean, Stephen?"

"There is a door there. If you don't like it, I suggest that you walk through the door."

"You can't be serious."

"I have never been more serious in my life."

In both situations, the local managers finally realized that I *was* serious. The most amazing thing is that, six months later, managers from both offices said, "Stephen, the open-plan office is one of the best things that ever happened." They agreed that open plan provided a better atmosphere, better communication and a better working environment.

The same thing happened when we were planning to move our employees in Cologne to a distinctive, modern building that was part of the Kranhaus complex in the city. Ralf Tillenburg, the CEO of our European insurance underwriting hub, was opposed to an open office plan.

"We don't do it this way," said Ralf, who was usually quite a reasonable fellow.

"Well, you're going to," was my response.

Several months later, Ralf told me that everyone in the office was delighted with the open-plan layout, and he wondered why they hadn't adopted it so much earlier.

* * *

The example of open-plan offices demonstrates that a corporate culture can transcend the local culture, but it doesn't stop differences in behavior in terms of how people use language. The value proposition that Catlin adopted was cross-cultural, but we could not change the way people speak.

German bluntness, Italian excitement and Asian indirectness were all part of the Catlin Culture. For example, a person born and raised in Britain might say, "Would you mind terribly, if it is not too much bother, to pass me that pencil, please?" An American colleague would probably say, "Please hand me that pencil." A German employee might just simply say, "Pencil." The Brit might think the German to be rude, but the German might think that the Brit was being terribly inefficient with words.

In 2013 we opened a shared services office in Wroclaw, Poland, which provided 'back office' services like IT support and accounts receivable. I paid a visit about eight months after the office was up and running. The minute I walked through the door, I knew it was a Catlin office. It was not just the décor, which was pretty similar to other Catlin offices, but the atmosphere was also consistent. You knew that it was a Catlin office because of the way people were talking, the way they were treating each other.

Those kind of office visits were important to making sure the Catlin Culture did not vary greatly from office to office. I felt it essential that employees see me as often as possible, not just because it was my name on the door, but because I thought it important that each employee – even those working in the mailrooms – have some sort of link to the CEO and founder of the company. I visited major Catlin offices with about 25 people or more each year, and I tried to get to each office every three years or so.

While I obviously met with local management during these office visits, I made sure that we also held a 'Town Hall' session with all employees. It gave me the chance to speak directly to the employees, and it gave them a chance to ask me any question they would like. What was even more important were the drinks receptions following each Town Hall. It allowed the employees to see that the CEO – along with other members of the management team – was just a normal human being.

* * *

Companies must cultivate a culture that works best for them and reflects the personalities and intents of the corporate leadership. For example, from what I have read, Steve Jobs appears to have been to be a ruthless person and therefore was ruthless with his staff. It appears that he didn't utilize the common courtesies of 'please', 'thank you' and 'sorry' very often. It seems as if he led by fear more than by respect.

Now, I can't argue with this type of culture because Apple is one of the greatest corporate success stories of the past 50 years. Apple has produced marvelous products, and furthermore the company has marketed them brilliantly. But, would I recommend this type of corporate culture? No, I wouldn't, but that's because I believe that – at the end of the day – corporate culture reflects the personality of the company's leadership. I don't think I'm the same type of person as Steve Jobs was.

* * *

The Catlin Culture even extended to the way we conducted meetings of the Group Executive Committee. During the final years of the company's existence, these meetings would usually be held in either Bermuda or Zurich, cities in which Catlin had established major offices. The company maintained houses in both places where traveling Catlin executives could feel as if they were at home rather than spending long stretches of time living out of a suitcase in a hotel room. It also means that executives spent time together during the evening rather than going their separate ways.

Benji Meuli says he will never forget his surprise when he was told that he would be staying at a private house in Bermuda, along with his colleagues, when he attended his first Group Executive Committee meeting. Benji notes that the other companies for which he had worked had now operated this way. He believes this was an 'inspirational' (his words, not mine) method to bring the leadership team together.

Every company holds management meetings that share a similar style: executives seated around a board table, listening to various presenters addressing different topics. Catlin was no exception. Most of the time, these meetings are fairly routine, and the system works pretty well. However, sometimes a presentation does not go so well, or there are major disagreements among members of the management team. All too often, there is not sufficient time during the meeting to review and discuss what has gone wrong and or why people have disagreed regarding a particular topic. At most companies, the executives either go home or back to their hotel rooms at the end of the day, and the problem often is either forgotten or not addressed until the next month's meeting.

However, that wasn't the case at Catlin. The members of the Group Executive Committee stayed in the same house after the meeting concluded, continuing the day's conversation over drinks and dinner. If a problem or disagreement encountered during the meeting earlier in the day had not come up in conversation by the second glass of wine, I would mention it. Sometimes we would end up staying up until 3 or 4 a.m., having a heated debate until the issue was resolved. Benji Meuli believes that this was an 'exceptional' – but effective – way in which to manage the company. By staying at the same house, the management team was forced to confront difficult issues in an informal setting, while it also bred a sense of cohesiveness among us.

*　*　*

What pleases me most about the Catlin Culture is that we managed to maintain it over the entire history of the company. A company with two employees is going to be a lot different than one with 2,500, but I believe – and I am supported by Catlin old-timers – that the culture never really changed.

I am not sure to this day how we managed to do it; it just happened. However, I assure you that I, along with Catlin's senior executives, worked really hard at making sure that our business was run the way we wanted it to be run and to ensure that our employees were empowered and fulfilled. To me, that's the secret to a successful company.

The person who first brought this phenomenon to my attention was Paul Swain, who joined Catlin as CEO in 1994. We probably had about 30 employees at the time. I really wanted to hire Paul after I interviewed him, but he turned me down. I learned through the headhunter that Paul had gathered from people in the market that I was an arrogant, dictatorial son of a bitch. The headhunter sat him down and explained that those people were wrong, and amazingly Paul did an about-face and ended up joining Catlin after all.

About six months later, I had the normal discussion you would have with any employee after a certain length of time. I said, "Tell me straight, am I the man you thought I would be when you originally declined the job?"

I was delighted when Paul said I was not that person in the least. What Paul said was, "If I have a criticism of you, you are too collegial. You run the business like a family, and that works so long as we stay this size, but you won't be able to continue this type of company culture if we get much larger."

I admire Paul greatly, but I am so glad that many years later he admitted that he was so wrong. The Catlin Culture endured.

20. ATTRACTING TALENT

You probably won't go wrong hiring people you like

A business that doesn't have good leadership probably won't succeed; it certainly won't stand a chance without a talented and engaged workforce.

That's why corporate culture is so important. If employees do not identify with the ethos of a company, they probably won't be engaged and thus perform to their maximum abilities. And, if they really don't like the culture, they'll probably quit and find someplace more enticing to work.

However, before you start worrying about retaining talented employees, you must first attract them.

Finding and attracting talented people has long been a problem in the insurance industry. Forty years ago, when I entered the business, virtually no one actually sought to work in insurance, even at Lloyd's. You just happened to find yourself there. In my case, I met a guy sailing who was looking for an entry-level employee at a Lloyd's managing agency. Some people were pre-ordained to join the market because their fathers – and sometimes their grandfathers – worked in insurance, but for the rest of us it was just chance that we ended up working in insurance rather than some other profession.

For years, insurance was considered by many in the financial services industry as a poor relation to banks. The most talented employees chose a career in banking; those who couldn't get a job with a bank often joined an insurer or insurance broker instead. I'm glad to say that is simply no longer the case.

One way of attracting talent in the insurance industry, just as any other field, is to lure quality people from competitors. In other words, you take notice of an impressive underwriter at another insurer, make a better offer, and hope you can lure him or her to your company. That's still very common. You read stories in the trade press all the time about a team of people moving from one insurer or broker to another. Catlin attracted a lot of talent over the years in this manner, and unfortunately a few of our best underwriters were enticed away by the competition. Again, this emphasizes the importance of a strong corporate culture. If an employee enjoys his or her work and feels valued by the organization, he or she is less likely to be seduced by a competitor.

Catlin had a unique method of identifying the employees that we wanted to hire, whether they were recent graduates or experienced professionals. We called it the 'Lesley Test'.

* * *

The Lesley Test is named after Lesley Denekamp. Over the years, Lesley went from being my personal assistant to group head of human resources and finally secretary to the Group Executive Committee, but all along the way Lesley was involved in a wide range of functions for Catlin. She probably knew the company better than anyone other than me – and sometimes better than me!

The Lesley Test was pretty simple. If Lesley did not like someone after interviewing them – if she didn't think they would fit in well – we simply didn't hire them. Twice over the years, I went against Lesley's judgment and hired someone she did not recommend; I was proved wrong in both instances. Lesley was absolutely fantastic at reading the underlying character of an individual. I knew that if Lesley said someone was okay, he or she would probably work out.

The Lesley Test did not mean that we would automatically become best friends with our employees. However, we worked on the basis that if you don't like and respect a member of the team, the workday can become very tedious. Where's the fun? How can you share a joke? The Lesley Test also measured a candidate's outward-facing people skills, because Lesley is great at interpersonal communications.

We did not want our workforce to be simply a bunch of clones. I take the view that a company is much better off having a catholic group of people with different backgrounds, different experiences … all the rest of it. If you have a diverse workforce, you're probably going to get different perspectives on the issues facing the company, and that can only be a good thing.

It all related to the Catlin value proposition of transparency, accountability, teamwork, integrity and dignity. If you find those characteristics in an individual, you're probably going to like them. The only thing left to do is to find out whether they have the skillset you need for the vacancy to be filled.

* * *

I would probably say this because I am an underwriter, but hiring underwriters is tougher than hiring back office employees. Good underwriters are quite rare beasts because you've got to have a mixture of skillsets. Being a boffin *per se* doesn't necessarily work.

Underwriters are complex people. They have to deal with brokers all day long. They must be presentable to clients and be able to listen to them; equally, they must be able to take shit from clients and brokers without overreacting. Good underwriters must have an innate ability to understand risk. When presented with a proposal, an underwriter must quickly assess the chances of a claim in terms of probability, severity and causation. Once the underwriter has done that, he or she must be able to determine a price. If a person can't think laterally like that, he or she will never become a good underwriter. There are so many things that an underwriter has to be good at and, generally speaking, very few underwriters possess all of those skills. Those who do are the real stars.

* * *

While so many people working in the insurance industry, including me, fell into it by accident, it's rather amazing that so many have achieved beyond their wildest dreams. I take great pride as I look back at many of the people who worked at Catlin and recall what they have accomplished. It's a fantastic feeling. What greater joy can you have than to watch people grow, evolve, mature and create value, not just for the company but for themselves and for their families.

I believe that one of the fundamental priorities of any business is to help people to achieve their potential. If people reached the ceiling in their particular roles at Catlin, we always tried to find them different positions within the company where they could retain their self-esteem and move forward doing something that suited their abilities.

Don't get me wrong; we sometimes made some big mistakes in the hiring process at Catlin. People just didn't fit in or work out. However, interestingly enough, our bigger problems were linked not with hiring, but with *firing*.

Several years ago, we commissioned an employee survey, and the results were overwhelmingly positive. Our employees seemed to be very happy. However, one criticism that was repeated across the company was that we tended to cling on to people who were not going to make the grade for far too long. We often gave them a second, third, fourth or even fifth opportunity. High-performing employees did not like that, and they told us so.

* * *

I am delighted to see that the insurance industry is now an employer of choice among students graduating from first-class universities around the world. Part of that success is that the industry over the years has done a much better job at communicating what we do and the value we can provide. However, we still have a long way to go.

We offered graduate recruitment programs at Catlin for nearly 20 years, and their popularity among candidates grew exponentially as young people's awareness of the insurance industry grew. A recognition has developed among university students that working in the insurance industry could actually be interesting; it's very much a people business. One advantage that insurers have over the investment banks is that, by and large, young people working in the insurance industry work socially acceptable hours compared with those working in junior positions in banks or even in accounting firms. While our employees sometimes worked into the evening, particularly during renewal periods, they hardly ever had to work all night.

What has also helped is that insurers are now paying graduates much better wages. When you compare what we now pay graduates versus what people in entry-level positions were making 40 years ago, it's simply a case of chalk and cheese.

In our last year of operations, Catlin's graduate training program attracted about 7,000 applicants, of which we selected only 35. Grades were of course a factor, but we were looking for something more from these young people. We quizzed the applicants about how they would handle situations that they would face once they joined the workforce and how their responses correlated with Catlin's five core values of transparency, accountability, teamwork, integrity and dignity.

In other words, although Lesley could not interview 7,000 graduates, we still were using a form of the Lesley Test.

Over the years, we expanded our graduate program to other countries, but one of our earliest – and most successful – graduate trainees came from China.

Paul Swain – who opened my eyes to the vast potential that China could offer insurers such as Catlin – suggested in 1999 that we try to recruit a graduate from a Chinese university. Paul contacted a university in Beijing, conducted an interview process there and selected Linmao Li, who was born in Manchuria. Paul didn't hire Linmao because he was Chinese; Paul hired him because he thought he would make a good Catlin underwriter.

Linmao moved to London, began training as an underwriter and worked for seven years at Lloyd's. When we established our operation in Hong Kong, Linmao was the ideal person to head the office and he later moved to our Shanghai office as head of China. Linmao, of course, spoke fluent

Mandarin and knew Chinese customs and culture, but most importantly he also understood the Catlin culture.

* * *

Diversity has become a hot topic in the insurance industry on a global basis. My view is that any employer should embrace employees from all genders, religions, nationalities and cultures. A truly heterogeneous workplace is far superior to one where everyone talks the same, looks the same and thinks the same.

Over the years, I observed that meetings attended by both men and women tended to be more productive than male-only meetings. The quality of the debate increased, people tended to treat each other with more respect and a greater range of opinions were exchanged.

Having said that, the environment at Lloyd's when I began working in the market was male-dominated to say the least. Women were not allowed in the Underwriting Room until the end of 1973, after I began working at Lloyd's. Looking back, that seems outrageous. However, women in the Room was actually a distraction for some of my colleagues. I had gone to a co-educational secondary school, so working alongside women was no big deal for me. However, I remember some guys actually complaining, "I don't know how I can concentrate with these women here." They were serious.

Much more must be done to increase the role of women in the insurance industry. There are now some women in high positions in the industry – Dame Inga Beale, the CEO of Lloyd's, is probably the most prominent example – but women are still grossly under-represented at the highest levels of the marketplace. During the latter years of Catlin, we had a 50/50 ratio between male and female employees worldwide, but the percentage of women fell away quickly as the pay grade increased.

There are all kinds of reasons why upper management is so male-dominated, but I think one of the reasons for this is that historically businesses have not provided enough support for working mothers. It is a huge challenge for a woman to have children and still retain their position in the workplace. Businesses don't make it as easy as they should for mothers. Children need parenting and support from both parents, but all too often the bulk of the burden is carried by mothers. Parents must sometimes prioritize care for their families ahead of their work, and a good employer should recognize and accommodate that need. We tried to do that at Catlin, although I cannot claim we did it as well as we could have done. I think the competitive nature of the marketplace too often supersedes doing the right thing.

When I joined Lloyd's, it had an atmosphere very much like a stuffy private club: few women, virtually no minorities and many people from a posh, upper-class background. Thankfully, Lloyd's – and the entire insurance industry for that matter – has moved on. The insurance industry is now based on meritocracy and an individual's capability; the industry now attracts people from all walks of life.

This can only be for the best.

21. Brand and Corporate Responsibility

A company's public identity must reflect its ethos

A company's brand should tell people quickly what the company is all about. Brand can mean logos and colors, it can include advertising, but a big part of a brand encompasses the quality of the products a company sells and the services it delivers. For instance, a major contributor to the Catlin brand was the fact that we paid valid claims fairly and, whenever possible, quickly.

A company must prove its performance and earn its reputation over time. Successful brands cannot be invented overnight; they mature. A brand will fail if a company's actions don't correspond with the image the brand presents.

* * *

The Catlin brand naturally began with the name 'Catlin'.

As I noted in Chapter 15, active underwriters at Lloyd's in the mid-1980s were essentially kings, and leading underwriters were placed on pedestals way beyond what was actually justified. So following market practice in 1984, I named the company I was forming after me. That's what one did at the time: the active underwriter's name was almost always included in the managing agency's name. The name of the agency wasn't that important in those days; the most important brand was the Lloyd's brand. The next most important was the name of a syndicate's active underwriter.

As I mentioned previously, the original name of the company that grew to become Catlin Group Limited was 'S.J.O. Catlin Underwriting Agencies Limited' (my full name is Stephen John Oakley Catlin). We soon dropped the 'S.J.O.' as superfluous. It probably did not help that the first letter I ever received as CEO of my own company was addressed to 'Mr. O'Catlin'.

If I were given the chance to correct errors of the past, I would not have named the company 'Catlin'. There are benefits to being eponymous, but there are also downsides. In retrospect, the benefits probably outweighed the downsides over time, but the latter were formidable.

The main benefit was that people associate the business with the founder, so I am still able to see almost anyone in the insurance industry on the back of my name. I remember going to see a regulator in India several years ago,

180

somewhat in fear and trepidation. The first thing the gentleman said was, "This is a great honor." You don't often hear regulators say that. I said, "What do you mean, sir?" He said, "I think this is the first time I have actually met somebody who has founded an insurance business." He was genuinely flattered and the meeting got off to a good start.

A downside is when the media reported: "Catlin says this …" or "Catlin says that …" The reader could assume that Catlin meant me as opposed to the business, so I often got accused of saying things I never actually said. It was probably someone else in the company.

The worst thing about having my name on the company's door was that I received most of the accolades. Several years after the company was founded, when I knew that the team was creating something really special, too many people thought that all this hard work was mine alone. I happened to be the team leader, but it wasn't proper for the team leader to get all the praise. The business was made up of all the people working for the company, not just me, so credit was due to them just as much as to me, even if my name was on the door.

I did suggest on several occasions that we rename the company, but it never happened. I raised the issue about five years after the company was formed, but the management team told me I was mad – in the British sense of the word. So I left it. I raised the issue again when Western General bought a majority stake in the company, but it was suggested that I could change my own name if I preferred; the company was going to continue to be called Catlin. It was pointed out, quite fairly, that we had already established a good brand … why would we want to change it? I tried it again in 2002 when we raised money from the private equity funds, and I essentially got the same response.

I gave up at that point.

I'm still not sure what I would have called the company if it hadn't been 'Catlin', but I do know I would have named it something beginning with the letter 'A' as opposed to 'Z'. I think there's a lot to be said for being at the front of the alphabet. And 'C' isn't too far away from 'A', so at least that had a benefit.

During the period in which I formed Catlin, the only person at Lloyd's who had the vision to avoid forming an eponymous company was Mark Denby, who called his agency Atrium Underwriting Ltd. Mark got it right; he named his company with a word beginning with 'A'.

You can be an entrepreneur without naming a company after yourself; Richard Branson has certainly proved that. He has done something which is really quite extraordinary. He has created a company, Virgin Group, that developed a brand that everybody knows, but nearly everybody also knows that it is Richard Branson who is behind the Virgin brand. That demonstrates that you can create a brand and a brand image driven by you and your own personality even if it is not actually named after you.

I don't think the public markets particularly like eponymous CEOs or chairmen. Robert Hiscox played it well, but it is interesting to observe that the share price of Hiscox Ltd. increased significantly after Robert retired. The business didn't change fundamentally when he stepped down. The idea that the company is better because he has left is absolutely wrong. He was the lifeblood of his business and was respected as such internally and externally. However, I do think that the public market has a fear of the eponymous. They have a fear of founders, in fact, but if the company is eponymous as well, it has two crosses to bear.

* * *

The Catlin brand began slowly. First, we had a name, my name. We began using cream-colored paper for our correspondence because, at the time, Lloyd's used cream-colored paper. So, the paper helped people identify Catlin as being part of the Lloyd's market. After a few years, we asked an agency to design a logo, which was red and grey. We later changed the grey to a rich shade of brown, which I believe gave our identity a bit more visual depth.

Someone, and I am not sure who it actually was, decided that we should give out umbrellas to brokers when it was raining. The umbrellas were originally red, grey and, of course, cream; we later substituted brown for the grey. Now, everyone likes a free umbrella, but at the time ours seemed to be the only ones in the City of London that were not black. They were easily recognizable, and people decided they had to have one. They were also extremely sturdy as opposed to some giveaway umbrellas which break the first time they are used.

We ended up giving away thousands of umbrellas each year, and they were worth every penny we spent. As Catlin expanded around the world, we introduced the umbrellas in each location, and soon you would see Catlin umbrellas on the streets of New York, Cologne, Zurich and Singapore as well as London. And, in London, Catlin umbrellas were clearly the 'brollies' of choice among insurance brokers. According to a study by Gracechurch Consulting conducted in 2013, 39 per cent of the London brokers surveyed said they had a Catlin umbrella. Amlin placed second with only 12 per cent.

* * *

In my view, a company's brand has to be consistent, no matter how many offices you may have or where they may be located. When we established our first European office in Cologne, the local management decided that they wanted to give away umbrellas and coffee cups that were quite different to what we used in London. They wanted to establish their own identity. It was one of the few times I remember blowing my top at a subordinate's decision. The Cologne office was a Catlin office, and it needed to show that it was part of the same company if we were going to nurture a successful global brand. Thankfully, the people in Cologne got the message, loud and clear. However, over the years I often had to make sure that some far-flung office did not tamper with the Catlin brand in an attempt to create its own identity.

Consistency is what sticks in people's minds. I still think that one of the most successful global brands is Heinz. It began using the 'Heinz 57' brand back in 1896, and it is still recognizable and trusted around the world more than a century later. That's what I wanted for Catlin. I think it is better to be consistent and somewhat conservative than to be creative but inconsistent. Not everyone would agree (particularly some former members of our marketing department who equated 'consistent' and 'conservative' with 'boring'!), but that's what I believe.

* * *

For the first ten years of Catlin's existence, we emphasized the Lloyd's brand as opposed to the Catlin brand. But in the mid-1990s, as Lloyd's was in the throes of a terrible crisis, agencies seriously began to build their own brands separate from Lloyd's. This was partly because the Lloyd's brand was thought to be tarnished, but it was also the result of corporate capital entering the marketplace.

Through the umbrellas, broker events and just word of mouth, the Catlin brand became established in London. However, as we evolved, I knew that we needed to really work on building and promoting our brand. By the mid-2000s, we had acquired Wellington and were aggressively expanding our international footprint, so we needed to find something special that would help communicate the Catlin brand worldwide. We wanted to associate ourselves with something that would grab people's attention. Some companies sponsor sports teams or symphony orchestras, but doing so costs lots of money and does not necessarily resonate internationally.

In early 2007, I hired John Carroll as Catlin's first head of marketing. John had worked for many years at HSBC, which has a fantastic brand. One of John's first duties was to increase the awareness of the Catlin brand.

I wanted him to find a sponsorship that would truly add value to the Catlin name. It took a bit longer than I had hoped, but John finally came to me with a proposal that would become the Catlin Arctic Survey.

The Catlin Arctic Survey was based on a simple premise. It was becoming clear to many scientists that the sea ice in the Arctic Ocean was disappearing faster than had been predicted due to climate change. You could try to measure the thickness of the ice by using airplanes or submarines, but those methods were not sufficiently accurate. You had to go to the Arctic physically and take first-hand measurements. Unfortunately, scientists had neither the training nor the skills necessary to survive in such a bitterly cold and hostile environment. However, if you trained experienced polar explorers to take the measurements and feed the data back to the researchers, you could get a much more accurate view of what was really going on.

The Catlin Arctic Survey had everything that I was looking for to build our brand. It was related to risk, the business that Catlin was in, and it showed that we were a socially responsible company. The project carried a sense of adventure. The photographs of the Arctic captured by the explorers – led by Pen Hadow – were truly awe-inspiring. The project could produce a lot of interest among our brokers and clients.

So I was surprised when our management committee gave the proposal a lukewarm response. I received enough support to take the proposal to the board of directors, but I received a similar reaction. Some of the directors were very supportive, but others weren't very comfortable with the project. Finally, Sir Graham Hearne, who was Catlin's chairman at the time, told me, "Stephen, every now and again, you have to put your head on the block. Is this one of those occasions?" In other words, I could go ahead with a promotional project that would cost millions of dollars each year, but my job could be in danger if the project did not succeed.

I had thought long and hard about the proposal and decided to go ahead. A couple of months later, when the Catlin Arctic Survey had been covered by newspapers and magazines around the world and was the subject of an eight-minute segment on the BBC 10 p.m. newscast and a 30-minute CNN documentary, nearly all of the directors called or emailed me to congratulate me for deciding to press on.

The Catlin Arctic Survey was hugely successful and created far more brand awareness than any one of us, including me, had ever anticipated. In fact, it had some very pleasant but unintended consequences. It made Catlin employees proud to be associated with a company that would sponsor such a socially responsible project. Many employees said things such as, "For the first time ever, I've gone back and talked about my work at home, and my children were interested." A project to create brand awareness also helped bring the company together in a way I hadn't anticipated.

The survey certainly built brand awareness. We got hundreds of thousands of hits on a special Catlin Arctic Survey website. The TV coverage we received over a three-year period was far greater than we ever expected. *Insurance Day*, the London-based insurance newspaper, published a weekly column, recapping the highlights of the survey. Photographs of the explorers were everywhere on the internet, nearly all of which included the Catlin logo sewn on the explorers' parkas and pasted onto the sledges they pulled.

The Catlin Arctic Survey particularly resonated with the university students who applied to our graduate training program. Young people are interested in working for companies that 'do the right thing', and suddenly Catlin was at the forefront of companies that demonstrated environmental responsibility.

* * *

Even though we expanded the Catlin Arctic Survey to include an Arctic 'ice camp' where scientists could conduct research first-hand, we realized after three years that the value of the survey as a brand-building tool was decreasing. It had become a bit old hat. We were struggling to find a similar but somewhat different project to sponsor when one of our underwriters in Sydney had a conversation with a friend during a backyard barbecue. His friend was interested in coral reef preservation and had helped to design a revolutionary underwater camera which could capture a continuous series of three-dimensional images.

The Catlin Seaview Survey was about to be born.

Getting a buy-in from management and the board was a lot easier this time around. We were spending more than a million dollars annually on the Arctic Survey, and the Seaview Survey would cost a similar amount. Was it worth the investment? Both Paul Brand and Rich Banas said, "What the hell are you talking about? Of course, we should do it." The board quickly agreed.

The Catlin Seaview Survey was a series of underwater expeditions to photograph and study conditions at coral reefs around the world. Like the Catlin Arctic Survey, the Seaview Survey produced captivating images that showed the beauty of coral reefs while broadcasting the message that these reefs, which are so important both ecologically and economically, are increasingly endangered by a range of factors, including climate change. Through an agreement with Google, many of the images were posted online as an underwater version of Google's 'Street View'.

Much to our surprise, we received as much if not more publicity from the Catlin Seaview Survey than we received from the Arctic Survey. Together, the two projects put Catlin in the limelight to an extent that none of us had anticipated. In a relatively short space of time, Catlin went from being relatively unknown to being very well known within the global insurance industry, and we increasingly became known outside of the industry for our sponsorship of environmental research.

* * *

Apart from gaining mass media coverage of the two projects, the surveys also allowed us to do some personalized marketing to important brokers and clients. Because of the inherent dangers, we could not invite guests to participate in the Catlin Arctic Survey, but we did take a group of broker executives to Svalbard, Norway, north of the Arctic Circle, to get a feel for what the survey participants were encountering. During the Catlin Seaview Survey, we invited brokers and clients to take part in a dive and see firsthand the life on a coral reef.

It seemed as if everyone who participated in one of these trips came home extremely impressed, having learned something new about the changing world in which we live. Several people said their experience represented the best business-related trip they had ever taken.

During the Seaview Survey trips, I would ask our guests on the final evening, "There's one thing I'd like you to do in return for coming here. If you've enjoyed the trip, please go home and tell your family, your friends and your colleagues what you have seen and what you have learned." And, they would do just that. I would receive emails telling me how fascinated families were to hear about these experiences. One broker told me that he had been "the life and soul of several dinner parties" by relating what he had seen.

In other words, the surveys raised people's consciousness about the environment. And, hopefully, the surveys raised their opinions of Catlin.

* * *

A big reason that the Catlin Arctic Survey and Catlin Seaview Survey were so successful in helping to build the Catlin brand was because they were seen as corporate responsibility efforts rather than simply marketing tools. What I have said about the relevance and value of insurance tied in perfectly with these two surveys. A lot of people saw the projects as an attempt by an insurance company to learn more about our changing environment and the risks that our children and grandchildren may face. It demonstrated that insurers could actually work to make our society better.

The one thing that we made absolutely clear was that Catlin was not getting involved in arguments regarding causation. In other words, we noted that our climate was changing and that certain features of our planet – whether it was the Arctic sea ice or warm-water coral reefs – were becoming endangered by climate change. However, we did not point fingers, and we did not tell people or companies how they should behave. We made it clear that our role was to obtain impartial scientific data and make it available to everyone to interpret.

To this day, insurance is all too often viewed as an evil necessity rather than a value-added product. If the Catlin Arctic Survey and the Catlin Seaview Survey helped change those false impressions, it's all to the good.

At about the same time as we became associated with the Catlin Arctic Survey, we realized that it was important to emphasize other types of corporate responsibility programs. We had always participated in Lloyd's-sponsored programs, but we also set out on our own. Over time, we established a worldwide corporate responsibility program, with each office given a budget and encouraged to finance and participate in projects that would benefit the local community.

One of our biggest successes was to build a partnership with what was a failing secondary school in the East End of London. We got closely involved with St. Paul's Way Trust School, donating not just money but our employees' time. John Carroll became both a school governor and trustee, and our marketing department worked with school administrators to help recruit students. After just three years, a school that had been declared 'failing' by UK education authorities had been transformed into an 'outstanding' school. Our role in the turnaround at St Paul's Way was small, but we are very proud of what we helped the school to achieve.

22. Regulation

Regulation is necessary; over-regulation is dangerous

Regulation of the insurance industry is very important. Insurance companies trade on a promise to pay valid claims, and it is the regulator's job to make sure that an insurer has the wherewithal to make good on that promise. If insurers are not regulated properly, history tells us that somebody is going to do something slippery and/or stupid – and the entire industry will end up with a black eye.

No one necessarily likes to be regulated, but in insurance it is certainly a necessity. I think most industry executives share this view. It's no surprise that when the Bermuda government decided to strengthen the quality of the regulation provided by the Bermuda Monetary Authority, insurers and reinsurers readily agreed to pay half of the cost.

* * *

At the start of my insurance career, regulation – at least in the UK – seemed to be of little consequence to most people working in the industry, and I had a feeling that regulators had little knowledge of how insurers really operated. Part of the problem had been that insurance had been historically lumped together with banks for regulatory purposes. That's nonsensical because, as I have previously pointed out, the dynamics of a bank's balance sheet are completely different to the dynamics of an insurance company's. Regulators now recognize the differences between the two industries.

I believe that insurance regulators sometimes lose sight of the fact that their primary duty is to protect the policyholders' interests, not the shareholders' interests. It should be irrelevant to the insurance regulator whether a company stays in business or goes bust. What should be relevant to the regulator is that the promise by the insurer to pay policyholders' valid claims is made good.

Improved insurance regulation has certainly enhanced the quality of the insurance industry, but insurers over the years have also been able to regulate themselves more effectively as they now have a much clearer handle on their exposures. Risk modeling is far better than it was ten or 20 years ago, and the manner in which the industry looks at the downside risk to capital is much improved. Management has a better understanding of how insurance and reinsurance portfolios can perform – or not perform – over the long term, largely because there is now greater actuarial capability within the industry.

I am sure that regulators would prefer to believe that these improvements are all down to them. Regulators have certainly been helpful, but I think most of the improvement is due to the fact that insurers are far more technical than they used to be. Investors require much more transparency and they are far more inquisitive than they were 20 years ago, and therefore obfuscating problems for any length of time is far more difficult today than it used to be. Problems within a particular insurance carrier surface more quickly, and that hopefully means less damage is done to the policyholder when difficulties do arise.

Does that mean that nothing will go wrong in the future? No, it doesn't. I dare say that in the next 25 years something bad will happen in the insurance industry that no one had previously considered. It will give everybody a headache. I don't think any amount of regulation today will reduce that risk because regulators can no more predict what might happen than insurers can.

* * *

The quality of insurance regulation differs greatly around the world. At Catlin, we were privileged to work with, in my mind, some of what I considered to be the best regulatory authorities in the world, including the Bermuda Monetary Authority, the Swiss Financial Market Supervisory Authority, the Monetary Authority of Singapore and various insurance regulatory bodies in the UK.

Insurance regulation in the US is a different kettle of fish compared with any other country. There is little federal regulation of insurance. Instead, there are insurance departments in each of the 50 states that are charged with regulating the insurers which are domiciled or 'admitted' in their respective jurisdictions. The National Association of Insurance Commissioners sets standards that each state can follow and provides support services. I believe some state insurance regulators – such as in New York – do a very good job; others aren't quite so good. In some instances, state insurance commissioners are elected officials (and you have to wonder what the voting public really knows about insurance regulation). In some other states, insurance regulation is headed by an individual who is a direct beneficiary of political patronage.

In Europe, regulators and insurers alike have been grappling with the implementation of the Solvency II directive for nearly a decade. Solvency II promised a new style of regulation through which the focus of insurance regulation would be changed from simply compliance and capital monitoring to the evaluation of insurers' risk profiles and the quality of their risk management and governance systems.

I have always been in favor of the concept of Solvency II because it forces insurers to describe the risks they have assumed on a holistic basis. I thought that was a very constructive move forward. However, Solvency II unfortunately got out of control and, in my opinion, we are now at a stage with Solvency II where one can't see the forest for the trees; it is almost like regulation gone mad. It's simply too complex, and I am not sure that all insurance company non-executive directors – the people really responsible for assuring that an insurance carrier is financially sound – can understand the myriad regulations under which insurers in Europe must operate today.

Now that Solvency II is finally up and running, insurers need to work with regulators to make sure that it operates from a common-sense point of view. That will probably take a long time.

In the meantime, regulatory costs – particularly for insurers subject to Solvency II – have skyrocketed. For example, the cost of regulatory compliance at Catlin rose by nearly 50 per cent between 2012 and 2014, more than double the growth in premium volume over the same period.

*   *   *

Is insurance regulation today better than it was 20 years ago? I would say 'yes' because regulation is much stronger and more effective. Has regulation gone over the top? Yes, in certain circumstances it has. In some cases, and I am specifically referring to Solvency II, regulation has ceased to be fit for purpose. In other words, it has lost sight of what it was trying to do in the first place.

For example, some regulators want to treat the local subsidiary of a global insurance company as if it were the holding company itself. A multinational insurance company may perform certain activities at the holding company level, such as investment management, reinsurance purchasing and many support functions. It can be dangerous if the regulator of each subsidiary believes it has the right to regulate these functions, which are not actually carried out by the company that the regulator is empowered to oversee. There needs to be better understanding as to where each legal entity fits into the entire insurance group and which regulator should be responsible for which activity.

It's still difficult for regulators in different jurisdictions to work together.

I believe that all too often regulators tend to look after their own parochial concerns, which can overtake the interests of a global business. In these cases, you often get a clash between what the holding company regulator wants and what the local regulator of a subsidiary wants.

I think the advent of 'colleges', where regulators from different jurisdictions meet, is a good step. Communication among different regulators is valuable. For several years, I spent two days each year in Brussels with insurance regulators from many nations to try to help regulators understand the problems that international insurers face and how regulators can work together. For example, the last time I attended this meeting, I tried to explain how it is in everybody's interest that surplus capital is held at a holding company level so it can be moved quickly to whichever legal entity requires additional capital at any given point in time.

Because of the breaches of regulation in the banking industry in particular, and in the insurance industry to a much lesser extent, tougher insurance regulation is here to stay. It's totally appropriate that insurance regulation has teeth as long as the regulators know when to bite and when to keep their mouths closed.

I made it my business to build personal relationships with the individual regulators around the world that Catlin dealt with. Nowadays, most companies will experience some regulatory hiccups along the way. It is important for an insurance company executive to recognize that a regulator has a job to do, and it is up to the industry to help that regulator carry out its duties as efficiently and as sensibly as is possible.

* * *

A lot is written about insurance fraud, and there will always be some unsavory people active in an industry where there's a promise to pay claims in the future in exchange for a premium paid upfront. You will never eradicate fraud completely in any industry because there is always going to be somebody, somewhere, who is going to lie, cheat and/or steal.

When I look back to the way some business was brokered and placed within the London market going back 20 to 40 years, it was at best sloppy and sometimes far worse. But, I don't see much evidence of that happening nowadays. That is a good thing. I think brokers have been forced by regulation to be much more open and transparent about what they are doing.

Enhanced regulation has encouraged and enforced greater transparency in the industry in terms of financial reporting, and that has significantly decreased the number of insurer insolvencies. Insolvencies were a fairly common occurrence during the first 20 years of my career, and they still do occur. However, when I look at one of the largest insolvencies in the UK – the collapse of the insurers backing the H.S. Weavers (Underwriting) Agencies Ltd. line slip – I believe that type of collapse would be very unlikely to occur today. Weavers and its insurers were possibly trading while insolvent for the better part of a decade. In addition, some of the problems that occurred at Lloyd's during the 1980s and 1990s could not recur today because of the establishment of the Franchise Board and proactive reporting requirements.

Will insurer insolvencies *never* happen again? I don't think I could say that, but they are much more rare today.

* * *

When addressing insurance regulation, one must also mention the major insurance rating agencies, such as A.M. Best Co., Standard & Poor's and Fitch Ratings. Rating agencies have become in many ways a pseudo-regulator. Some would argue that is good, and some would argue that is bad. I think the combination of good regulation alongside informed rating agencies is an effective combination.

While the rating agencies generally do a pretty good job, there have been some problems. How they regarded subprime investments before the financial crisis is a good example of where they have not done such a good job.

While there are several rating agencies, one cannot assume they are all the same. They're not. They have different methodologies and different capital models. For example, the capital loads that some rating agencies assign to certain types of special situation investments are so great that it discourages the insurer from investing in these areas, which is a shame. While one could reason that this type of policy results in a safer investment portfolio, it also deters diversification, and I believe that diversification in an investment portfolio is a good thing.

Another problem that rating agencies can create is their reliance on risk models. If everyone uses the same risk model and the model proves to be wrong, everyone winds up in the soup. However, rating agencies often encourage this type of uniform behavior. As I said earlier, models can be valuable tools and are now part of the underwriting process, but they should never solely drive the underwriting decision.

I respect the fact that rating agencies are constantly trying to up their game. They are certainly making better use of data. Their independence is quite valuable in assessing the quality of an insurer.

In terms of dealing with rating agencies, it's very much like dealing with regulators. They tend to treat you in the same manner you treat them. If you're open, transparent and constructive in your relationship with the rating agencies, they will act in the same way.

23. International Insurance/ Reinsurance Markets

Insurance is now a truly global industry

I began this book by warning that it could be somewhat London-centric. I spent the bulk of my career working at Lloyd's, but as Catlin expanded I obtained considerable exposure to other insurance and reinsurance markets around the world.

Once upon a time, London was truly the center of the insurance world, particularly the reinsurance market. Sure, Munich Re, Swiss Re and other large European reinsurers played a major role, and there were several major reinsurers based in the US. However, the world pretty much looked to London for leadership in reinsurance.

That's no longer the case. Just as I foresaw the fact that insurance would increasingly be purchased from local markets, the reinsurance market has also become more fragmented.

Bermuda became a center for catastrophe reinsurance in 1993, following Hurricane Andrew, as companies like Renaissance Re, Partner Re, Mid Ocean Re and Tempest Re were established on the island, rather than in London, Europe or the US. Then, over time, regional reinsurance centers have formed and are still growing. While Swiss Re had long been based in Zurich, many other companies – including Catlin – formed reinsurance subsidiaries there earlier this century to write protection for European insurers. Likewise, more than a dozen companies in Singapore now write reinsurance for Asian cedants. And, over the past several years, a growing reinsurance market for Latin American business has sprung up in Miami. Perhaps in the future we will see burgeoning reinsurance centers spring up in cities like Shanghai and Mumbai.

* * *

The US insurance market is different to the London market in many ways, but they share one similar trait. Both markets sincerely believe they are at the center of the global insurance industry. A lot of Brits will tell you that London has to be recognized as the true heart of the insurance marketplace because the Marine Insurance Act 1906 is the basis for insurance law and practices in many countries around the world. Indeed, a Brit could even argue that much of the damage from the 1906 San Francisco earthquake was paid for by Lloyd's and other London-based insurers.

Not long ago, I attended a meeting in Washington, DC, held by a consulting firm. There were lots of really intelligent people sitting around a table, discussing how insurance business could be brought back to the US. I was shocked, however, by their attitude. The prevailing belief around the table was that if Congress lowered the US corporation tax, the whole of the insurance industry would flock to America ... because that is where it belongs.

I wanted to try to accept this argument. The US represents about 40 per cent of the world's property/casualty insurance premiums, according to a 2015 Aon study. There are certainly some large insurance companies that are domiciled in the US, including Berkshire Hathaway, American International Group and Liberty Mutual.

However, when I thought about it more, I realized that there are three main concerns an insurance company has when selecting a domicile. Tax is certainly one of them, but so are capital requirements and regulation. Capital requirements vary greatly from state to state. So, while a low-tax regime could be uniformly applied across the 50 states, uniform capital requirements would be impossible. Insurance regulation, of course, is inconsistent across America, again depending on which state an insurer is domiciled or admitted.

While America is probably the most important insurance market in the world in terms of sheer premium volume, I don't think you can say it is the center of the insurance industry. In fact, I am surprised by just how much American business is placed with non-US insurers. I think this was made clear following 9/11. According to research conducted by investment firm Dowling & Partners, US-based insurers and reinsurers paid only 36 per cent of the insured losses arising from the tragedy.

Insured 9/11 losses ($bn)

Category	Losses paid	Percentage
US primary insurers	5,659	21.1%
US reinsurers	4,109	15.3%
European primary insurers	3,865	14.4%
European reinsurers	5,506	20.5%
Bermuda reinsurers	2,479	9.2%
Lloyd's syndicates	2,844	10.6%
Japanese reinsurers	2,388	8.9%
Total	26,850	100.0%

Source: Dowling & Partners

This is a good example of how risk is effectively spread across the world's various insurance and reinsurance markets.

* * *

Possibly the biggest difference between the London and US markets is the level of concentration. The London insurance market is concentrated within the 'Square Mile', or the City of London. There is substantial opportunity for face-to-face dealing because everyone in the market is no more than a ten-minute walk away.

In the US, there is no single insurance market as there is in London, so there really isn't a 'marketplace' as such. Insurance is carried out from coast to coast. The way business is conducted is very different to London. There is relatively little face-to-face negotiation. Instead, most business is placed by phone, fax and, within the past 20 years, email. US insurers must actively go out and seek business; in London, the business traditionally comes from brokers to underwriters, without the underwriters having to do very much. If you speak to any Brit who has worked Stateside, they will probably say that people in the London market should try working in America just so they realize how tough it is to go out and attract business rather than having it brought to you.

To me, however, what the US market lacks is the ability to syndicate risk. In London and at Lloyd's, various underwriters can subscribe to the same risk, following the same policy form and with one underwriter serving as a claims lead. Hundreds of millions of dollars in capacity – even more in some cases – is readily available depending on the risk. Such an insurance program is impossible to construct in the US. You would have to place the program in many layers, with each insurer using its own policy wording and handling its own claims.

I don't wish to be parochial, but I would prefer the 'holistic' London program if I were an insurance buyer.

* * *

The origins of the Bermuda market, as we know it today, began shortly after Catlin was established. Bermuda was already known as the home of many US corporations' captive insurers, but the commercial insurance business in Bermuda at that time was not taken very seriously. Regulation was lax, and so was capitalization. That all changed in the late 1980s, a time when it was virtually impossible for big corporations to buy meaningful excess casualty insurance capacity in the US, when US companies banded together to form ACE Limited and then EXEL Limited, now XL Group Ltd. While neither company was domiciled in Bermuda, both based their operations there and specialized in writing excess liability insurance. They grew quickly, and after several years began writing various classes of property and casualty business.

In my view, ACE and XL during the late 1980s changed the reputation of the Bermuda market. Then, in the months following 1992's Hurricane Andrew, eight major catastrophe reinsurers were formed in Bermuda, largely because ACE and XL had demonstrated the advantages of the marketplace so well. Likewise, there was another flurry of insurer/reinsurer formations after 9/11 in 2001 and still more following Hurricane Katrina in 2005.

In my view, Bermuda became a true insurance marketplace around 2002. From 1986 onwards you could go to Bermuda to buy excess liability insurance if you were a US corporation, and from 1993 onwards it became a center for catastrophe reinsurance. The companies which sprang up after 9/11, however, really made Bermuda the multi-faceted marketplace it remains today.

As time passed, Bermuda has strengthened its position, especially with regard to the quality of regulation. Bermuda had been known as a domicile with relatively light-touch regulation, which I believe frankly is dangerous. Regulation needs to be fit for purpose, and weak regulation ends up being a disaster because the mud sticks to everybody.

The Bermuda Monetary Authority is now regarded as one of the better insurance regulators worldwide. It was a real coup in 2016 when Bermuda was awarded Solvency II equivalence, which means that the regulation in Bermuda is considered by the European Union to be equivalent to EU regulation under Solvency II. Only Bermuda and Switzerland have been so recognized at the time of publication.

That does not mean that Bermuda does not have its problems. One is the characterization of Bermuda as a tax haven. Companies domiciled in Bermuda do not pay income tax, but that does not mean that Bermuda is a tax haven. Bermuda simply chooses to raise taxes through other means. The percentage of GDP that is taxed is not that much lower in Bermuda than in the US. However, some US politicians continue to make political gravy by complaining about the so-called tax advantages enjoyed by companies based in Bermuda.

In addition, Bermuda suffers from budgetary problems as well as tensions between local Bermudians and the expatriates who work for insurance companies. Operating costs in Bermuda are already among the highest in the world.

Despite these problems, Bermuda is here to stay as an insurance/reinsurance center. I have been privileged to serve as the chairman of the Association of Bermuda Insurers and Reinsurers (ABIR). And, I was personally delighted when XL Catlin in 2016 chose to move the domicile of its parent company from Ireland to Bermuda. For those of us who had worked at Catlin, it was like coming home again.

24. CLOSING THE PROTECTION GAP

Making sure more people can recover from natural catastrophes

In the late afternoon on Tuesday, January 12, 2010, a magnitude 7.0 earthquake rocked the Caribbean nation of Haiti. The quake, which was centered just 25 kilometers from the capital city Port au Prince, was one of the greatest humanitarian disasters of the 21st century. No one knows exactly how many people died, but estimates range from 100,000 to more than 300,000. Approximately 1 million people were displaced.

The property damage was extensive. According to a report from the United Nations, at least 50 per cent of all homes and buildings in Port au Prince were destroyed and another 25 per cent were damaged beyond repair. Across the country, about 250,000 residences and 30,000 commercial buildings were destroyed or suffered so much damage that they required demolition. More than 1,300 schools and 50 healthcare facilities were among the buildings destroyed. Swiss Re estimated that property damage from the catastrophe amounted to $10 billion.

Aid flowed to Haiti from around the world. Significant aid came from the US, where former presidents Bill Clinton and George H.W. Bush co-chaired efforts to raise funds. Within two years, the UN estimated that some $4.5 billion in aid and donations had been pledged, although less than 50 per cent of the amount had actually been delivered.

One would assume that the insurance industry would have been a major contributor to the rebuilding of Haiti, which is considered to be the poorest nation in the Western Hemisphere. However, it wasn't. Of the estimated $10 billion in property damage sustained, only $100 million to $200 million was insured. At the time of the earthquake, Haiti spent about an estimated 0.3 per cent of its meager gross domestic product on non-life insurance. By comparison, the non-life insurance spend in the US was about 4.2 per cent of GDP in 2015, according to Swiss Re, while European nations spent 2.7 per cent and Asian nations spent 1.7 per cent of GDP on non-life insurance.

* * *

There are too many countries like Haiti, where a serious 'protection gap' exists. Around the world, it is estimated that 70 per cent of economic losses from natural catastrophes – such as windstorms, floods and earthquakes – remain uninsured. Among low- or middle-income nations, the protection gap exceeds 90 per cent. For the world's poorest 100 nations – including Haiti – the gap is greater than 97 per cent.

While most people in developed countries accept insurance as a given, the protection gap can even be found in the US. Should a major earthquake strike California, it's estimated that the protection gap could range from 50 per cent to 90 per cent. Take 'Superstorm Sandy', which walloped the East Coast of the US in November 2012: insurance covered less than 50 per cent of the total damage.

When it comes to developing and low-income countries, where the protection gap is the greatest, there are good reasons why insurance penetration has lagged so much behind developed nations:

- Governments and the private sector simply cannot afford to buy protection;
- Regulatory frameworks in some nations impede insurance market development;
- Likewise, the structure of commercial markets in some countries make it difficult to distribute insurance products easily;
- There is not sufficient or appropriate data to model risks so therefore insurance is not readily available; and/or
- There is a general lack of awareness or understanding of the benefits that insurance could provide.

What's more worrying is that the protection gap will widen before it can be narrowed. Due to climate change, an estimated 100 million people could fall below the poverty line by 2030 without appropriate climate-resilient development. And, if global warming keeps increasing at its current pace, global economic losses could exceed $50 trillion over the coming decades.

* * *

In Chapter 1, I spoke about the value of insurance, and how its value is probably best demonstrated following a natural catastrophe. It has been proven time and time again that when a large portion of a loss is insured, there is less human deprivation, faster economic recovery and a lower cost to the taxpayer. Surely that's a desirable outcome for everyone concerned?

However, as I also stated previously, the insurance industry is rather lousy at communicating the value of its products and services. We are not particularly trusted and we don't often try to be heard.

For an economically fragile country such as Haiti, insurance has true value:

- Obviously, insurance can provide financial risk transfer, which provides protection by absorbing losses that would otherwise be borne by the government and the private sector of affected nations; and
- Furthermore, the insurance industry can also play another important role. We as insurers and brokers know much more about potential exposures than any other sector. Therefore, we can contribute to a better understanding of risk and the implementation of more effective risk reduction and resilience strategies. In other words, the insurance industry can help countries like Haiti identify, assess, prevent and reduce risk.

* * *

The scale, scope and complexity of the protection gap will require a joint effort from the private and public sectors if this gap is indeed to be closed. Recent international frameworks, such as the 2015 Paris climate change agreement (COP 21), the Sendai Framework of Disaster Risk Reduction and the United Nations' 2030 Agenda for Sustainable Development, recognize the role that insurers can play in closing the gap. However, if an individual insurer or broker attempts to make suggestions unilaterally, governments immediately assume that the insurer or broker is acting purely out of self-interest. What is needed is for the insurance industry to propose a solution in a unified manner.

Such an effort was the brainchild of Rowan Douglas, CEO of capital, science and policy practice at broker Willis Towers Watson. Rowan's idea was to bring together governments, international organizations and the insurance/reinsurance industry to enable the development of insurance-related capabilities and disaster resilience at a national level.

Rowan's dream is now a reality. The Insurance Development Forum was formally established in early 2016 with the aim of extending insurance and risk management principles to strengthen resilience against disasters and protect more people from the economic shocks created by catastrophe, climate and other risks.

The IDF is a truly unique initiative as it is being led by the insurance industry, co-sponsored by the UN and the World Bank. I am honored to have been appointed as chairman of the IDF, along with two co-chairs: Helen Clark, the former prime minister of New Zealand and the administrator of the UN Development Program, and Joaquim Levy, chief financial officer of the World Bank. Helen stepped down from her role with the UN Development Program in April 2017, and a successor as co-chair of the IDF had not been appointed at the time this book was published.

One of my first tasks as IDF chairman was to enlist the support of insurers, reinsurers and brokers. Utilizing relationships that I had made over the years, the IDF's steering committee represents a virtual 'who's who' of the property/casualty insurance industry, including executives from insurers, reinsurers, brokers and trade associations:

- Dame Inga Beale, CEO of Lloyd's;
- Albert Benchimol, president and CEO of AXIS Capital of Bermuda;
- Greg Case; president and CEO of Aon;
- Jean-Louis Davet, CEO of MGEN, the Paris-based mutual group;
- Denis Duverne, chairman of AXA of France;
- Dan Glaser, president and CEO of Marsh & McLennan;
- John Haley, CEO of Willis Towers Watson;
- Torsten Jeworrek, CEO-reinsurance of Munich Re;
- Denis Kessler, chairman and CEO of SCOR;
- Christian Mumenthaler, CEO of Swiss Re;
- Christopher Swift, chairman and CEO of The Hartford;
- Maurice Tulloch, chairman of Aviva Global Insurance; and
- Rob Wesseling, president and CEO of The Co-operators Group of Canada.

Additionally, Mark Carney, the governor of the Bank of England, is a member of the steering committee in his role as chairman of the Financial Stability Board, an international body that monitors and makes recommendations about the global financial system. Several UN officials also serve on the committee.

Among the insurance trade associations and other groups working with the IDF are the Geneva Association, the International Insurance Society, the Association of Bermuda Insurers and Reinsurers, and the International Cooperative and Mutual Insurance Federation.

As I write this, the IDF is still in an embryonic state, but we have already set a daunting goal. We hope to help achieve the target set in 2015 by the G7 nations to ensure that insurance protection against climate-related risks is extended to 400 million additional people worldwide by 2020. The IDF hopes to achieve this by putting in place what we call a 'technical assistance facility', an advisory and assistance platform supported by the insurance industry, the UN and the World Bank.

This facility will help governments:

- better understand the risks that their individual countries face; and
- develop and deploy effective risk transfer solutions that are tailored to each country's unique circumstances and challenges.

While I obviously have a vested interest, I am confident that the IDF – in partnership with international organizations, the insurance industry and other parts of the private sector – can make a real difference in closing the protection gap, building resilience to natural catastrophes and climate risk, and increasing prosperity for people around the world.

25. The Challenges of Tomorrow

The industry faces threats on several different fronts

If the insurance industry is to remain relevant to society over the next 20 or 25 years, it must embrace the new risks to which society will be exposed. We must be at the forefront of understanding those risks and finding solutions to mitigate them. The big obstacle, however, is that insurers' thinking tends to focus on what has happened in the past rather than what might happen in the future.

Insurers must look forward to where the world is heading. Our society is a very different place today than when I joined the insurance industry in 1973. Personal computers, the internet and emails were unheard of. Fax machines were cutting-edge technology. Climate change was not a major worry.

We as an industry must do a better job of thinking ahead. Social behavior will undoubtedly change over the next several decades. Manufacturing will change with the growing use of robotics, which could result in increased unemployment. The white-collar workforce will also be impacted by the advance of technology. People will continue to live longer. Mass transportation will change as driverless cars quickly become a reality.

As the world changes, the products and services that insurers sell must keep pace. It's unavoidable if we as an industry are to remain relevant.

Historically, insurance has primarily been driven by property coverage, and we in the industry still spend much of our time talking about property catastrophe business. Casualty insurance has increased dramatically during the past half-century, and non-property risks will continue to increase in importance. If you assess the value of Fortune 500 companies over the past 50 years, I reckon that 80 per cent of that value was attributable to physical assets, such as property and equipment. If you look at a similar group of companies today, possibly 80 per cent of their value is associated with soft assets such as intellectual property rights or data, not physical assets.

Management's biggest worry was once that the factory would burn down. Today, some of the biggest worries relate to competitiveness, data retention and cyber security. Do insurers really spend enough time thinking about those things?

Thankfully, risk management and loss prevention has improved immeasurably over the past 40 years. Health and safety, both in the workplace and at home, is much improved. Airplanes are safer, and so are ships and cars. Buildings are constructed to withstand hurricanes, earthquakes and other natural perils.

We as humans, though, do not have any real control over elemental perils. Whether it's due to climate change or just random chance, the frequency of elemental losses appears to be increasing. So, as values continue to rise, the potential economic loss – in other words severity – will also increase.

* * *

To me, the elephant in the room today is what we call the 'cyber' issue. The growing interconnectivity of computers, their ability to learn from each other and the fact that the world's economy has become absolutely dependent on the internet raises huge new challenges for the insurance industry.

Rarely a week passes that we don't see a headline relating to data theft at a big corporation. But what are the implications of an even bigger event? No one has succeeded in knocking out the internet – at least not yet.

I realize that experts say it could never happen. However, insurers in the past have had to pay a lot of losses 'that could never happen'. Who would have thought that someone would have such a twisted mind to hijack airplanes full of innocent passengers and deliberately fly them into skyscrapers?

So, we must continue to contemplate and model the unknown and unthinkable, even though it is much easier said than done. To my mind, the potential systemic risk arising from a collapse of the internet is the greatest exposure I've ever considered during my insurance career. When insurers have modelled true catastrophic losses in the past, they have modeled elemental risks that, by their very nature, are relatively localized. (Some progress is being made towards modeling the global fall-out from disasters, such as the interruption to auto parts supply caused by the floods in Thailand.) However, the interconnectivity of data systems worldwide means that a severe cyber breach will affect companies from the US to China – and everyone in between – at a whole new level.

The real challenge for the insurance industry is how insurers can offer meaningful cyber insurance coverage to clients – both in terms of scope and policy limits – without bankrupting themselves. There is no doubt in my mind that only governments could provide ultimate financial protection if and when society faces a truly catastrophic cyber-related loss, such as complete disruption of the internet for a prolonged period. There is simply not enough capital in the insurance industry to pay the resulting losses.

For context, the industry currently thinks nothing of providing $2 billion in coverage for a physical damage exposure, but the most insurers currently can provide for a cyber exposure is $500 million – and that coverage is extremely restricted. In fact, it's hard for most businesses to get even $100 million in limits.

Of course, plugging this cyber coverage gap will be extremely difficult, especially if insurers look back on their experience with asbestos and pollution claims. Policy wordings will be crucial. Tom Bolt, the former director of performance management at Lloyd's and now CEO of Berkshire Hathaway International Insurance, has said that insurers in the near future must draft clear language in each and every policy they underwrite to make it absolutely clear whether cyber risk is included or excluded and to what extent. His hypothesis is that any policy that is 'silent' as to whether cyber risks are covered could be interpreted by US courts to include coverage. I agree with Tom's thinking.

It is going to take the finest legal brains to work out how insurers can protect themselves from potential cyber claims they never intended to insure. It's a huge challenge.

* * *

Several years ago, I suggested that the best way to cover cyber claims would be a TRIA-like system. I was referring to the US Terrorism Risk Insurance Act, originally enacted in 2002, which created a public/private system for paying claims arising from terrorist acts on US soil. The commercial insurance industry is responsible for paying a certain level of claims arising from a terrorism incident, after which the federal government takes over. TRIA has since been superseded by the Terrorism Risk Insurance Program Reauthorization Act of 2015, which has extended this mechanism through 2020.

However, I have since concluded that a TRIA-type solution simply will not work for cyber losses. The more I thought about it, I realized that these risks are global, not just confined to one country. For example, what happens if US companies incur cyber-related losses instigated, for example, by a group of Russian hackers. Would the US government's TRIA-type program foot the bill, or should it be covered by a Russian program? The two governments would undoubtedly argue over who should pay.

I still think – for an Armageddon-type episode – only governments will have the wherewithal to compensate companies for cyber-related losses. However, this is an issue that most governments are unlikely to consider in the near future.

* * *

Another, unrelated challenge that insurers and brokers must face is rising costs. Expense ratios for nearly all insurers are rising. Why is that? It's largely because insurers are expected to do more. Forty years ago, there weren't all that many lawyers or actuaries working for insurance companies. IT departments did not exist. Now, they're essential, and they're also expensive. Once upon a time, we didn't have pricing models or reserving models. We now do, and they cost plenty. I noted earlier that Catlin's regulatory-related costs increased by nearly 50 per cent over a three-year period. Our premium volume increased by only about half that amount, even though Catlin was growing much more quickly than many of its competitors.

The cost of doing business is going up by so much that I fear there will no longer be room for small players in our industry. Insurance has always been home to small 'niche' players, those that only underwrite a small number of business classes but write them very well. However, I doubt if many of the niche players will be able to thrive because their costs will probably increase faster than their premium volume. The good news is that there are plenty of companies out there that will want to buy a smaller business with a high-quality niche portfolio.

This goes back to what XL's Mike McGavick and I discussed several years ago in Brussels. The marketplace will consolidate. It already has begun to do so, and consolidation will continue for the foreseeable future.

As time moves on, insurers that are not of a sufficient size and that do not add significant value will find the going tough.

* * *

As I noted in Chapter 8, the industry must sort out the process problem – quickly. If we don't, someone else will surely do it for us, and we probably won't like their solution. We are simply inefficient as an industry. We enter data three or four times instead of once, increasing costs and creating greater probability of errors. When I began working in insurance back in 1973, I thought the process being used was archaic; it's probably not much better today.

The process problem is a much bigger issue than some people acknowledge or even realize. The cost of process must decrease. For that to happen, process must become much more efficient. The personal lines segment of the market has done a much better job than the commercial lines segment because of the commodity nature of that business. But data and data collection remain a challenge throughout the industry that no one has yet cracked properly.

I have always held the view that brokers play a valuable role by providing advice to the client, structuring the solution and, most importantly, providing choice. Insurers can only sell the products they individually offer; they would find it difficult to construct bespoke products to meet the specific needs of individual clients, but brokers can help the client by contacting a wide variety of insurers.

However, brokers can no longer steadfastly believe that their role in processing the business after it is placed is another value-added service. Their process capabilities are poor. However, if they lose control of the process to a company like Microsoft or Google, they also risk losing control of their clients.

* * *

I wish I had a dollar for every time I have read an article or participated in a discussion about insurance market cycles. The subject is truly inescapable. Over the years, I have heard many 'experts' say that cycles would eventually become shallower.

Guess what? They haven't.

As I write this in mid-2017, insurers find themselves in a marketplace where the level of pricing is close to unsustainable. Absent a major catastrophe, it could take several more years to get to a situation in which the industry has negative cash flow and equity levels begin to fall. When that happens, you will see capital flee the marketplace, supply will dry up and – assuming that demand does not change – prices will finally rise. The question is when will this happen?

The trick of riding out a down cycle is to make certain that your capital is still intact when the market finally does turn. Then, you're going to want to raise new capital. Raising new capital is a hell of a lot easier than replenishing capital. The appetite for new capital is far, far greater than the appetite for replenishing capital.

Cycles can turn in one of three ways. The first is through inward pressure, which is the scenario that I cited above. Cycles have also turned on the back of a major catastrophe, such as Hurricane Andrew in 1992 or Hurricane Katrina in 2005. A third possibility is some massive deterioration of legacy liability – such as asbestos – which hadn't been foreseen.

Luckily, individual product lines have tended to have their own cycles, and it's often not the case that all classes of business head in the same direction. Casualty rates could be rising, while marine hull pricing could be plummeting.

Every now and again, you get a perfect storm where every class of business heads south at the same time. The year 1999 was a good example; I have never seen a market that was so uniformly bad for insurers. A lot of people think that 9/11 turned the market, but prices were already starting to increase by early 2001. By the time 9/11 occurred, there was already an appetite to raise rates.

At the moment, we are moving rather swiftly to a 1999-type environment. If current market conditions continue, either the market will eventually turn because a dearth of capital or a major event will speed the correction. However, until that happens, some companies may either go out of business or be in such bad shape that they will be unable to raise capital once conditions improve.

* * *

Another topic that perhaps has been over-debated is the future role of so-called alternative capital in the marketplace. Does it pose a threat to traditional insurance and reinsurance companies? I have never really worried about it.

When you discuss alternative capital, you must look at it as two groups. First, there are pension funds and similar vehicles that have begun investing in the insurance industry because it offered diversification as well as a better potential return in an era of low interest rates. I believe this type of alternative capital is here to stay.

Then there is the alternative capital that is being supplied by reinsurance vehicles sponsored by hedge funds and similar entities; I would label that kind of capital as 'opportunistic' to say the least. How long will this type of capital stick around?

If interest rates do rise, my guess is that hedge funds will look for non-insurance investments that can offer attractive returns with a much lower level of risk. Secondly, there are elements of tax arbitrage associated with this type of capital, and I think these loopholes will probably close over time. Thirdly, we have seen a lower than average incidence of natural catastrophes over the past several years. What will these types of reinsurers do if suddenly there is a truly major event or a series of moderate catastrophes such as in 2011? Finally, if reinsurance rates fall to bargain-basement levels, will this form of alternative capital withdraw from the industry and look for a better return elsewhere? Once upon a time, these vehicles were producing 25 per cent annual returns on equity. They could take the view that, if you achieve that type of return for five years in a row, you could afford a really bad year.

Nowadays, though, the returns aren't that high, possibly in the single digits, so the return period to recover from a major loss is much longer.

I am not against this type of alternative capital. We at Catlin bought protection from hedge fund-type reinsurers, and they are now part of the industry's landscape. How long will they stay around? That's anyone's guess.

What I hope is that any type of 'alternative capital' vehicle will honor the promise to pay. Most of the disputes that have involved these types of vehicles are subject to arbitration, so details of the outcomes are not publicly known, but there have been reports that some cedants have had a difficult time collecting after a major event. It's not uncommon to hear about payment disputes with traditional reinsurers, but traditional reinsurers usually seek a long-term relationship, so a resolution of the dispute is usually possible. The type of relationship that alternative capital seeks still isn't totally clear.

I do not see alternative capital as posing a threat to the industry. Rather, this type of capital should be welcomed, particularly when it is really needed, never forgetting the value of relationships that exist in the traditional reinsurance market.

*   *   *

So, the property/casualty insurance industry faces a great many challenges. Some will be difficult to address – particularly those posed by cyber exposures and by process – but they are not insoluble.

Insurers must learn to look ahead even though their instincts are to look to the past.

*   *   *

As this book entered the final stages prior to publication, Lloyd's announced that it will appoint Bruce Carnegie-Brown as its next chairman. I sincerely wish Bruce well and hope that his chairmanship is a success.

Bruce comes to Lloyd's at a particularly challenging time as its relevance in the international property/casualty insurance marketplace is being increasingly questioned. Some would go so far as to say that its future is in doubt. The issues that Bruce will need to address include relationships with regulators, capital providers and brokers (which are at a lower point than they have been previously). The new chairman will also have to evaluate the leadership within the Corporation of Lloyd's as many key members of staff have resigned or retired over the past 18 months.

Above all else, the new chairman will have to address the major problems of process and expenses, which are especially important in the context of Lloyd's. The expense base of syndicates writing business at Lloyd's is now approximately 40 per cent, which is a level that is unsustainable over time. Expenses and process are problems for which Lloyd's has tried to find solutions for years, but they now need to be addressed urgently if Lloyd's is to maintain a pre-eminent position in the industry.

At the same time, I have decided to retire from XL Catlin after being part of the integration process for the past two years, although I will remain a consultant to the company for the foreseeable future. The integration of XL and Catlin, while complex, has been successful, and XL Catlin is in a great position to take advantage of opportunities as they arise. I wish Mike McGavick and the entire XL Catlin team well.

It's perhaps fitting that this book is published as I come to a crossroads in my career. I worked for the same organization – first as Catlin, then as XL Catlin – for nearly 33 years, a pretty remarkable run. As I now look back on nearly 45 years in the insurance industry, I have been extremely fortunate, and I remain grateful to so many people who have supported me, mentored me and challenged me all the way through. I cannot thank all of them enough.

I am now keen to find other ways to give back to the industry which has provided me with so much. I hope to remain closely involved with the Insurance Development Forum, and I have no doubt that other new challenges await me.

I began this book by talking about the value of insurance. The value of the products that we as insurers and brokers offer to the public has not waned, and indeed I believe it can be successfully argued that insurance has never been so important. I genuinely hope that readers now have a better understanding of the significance of the insurance industry and the value it generates for the common good.

Afterword

Mike McGavick
Chief executive officer, XL Catlin and XL Group Ltd

It is a joy for me to add some thoughts at the end of this remarkable volume. In *Risk & Reward*, Stephen Catlin has given us the gift of his insights into the insurance and reinsurance marketplaces, his key ideas about leading complex businesses, and has even peered into the future of the sector and shared what he has foreseen.

That substance alone would have been a full reward for the reader's risk of purchase and time spent.

But, Stephen has done something even more generous and less obvious in the way in which he has written this book: Stephen's wonderful and often exceptional personal qualities are also fully present. We see the humor, the love of his family, and the deep sense of commitment and duty he feels toward his colleagues fully woven into these pages. This changes everything. For my money, there is more to be learned by focusing on these personal qualities and devotions when you re-read this book.

If read in this context, you can easily understand why Stephen commands such loyalty, trust and respect.

There is such profound loyalty to Stephen because he always gave it in such full measure to those who worked with him.

There is such trust in Stephen because he always knew and displayed that trust is earned in all actions, large and small, every day.

And there is such regard for Stephen because he has the unique gift not only to understand the industry and the larger business world as it was at any given moment, but also to see the changes that would come and act ahead of others.

It is, for me, the central lesson of *Risk & Reward*.

When Stephen saw the difference capital sources could make, he entirely changed his approach and endured great risks along the way: from accepting private equity ownership to an IPO to M&A and to bold debt approaches. When Stephen saw the advantages offered by Bermuda, he pursued them for his firm, far ahead of the rest of London. When Stephen saw the customer preferring to purchase locally rather than in London, he transformed his business to become a global operation. And when the winds of consolidation were just whispering, Stephen moved boldly, and XL Catlin exists as a result.

Each of these actions carried extraordinary personal risk, which Stephen covers in the book but, as ever with him, he did not dwell on it ... as though it is just a matter of fact. Well, let's dwell on that for a moment.

Stephen put his family home on the line to start the business. Read it again: his home on the line! And, in doing so, he nearly lost everything when the bureaucracy blocked his plans until the very last moment. Imagine how slowly and painfully time moved throughout that process.

He accepted private equity capital only to see the short-termism of that capital conflict with his leadership of the firm, nearly being driven out of the business he had built! Imagine, again, your thoughts as you sleep fitfully with that risk for weeks on end.

Stephen built operations all around the world while being constantly second-guessed by investors, and thus he was burdened with a depressed share price. Imagine the many meetings with his board and his colleagues, having to constantly reassure them that this situation was worth enduring while no doubt worrying that this work would never be fully appreciated.

And imagine, in the end, choosing to trade all that you have built and led so that the firm could thrive as part of an organization that was larger and more capable. While Stephen does describe his emotions on this decision, even there he has spared the reader the true depth of the emotional trauma and the truly remarkable sacrifice he knowingly made to further his colleagues' future opportunities and serve his duty of care to his shareholders. Of this bit, I know for sure. I was there side by side with him throughout.

Of course, now that he has spent a grinding couple of years seeing to it that XL Catlin is well and truly launched, Stephen is restless again. It is reassuring that he will be with us as a colleague through the end of 2017 and then still helping beyond that. And, it is a testament to Stephen's insatiable thirst to make a difference that he is already imagining new and better things. It will be wonderful to watch what comes next.

Finally, for me personally, getting to know and work so closely with Stephen has been an enormous delight. His insight and determination, his wit and joy of life, are the stuff of legend. Read properly, the story of Stephen's life and his work is a proxy for the sector's changes throughout his lifetime, except that Stephen has always been a step ahead. It is not often one gets the privilege of working side by side with such a person while actively engaged in extraordinary work. I have had that blessing, and I am eternally grateful.

What character! And what a character.

Thank you, Stephen, from me and from all your colleagues at XL Catlin.

Mike McGavick
Bermuda
June 2017

ACKNOWLEDGEMENTS

The authors would like to thank many people whose encouragement and help has made this book possible.

The idea that led to *Risk & Reward* came from Mike McGavick, chief executive officer of XL Group Ltd., who urged Stephen "to tell his story". While it has taken more than 18 months from the time of Mike's suggestion for this book to become a reality, Mike and other colleagues at XL Catlin continued to provide great support for the project all along the way.

Brian Evens, Stephen's boss for more than a decade when he began working at Lloyd's, is mentioned frequently within these pages, but words cannot describe the impact that Brian had on Stephen's career. Brian cannot be thanked enough.

While this book is dedicated to all the employees who helped build Catlin Group Limited into a leader in the global insurance industry, the authors would like to express special thanks to the members of Catlin's Group Executive Committee during the company's final years: Richard Banas, Paul Brand, Paul Jardine, Andrew McMellin, Benji Meuli, Jo Mier and Adrian Spieler. Likewise, we express our thanks to the insurance professionals around the world who helped Catlin grow and succeed and who continued to extend their friendship to the authors following Catlin's acquisition by XL.

This book benefitted greatly from incisive comments made by friends and former colleagues: Lesley Denekamp, Paul Jardine (again), Nick Lyons, Benji Meuli (again), Graham Pewter, Dan Primer and Paul Swain. We are extremely grateful for the time this group took out of their busy schedules to read the manuscript and for their helpful suggestions.

Nicki Cockell, who has been Stephen's personal assistant for nearly 15 years, never ceased to provide invaluable help and advice to both of the authors. Thank you, Nicki.

Garry Booth is not only an insurance journalist *extraordinaire*, but also a gifted editor. Thanks to Garry's editorial talents, *Risk & Reward* reads immeasurably better than originally written.

For many years Emperor Design helped Catlin communicate with its shareholders. It was only natural that we worked with Emperor again to design and produce this book. Our thanks go out to the Emperor team, led by Bart Hallett and Steve Kemp, and which included Emma Pike, Marc Jenks, Robert Meredith and Louise Johnson-Bellot.

Last, but certainly not least, we would have never been able to complete this book without the love and support of our families. We are fortunate to have sympathetic and understanding wives in Helen and Barbie, as well as children and grandchildren who graciously overlooked all the times we have been too busy to be with them. We cannot thank them enough.

* * *

On a personal note, Stephen Catlin would like to thank Jim Burcke for his enormous help and support in co-writing *Risk & Reward*. Jim's writing skills far exceed Stephen's, and Jim has that rare skill of being able to write in the same style as his subject speaks. This book would never have been published without Jim's hard work and talents. Jim, I will always be grateful.

Appendix 1

Glossary of Terms

This is not intended to be a comprehensive glossary of insurance terms. Instead, the following is a glossary of terms that have been included in this book. There are many excellent glossaries of insurance terms available online or in print. The authors found the online glossaries on the International Risk Management Institute Inc. and the Lloyd's websites particularly useful.

Active underwriter
The individual with principal authority to accept insurance and *reinsurance* risk on behalf of the members of a *Lloyd's syndicate*.

Actuary
A person who compiles and analyzes statistics and uses them to calculate insurance risks and *premiums*.

Attritional loss ratio
The *loss ratio* excluding catastrophe losses, large single-risk losses and movements in *loss reserves*. The attritional loss ratio is a measure of underlying underwriting profitability.

Average
The principle used in insurance to calculate a claims payment in cases where the limit of the policy is less than the actual value of the property or good insured (in other words, the property or good is underinsured). If a partial loss occurs, the claims payment will be proportionate to the percentage of the underinsurance. For example, if a building valued at $1 million is insured for only $500,000, the insurer is liable to pay only half of the value of any damage claim.

Binding authority
An agreement between an insurer (or *Lloyd's syndicate*) and a *coverholder* under which the insurer delegates its authority to the coverholder to enter into a contract of insurance.

Blue-water hull insurance
A form of *marine insurance* covering damage sustained by vessels traveling on large bodies of water, particularly oceans. Brown-water hull insurance covers vessels traveling on inland waterways or close to shore.

Box (or underwriting box)
The desks in the Lloyd's *Underwriting Room* used by a *Lloyd's syndicate* at which it transacts business.

Broker
An insurance intermediary that represents the policyholder rather than the insurer. See also *retail broker* and *wholesale broker*.

Business interruption insurance
A form of commercial *property insurance* covering the loss of income suffered by a business when damage to its premises by a covered cause of loss causes a slowdown or suspension of its operations.

Captive insurer
An insurance company that primarily underwrites coverage for the risks faced by its owners or participants or a sponsoring association.

Casualty insurance
See *liability insurance*.

Caveat emptor
Or 'let the buyer beware'. The contract law principle that places the onus on a buyer to perform due diligence before making a purchase. In insurance, the legal doctrine of *uberrima fides* (meaning 'utmost good faith') is commonly used whereby all parties to an insurance contract must deal in good faith, making a full declaration of all material facts in the insurance proposal.

Cedant or ceding company
An insurer (or reinsurer) that pays a premium to transfer a portion of its risk portfolio to a reinsurer.

Claims-made form
A *liability insurance* policy providing coverage that is triggered when a claim is made against the policyholder during the policy period, regardless of when the wrongful act that gave rise to the claim took place. If a retroactive date is applicable to a policy, the action that gave rise to the claim must have taken place on or after that date.

Combined ratio
The sum of the *loss ratio* and the *expense ratio*.

Contract certainty
A situation in which the terms of an insurance or *reinsurance* contract are agreed before its inception date, rather than being negotiated afterwards.

Corporation of Lloyd's
The entity responsible for the management of the activities at Lloyd's. The Corporation of Lloyd's does not underwrite insurance or *reinsurance* itself but provides the licenses and other facilities that enable insurance and *reinsurance* to be underwritten by *Lloyd's managing agents* acting on behalf of *Lloyd's members*.

Cover note
A document issued by a broker pending the issuance of a policy that confirms that coverage has been bound.

Coverholder
An insurance intermediary authorized by an insurer to enter into contracts of insurance in the name of the insurer, subject to certain written terms and conditions. A coverholder is often described as having *binding authority* for an insurer because it has the ability to 'bind' the insurer to a certain risk.

Deductible
The amount that is deducted from some or all claims arising under an insurance or *reinsurance* contract. The practical effect is the same as an 'excess' in that the policyholder must bear a proportion of the relevant loss.

Directors' and officers' liability insurance (D&O)
A type of *liability insurance* covering directors and officers for claims made against them while serving on a board of directors and/or as an officer. These policies commonly cover claims resulting from managerial decisions that have adverse financial consequences.

Distribution
The method used by an insurer to attract business from policyholders; for example, through *brokers*, through agents representing only one insurer or through direct contact with the client (a direct-writing insurer).

Earned premium
See *premium earned*.

Endorsement
A document that is attached to a policy, *signing slip* or *cover note* that makes changes in the terms of the insurance or *reinsurance* contract to which it refers.

Equitas
The independent company established as part of the Lloyd's *Reconstruction and Renewal program* to reinsure and run off the 1992 and prior year liabilities of Lloyd's syndicates.

Excess-of-loss reinsurance
See *non-proportional reinsurance*.

Expense ratio
The percentage of *premium* used to pay an insurer's or reinsurer's costs of acquiring, underwriting and servicing its underwriting portfolio. While there are various ways of computing an expense ratio, most typically all expenses are divided by *net premiums earned*.

Facultative reinsurance
The *reinsurance* of part or all of a single insurance policy; each transaction is negotiated separately. The word 'facultative' connotes that both the primary insurer and the reinsurer have the faculty or option of accepting or rejecting the individual submission (as distinguished from *treaty reinsurance*, where the parties have an obligation to cede and accept).

Following underwriter
An underwriter of a syndicate or an insurance company in the *London market* who agrees to underwrite a proportion of a given policy, following terms set by another underwriter called the *lead* or *leading underwriter*.

Gross premiums
The total amount of *premiums* written by an insurer during a period.

Incurred losses
The total amount of paid claims and loss reserves associated with a particular period. It does not ordinarily include *incurred-but-not-reported losses*.

Incurred-but-not-reported losses (IBNR)
Estimated losses that an insurer or reinsurer, based on its knowledge or experience of underwriting similar contracts, believes have arisen or will arise, but which have not been notified to the insurer or reinsurer at the time of their estimation.

LMX spiral
The situation that arose in the *London market* during the 1980s whereby insurers and reinsurers purchased *excess of loss reinsurance* coverage from each other, leading to claims 'spiraling' from one underwriter to another many times over.

Lead or leading underwriter
The underwriter in the *London market* whose syndicate or insurance company is responsible for setting the terms of a policy that is subscribed by more than one syndicate or insurer. This underwriter generally has primary responsibility for handling any claims arising from such a policy.

Liability insurance
Insurance covering the policyholder against claims from third parties, primarily as a result of bodily injuries or property damage.

Line
The proportion of an insurance or *reinsurance* risk that is accepted by an underwriter or which an underwriter is willing to accept.

Lloyd's Central Fund
A fund maintained by Lloyd's which, at the discretion of the Council of Lloyd's, may be drawn upon to meet any valid claim that cannot be met by the resources of any underwriting member. It is funded by *Lloyd's members'* annual contributions and subordinated debt issued by the *Corporation of Lloyd's*.

Lloyd's managing agency
An underwriting agent responsible for managing a *Lloyd's syndicate* or multiple syndicates.

Lloyd's member or 'Name'
Capital providers – both individuals and companies – who provide financial backing to *Lloyd's syndicates* underwriting insurance and *reinsurance*. Prior to 1994, all Lloyd's members were individuals who had unlimited liability for the risks underwritten by the syndicates they supported. Today, most of Lloyd's capacity is supplied by corporations that provide financial backing to syndicates on a limited liability basis.

The term 'Lloyd's Name' refers to individual Lloyd's members underwriting with unlimited liability.

Lloyd's members' agency
An underwriting agent appointed by *Lloyd's members* to provide certain services, including advising members regarding the syndicates on which to participate, the level of participation on such syndicates and liaising with the relevant *Lloyd's managing agency*.

Lloyd's syndicate
A *Lloyd's member* or group of members underwriting insurance business at Lloyd's to which a syndicate number is assigned. A Lloyd's syndicate basically operates as an insurance company within the Lloyd's marketplace.

London market
Insurance business carried out in the City of London at Lloyd's and by specialist insurance companies.

Long-tail coverage
Classes of insurance – primarily *liability insurance* – where claims may arise many years after the policy period has expired.

Loss ratio
The percentage of *premium* used to pay an insurer's or reinsurer's loss costs. While there are various ways of computing a loss ratio, most typically all losses and movements in *loss reserves* are aggregated and then divided by *net premiums earned*.

Loss reserves (or simply reserves)
The amount of money set aside by an insurer or reinsurer to meet outstanding claims, *incurred-but-not-reported losses* and any associated expenses.

Managing general agent (MGA)

A specialized type of *wholesale broker* that operates under a *binding authority* from an insurer. Accordingly, MGAs often perform certain functions usually handled only by insurers, such as underwriting and pricing policies, binding coverage and managing claims. MGAs are a type of *coverholder*.

Marine insurance

Insurance providing coverage for the transportation of goods either on the ocean or by land, as well as damage to vessels and the liability to third parties arising out of the process.

Members' agent

See *Lloyd's members' agent*.

Name

See *Lloyd's member*.

Net premiums

The amount of *written premiums* or *earned premiums* less the amount paid for reinsurance protection (and in some cases broker commissions and related expenses).

Non-proportional reinsurance

A type of *reinsurance* in which losses in excess of the ceding company's retention are paid by the reinsurer, up to a maximum limit. Also known as *excess-of-loss reinsurance*.

Occurrence form

A *liability insurance* policy covering claims that arise from damage or injury that took place during the policy period, regardless of when claims are made. See also *claims-made form*.

Placing slip

A document created by a broker that contains a summary of the terms of a proposed insurance or *reinsurance* contract which is then presented to underwriters for consideration. Underwriters may delete, amend or add terms on a slip as they consider appropriate when giving a quotation or an indication that they would underwrite the contract.

Premium

The amount of money paid to an insurer or reinsurer for the coverage provided by a policy.

Premium earned (or earned premium)

The portion of the *premium written* allocatable (usually on a proportional basis) to the time already elapsed during a policy period. See also *gross premiums* and *net premiums*.

Premium written (or written premium)

The amount of *premium* accounted for by an insurer or reinsurer when the policy is issued. It is usually equal to the total premium payable for a policy.

Property insurance

A form of first-party insurance that indemnifies the owner or user of property for loss or damage caused by a covered peril, such as fire, explosion or weather-related causes.

Property/casualty insurance

Insurance that generally covers risks that result in loss to goods and property or claims filed by third parties against the policyholder. Examples include *property insurance*, *liability* or *casualty insurance*, auto insurance, aviation insurance, *marine insurance*, credit and surety insurance, as well as many others. In some countries, property/casualty insurance is called non-life insurance, to distinguish it from life, health and medical coverages.

Proportional reinsurance

A type of *reinsurance* in which the reinsurer agrees to reimburse a given percentage of a *cedant's* losses in exchange for a given percentage of the original *premium*.

Protection and indemnity (P&I) insurance

Liability insurance for many types of maritime liability risks associated with the operation of a vessel. P&I insurance is most commonly underwritten by P&I clubs, which are mutual insurance associations that underwrite coverage on behalf of member ship owners.

Quota share reinsurance

A form of *proportional reinsurance* in which the buyer cedes to a reinsurer a specified percentage of all *premiums* received, either for a portion of its portfolio or the entire portfolio. In exchange, the reinsurer is obliged to pay the same percentage of any claims and specified expenses arising.

Reconstruction and Renewal program

A comprehensive restructuring plan proposed by Lloyd's in the aftermath of large losses in the late 1980s and early 1990s. The plan had two major components: an offer to *Lloyd's members* to settle litigation arising from the losses, and the creation of *Equitas* to reinsure and *run off* the 1992 and prior year liabilities of Lloyd's syndicates. The plan was approved by members and implemented in September 1996.

Reinstatement premium

A *premium* charged for the reinstatement of insurance or *reinsurance* coverage reduced or exhausted by loss payments during the policy period.

Reinsurance

A contract under which an insurer agrees to pay a *premium* to another company in exchange for the promise to pay specified types and amounts of underwriting loss incurred by the buyer (known as the *cedant*).

Reinsurance to close

A *reinsurance* contract that closes a year of account of a *Lloyd's syndicate* by transferring the responsibility for payment of all liabilities pertaining to that year of account to a subsequent year of account of either the same syndicate or different syndicate.

Reservation of rights

Notice by an insurer that coverage for a claim may not apply. Such notification allows the insurer to investigate the claim without waiving its right to later deny coverage based on information revealed by the investigation.

Retail broker

An insurance *broker* that deals directly with a policyholder, as opposed to a *wholesale broker*.

Retrocession

A transaction in which a reinsurer transfers risks it has reinsured to another reinsurer. In other words, the *reinsurance* of reinsurance.

Run off

The management of insurance or *reinsurance* portfolios that are no longer being underwritten. Principal run-off activities include claims settlement and reinsurance recoveries.

Signed lines

The percentage of a policy that an underwriter has agreed to accept. The amount of a Lloyd's *syndicate's* signed line should be shown in a table in the policy, where one is issued.

Signing slip

A document, usually used at Lloyd's and in the *London market*, that is created by a *broker* after a quote has been accepted from an underwriter. It is a refined version of the final *placing slip* and shows underwriters' stamps, *signed lines* and underwriting references. As long as it shows the underwriters' stamps, *signed lines* and underwriting references, a *placing slip* may be used as a signing slip.

Slip

See *placing slip* and *signing slip*.

Special purpose syndicate

A *syndicate* at Lloyd's established solely to underwrite *quota share reinsurance* of another syndicate's business for a year of account.

Subscription market

An insurance market in which the underwriting of a policy is shared among different entities. Usually, the policy is negotiated by a *lead underwriter* which sets the rate, terms and conditions of the policy. Other underwriters then follow the leader, each agreeing to assume responsibility for a certain percentage of the policy.

Syndicate

See *Lloyd's syndicate*.

Treaty reinsurance

A form of *reinsurance* in which the *cedant* agrees to cede certain classes of business. In exchange, the reinsurer agrees to accept all business qualifying under the agreement, known as a 'treaty'.

Wholesale broker

An insurance *broker* that acts as an intermediary between a *retail broker* or agent and an insurer. The wholesale broker usually has little or no contact with the policyholder. Wholesale brokers are usually used to place complex, specialized or difficult-to-place risks.

Written premiums

See *premiums written*.

Appendix 2

Catlin Group Offices

at 30 April 2015

At the date of its acquisition, Catlin Group Limited operated 55 offices in 25 countries.

Australia
Melbourne, Sydney

Austria
Innsbruck, Vienna

Belgium
Antwerp

Bermuda
Hamilton

Brazil
São Paulo

Canada
Calgary, Montreal, Toronto, Vancouver

China
Beijing, Hong Kong, Shanghai

Colombia
Bogotá

Denmark
Copenhagen

Dubai
Dubai

France
Paris

Germany
Cologne, Munich

India
Mumbai

Italy
Genoa, Rome

Japan
Tokyo

Malaysia
Kuala Lumpur

Netherlands
Rotterdam

Norway
Bergen, Oslo

Poland
Wroclaw

Singapore
Singapore

Spain
Barcelona, Madrid

Sweden
Stockholm

Switzerland
Lausanne, Zurich

United Kingdom
Colchester, Guernsey, Ipswich, London

United States
Annapolis, Atlanta, Boston, Chicago, Cleveland, Columbus, Hartford, Houston, Lexington (Kentucky), Miami, New York, Philadelphia, Scottsdale, Summit, Walnut Creek, Woodland Hills

About the Authors

Stephen Catlin began his insurance career in 1973, joining B.L. Evens & Others on Syndicate 264 at Lloyd's of London. In 1982 he became deputy underwriter, specializing in the excess of loss and energy accounts where he was supported as a market leader. He founded Catlin Underwriting Agencies Limited in 1984, which later became part of Catlin Group Limited. Stephen served as the Catlin Group's chief executive throughout its history and was the active underwriter of Lloyd's Syndicate 1003 and later Syndicate 2003 until May 2003.

He was appointed executive deputy chairman of XL Group plc in May 2015 upon the completion of XL's acquisition of Catlin Group Limited to form XL Catlin. XL announced in April 2017 that Stephen will retire effective December 31, 2017, although he will remain a special advisor to XL CEO Mike McGavick.

Stephen has served as the Lloyd's nominated director of Equitas Holdings Limited; chairman of the Lloyd's Market Association, the trade association representing the interests of Lloyd's underwriters and underwriting agents; a member of the Council of Lloyd's; and a member of the Lloyd's Franchise Board. He also served as president of the Insurance Institute of London and chair of the Association of Bermuda Insurers and Reinsurers (ABIR).

He was selected by Ernst & Young as the 'UK Entrepreneur of the Year' in 2011.

Stephen is currently Chair of the Insurance Development Forum and a Visiting Fellow at the Oxford University Centre for Corporate Reputation.

Stephen was inducted into the International Insurance Society's Insurance Hall of Fame in June 2015.

* * *

James Burcke has been involved with insurance industry communications for more than 35 years. He most recently was head of corporate affairs for Catlin Group Limited in London. Prior to that, he was head of communications for Equitas Holdings Limited.

James was previously editor of *Business Insurance* magazine in the US and editorial/managing director of Reactions Publishing Group in the UK. He was also an editor at daily newspapers in Michigan and Kentucky. He received bachelor's and master's degrees from the Medill School of Journalism at Northwestern University.

INDEX